MAKER OF MODERN
GOA

MAKER OF MODERN GOA

The Untold Story Of
PRATAPSINGH RANE

VIJAYADEVI RANE

Published by
Rupa Publications India Pvt. Ltd 2024
7/16, Ansari Road, Daryaganj
New Delhi 110002

Sales centres:
Bengaluru Chennai Hyderabad
Jaipur Kathmandu Kolkata
Mumbai Prayagraj

Copyright © Vijayadevi Rane 2024

The views and opinions expressed in this book are the author's own and the facts are as reported by her which have been verified to the extent possible, and the publishers are not in any way liable for the same.

All rights reserved.

No part of this publication may be reproduced, transmitted, or stored in a retrieval system, in any form or by any means, electronic, mechanical, photocopying, recording or otherwise, without the prior permission of the publisher.

P-ISBN: 978-93-5702-631-4
E-ISBN: 978-93-5702-918-6

First impression 2024

10 9 8 7 6 5 4 3 2 1

The moral right of the author has been asserted.

Printed in India

This book is sold subject to the condition that it shall not, by way of trade or otherwise, be lent, resold, hired out, or otherwise circulated, without the publisher's prior consent, in any form of binding or cover other than that in which it is published.

*To the people of Goa, who gave Pratapsingh Rane
the opportunity to serve and develop the state*

CONTENTS

Foreword / ix

Introduction / xiii

1. Early Life: 1939–1969 / 1
2. Stepping into Public Life: 1969–1977 / 31
3. Face of the Congress in Goa: 1977–1980 / 62
4. Chief Minister: 1980–1990 / 81
5. The Turbulent Decade: 1990–2000 / 125
6. The Later Years: 2000–2022 / 151
7. Thoughts: Looking Back, Looking Forward / 182
8. The Man behind the Leader / 206

Acknowledgements / 237

Index / 239

FOREWORD

'Any man can be a father but it takes a special person to be a dad.'
—VISHWAJIT PRATAPSINGH RANE

For the people of Goa, Shri Pratapsingh Raoji Rane is a remarkable politician and administrator. He is the state's most enduring leader who has been Goa's chief minister (CM) a record six times and a Member of the Legislative Assembly (MLA) for an astounding 50 years. Pratapsingh Rane has never lost his seat over 11 consecutive elections. These career statistics are extraordinary. They place Pratapsingh Rane in the front rank of post-Independence Indian politicians.

For me, his proud son, my father has been my political and personal role model, my leader, mentor and friend. Without his guidance, I would have never stepped into the maze of Goan politics. I don't just carry my father's legacy; I remain constantly inspired by him.

Yet many outside Goa and, indeed, even a new generation of young Goans might not be aware of just how enormously Pratapsingh Rane has shaped the destiny of one of India's youngest and smallest states. His far-sighted leadership enabled Goa to rise from union territory (UT) to full statehood, eventually emerging as one of the country's most progressive and well-governed states. For decades, he was the voice of reason and stable governance in

Goa and beyond. Today, you will find Pratapsingh Rane's stamp across almost every sector of Goa: from education to infrastructure, industry to health, and from tourism to the arts. He is, as this book reveals, a true builder of modern Goa.

Many may have seen the Hindi film *Swades*, in which an idealistic young man gives up his comfortable life in the United States (US) to eventually help set up a hydroelectric power generation plant in rural India. My father's life, to some extent, mirrors the journey of that protagonist Mohan (played by superstar Shah Rukh Khan), as my father too, after being educated abroad, dedicated every fibre of his being to the people of Goa.

In the pursuit of the common good, my father represents a unique spirit of bipartisanship. A leader from an era of consensual politics, when public figures enjoyed ties of comradeship across party lines, my father, a lifelong Congressman, still maintained friendly relations with many senior leaders of the Bharatiya Janata Party (BJP), including former Prime Minister (PM) Atal Bihari Vajpayee. When Vajpayee visited Goa, my father had no hesitation in hailing him as a true statesman. These links have endured to this day. The heart-warming concern of my leader PM Narendra Modi towards my father—the PM publicly recalling the times when Pratapsingh Rane and Narendra Modi as CMs of Goa and Gujarat, respectively, worked together in national forums—has meant a great deal to my family and to me. I continue to draw inspiration from the PM's warmth and sensitivity towards all those he comes in contact with.

Prime Minister Modi, like my father, earned his spurs as a CM committed to good governance. When Modi was the CM of Gujarat and my father the CM of Goa, the two shared an excellent rapport at various Planning Commission meetings and national forums. They belonged to different parties, yet forged an understanding based on always keeping the common good at the heart of state administration. It is this enduring friendship that I take pride in recalling.

Yet it's not only Pratapsingh Rane the politician who is an outstanding figure. It is my father's human side, remarkably untouched by power and privilege, that makes him such a special person. Through his long journey in public life, his wife, my mother Vijayadevi Rane, has been his constant companion. She has been the wind beneath his wings. Without her strengthening and energizing presence, I doubt if my father would have been able to embark on his lifelong mission to serve the people of Goa. It is her unstinting support that has shaped his life and career. Which is why it is only appropriate that she is at the heart of this book. This is the untold story of Pratapsingh Rane but it is also a story of my parents' 55-year-old relationship, the love story of Pratap and Vijaya, which has so admirably weathered life's changing seasons.

My father's life also reveals what it takes to win the real affection of people over generations and touch the hearts of everyone a leader comes in contact with. I believe it is his deep engagement with every human being he meets which gives him a luminosity that marks him out as not just a top-flight politician, but a statesman rooted among the people. I hope this book will give the reader a sense of Goa's unique place in India. I also hope readers will gain an insight into the life and work of my father Pratapsingh Raoji Rane, a devoted son of Goa and of India.

Vishwajit Pratapsingh Rane

INTRODUCTION

Goa may be India's smallest state, but it is one of India's biggest brands. The appeal of Goa both at home and abroad is unparalleled, as millions of tourists both international and domestic flock to Goa's shores to enjoy its stunning palm-fringed beaches. Yet under the tourist brochure images of the state, there is a cultural and historical depth that tourists perhaps don't see. Different religious faiths have co-existed in Goa for centuries, a dizzyingly rich variety of art forms flourish here, and East and West have mingled to create a unique outlook that is both rooted and open to the world.

When India became independent in 1947, Goa remained under Portuguese colonial rule. Goa was liberated only in December 1961, 14 years after India became free. In terms of development, Goa had a lot of catching up to do in bringing modern amenities to its people. It is a tribute to the early administrators of post-Liberation Goa that today, the state has the highest per capita income in India and has consistently maintained high levels of literacy, public health and exemplary communal harmony. Goa is a place where the Latin spirit of the Portuguese and the inclusive spirit of the Konkani language have combined to create grace in everyday life, respect for each other's traditions and a shared commitment to preserve Goa's ecological heritage.

The transformation of Goa from a Portuguese colony to a self-reliant Indian state owes a great deal to its early chief ministers (CMs), of whom Pratapsingh Rane is the foremost example. As

Goa's longest serving CM for 15 years, sworn in as the CM as many as six times, it was Pratapsingh who oversaw Goa's transition from a Union Territory (UT) to a full-fledged state—India's twenty-fifth state—in 1987. He was not only the longest serving CM but the first CM of the Goa state. Rane's unbroken tenure of a decade from 1980 to 1990 provided the state with much needed stability and governance and laid the basis for its entry into the twenty-first century. Pratapsingh's two consecutive full terms as the CM and the stable government of these years stand in sharp contrast to the 1990s when instability became chronic, when there were repeated defections and a dozen governments replaced each other in a volatile game of musical chairs from 1990 to 2000.

Goa's present-day politics tends to be rough and ready. Defections are the order of the day and the '*Aya Ram Gaya Ram*' syndrome bedevils public life. Pratapsingh is an exception to this norm. He has remained in the Indian National Congress (INC) for almost half a century, having joined the party in 1977. As a politician, both in Opposition and as CM, he consistently pursued the politics of development and reform, rather than of short-termism or debilitating intrigue.

Pratapsingh's life is one of idealism and duty. Schooled in Poona (now Pune) and holding a degree in business management from Texas A&M University, United States (US), he joined Tata Engineering and Locomotive Company (Telco) on his return to India. Yet, after a family tragedy, he gave up a life of corporate success and daily comfort to return to Goa to work on his family's ancestral lands. When asked to join politics by Goa's first CM Dayanand Balkrishna (D.B.) Bandodkar, he did so because of his fervent wish to work to uplift the people of Goa. Having lived and worked in the US and in other parts of India, he witnessed first-hand the lack of basic amenities in Goa and made an idealistic choice to join politics to bring to the state the development it was thirsting for.

His beginnings in politics shaped the kind of public figure he became: he was not in politics for self-aggrandizement or after power for its own sake. Endowed with vast estates in north Goa, he did not lack for his own resources and did not crave the trappings of official positions. His mission was to work to bring education, health, transportation and industry to Goa and to build it up as a model state. Perhaps this sincerity of purpose is the reason why Pratapsingh has never lost an election, winning a remarkable 11 consecutive elections from his constituency, a Member of Legislative Assembly (MLA) for over 50 years. Eleven consecutive wins (not a single defeat in 50 years) is a record that few Indian politicians hold. Even former Prime Minister (PM) Atal Bihari Vajpayee, who won 10 elections from 1957 to 2004, famously failed to get elected to the Lok Sabha twice, in 1962 and 1984.

Pratapsingh started Goa's first public bus service—the Kadamba Transport Corporation Ltd., built all weather roads connecting every village, started an electrification drive with the slogan of 'two points for every house' so that every home would get at least one or two electricity connections. He brought in several pioneering laws such as The Goa, Daman and Diu Town and Country Planning Act, 1974, when he was the law minister in the Shashikala Kakodkar government, by which towns and villages were carefully planned, industrial estates separated from residential areas, and each village provided with a playground and space for shrines. The Goa Right to Information (RTI) Act of 1997 predated by some years the centre's own RTI Act. The Goa Rural Employment Guarantee Scheme of 2006 was also passed by the Pratapsingh Rane government. He brought in laws such as the Goa Prevention of Defacement of Property Act, 1988, which today protects the state's skyline from being spoiled, and the Prohibition of Smoking and Spitting Act, 1997.

Pratapsingh Rane was the first CM to visualize Goa as a tourist destination and urged the then Indira Gandhi-led government to hold a Commonwealth Heads of Government Meeting (CHOGM) weekend retreat in Goa. The Retreat, held in 1983, gave a big push to Goa's tourism profile. Goa was placed on the national and international map. Rane's successive governments also went all out to encourage industry in Goa, while at the same time looking after the needs of rural communities. Himself a passionate agriculturalist, Rane was keenly alive to Goa's irrigation and drinking water supply needs. He completed the Anjunem Irrigation project in 1989 and moved full speed towards the completion of the Selaulim Dam.

Recognizing the need to bolster Goa's connectivity with the rest of the world, Pratapsingh Rane oversaw an increase in flights and train transport and laid the blueprint for the Mopa airport in Goa, today regarded as a first-rate airport. He built schools and colleges across Goa, established the Goa University and the Goa Institute of Management (GIM). He made an all-out effort to promote Goa's arts and, in 1983, built the iconic Kala Academy building in Goa, as well as smaller cultural centres known as Ravindra Bhavans across Goa. As Speaker of the Goa Assembly, he upgraded the assembly library. As Leader of the Opposition (LoP), his interventions were substantive; he was never unruly or intemperate. No wonder that Pratapsingh Rane was honoured with the title 'Goa's Legislator of the Millennium' by the Goa Assembly in 2001.

He was able to pull off so much all-round development work because of his personality and style of working. Unassuming, reserved, courteous, impartial and rule-bound while at the same time, highly disciplined and hard-working, the words 'a thorough gentleman' are often used for him. His officers emulated his hard work and daily discipline, his peers respected him and the people appreciated him for the sincere and honest CM he was. When he made offers of rehabilitation to those whose homes were displaced by the Anjunem Dam, his words were trusted. When he started the state bus service and electrification drives, people saw that he kept his word.

Pratapsingh represents a bridge between the old and new Goa, between past days of a gracious, easy-going gentility to the boisterous politically competitive Goa of today. He created a roadmap for the future development of the state by focussing on governance and administration. Goa's official culture today remains largely impartial and disciplined. Goa's lively civil society, its writers, performers, architects, eco-warriors, academics and RTI activists show that a civic culture has been nurtured. Vibrant village panchayats, the benign peace that reigns between religious communities and a law-abiding public show that post-Liberation modern Goa has been built on strong foundations.

None of this means that Goa's challenges are over. Far from it. Hard choices still have to be made on development and protection of the environment; youth unemployment remains high; there are miles to go in the tasks of job creation, attracting industry and building infrastructure. Politics takes its own toll. High levels of corruption, fractious instability and short-termism threaten to paralyse development. Yet as new administrations grapple with Goa's problems, the 'Rane Model of Development' can provide pointers on how to harness the energies of the state. That's why at a time when governance expertise is much needed across India, when governance is the mantra that many swear by but don't often practice, the story of Pratapsingh Rane needs to be told. It is not just his story; it is the story of the making of modern Goa.

ONE

EARLY LIFE: 1939–1969

*'My father tried to give me and all my siblings the best possible
education. But I was a naughty child,
so he gave me some thrashings too.'*

Goa. On the shores of the Arabian Sea, criss-crossed by rivers and bordered by the slopes of the Western Ghats. Where sea, river, forest and hills meet and mingle to create what writer Graham Greene has called 'a deep country peace'.

White-painted churches rise through coconut trees. Ancient temples dwell in dense forests. Wayside shrines across the landscape imbue the place with a spiritual calm that is irresistible to the visitor. The tourist brochures of seaside shacks and bars, the media stereotypes of the 'holiday state' and dusk to dawn beach parties hardly capture the social, cultural and historical depth of Goa. Here, there is a magical golden glow to the sunshine, and in remote interior villages where the rivers run—Mandovi and Zuari, Chapora and Mapusa—candles flicker in the quiet twilight and soft temple bells ring making the atmosphere quite transcendental.

Goa is surrounded and, in a way, defined by water—the endless expanse of ocean and white sand beaches stretching along the coast and a network of rivers circling towns and villages. In the days when there were no bridges, Goa formed an emerald-green archipelago, the life of each hamlet centred around its own unique shrines and cultural traditions. There are sacred groves throughout Goa. These are forest-shrines located deep in the heart of primaeval natural vegetation, invisible to outsiders, surrounded by streams, natural springs and ancient undisturbed trees. Local communities have protected these groves for decades, practising age-old forms of nature worship in these sacred woodlands.

There is music in the air of Goa. The Latin spirit from the Portuguese, the bubbling merriment of the Konkani language, the traditional songs of ancient Hindu deities, church hymns, temple chants and *kirtans* fill every village with melody and song. Falling water seems to hum a tune, palms seem to whisper in cadence and Mother Nature seems to smile in Goa.

Goa was once the ancient Gomanchala of the Vedic period. The often-heard mythology about Goa is that it's the land of Parashuram. Parashuram, brave and righteous but driven to vengeance by the death of his father, was so feared that some people went to a holy sage and begged him to send Parashuram away. But where would Parashuram live? So, the fierce fighter climbed up the Sahyadri mountains and shot his arrow down towards land. His arrow went racing through the air, travelled a vast distance and landed in an expanse of water. Miraculously, the waters drew back to reveal the land of Goa, beautiful and tranquil, surrounded by still, calm water that brought peace to the warrior and continues to bring peace to all who come here.

To the north of Goa lies the hilly forested area known as Sattari. It's a place of rugged beauty, the tree-clad hills of the Western Ghats rising from broad valleys. Forests are dense, and we can hear songbirds in the day and the haunting cry of jackals at night. The Valvanti River (or Mhadei as it is also called)—its water fresh and sweet in this region—curves through the terrain, sustaining fields and orchards. In villages along the foothills, multicoloured bursts of bougainvillea cling to neat, graceful homes. Forests are full of timber. Mango and cashew orchards dot the landscape. This is the land of the Ranes. And I came as a young bride to this beloved place of my husband of 55 years, Pratapsingh Rane.

Fearless Warrior Clan

The Ranes have descended from the Rajputs of Rajasthan and have dominated Sattari since the sixteenth century as landlords or *bhatkar*s of the region. We are Kshatriya-Marathas, warrior clans with roots across the Deccan. We are a hardy, robust and aristocratic people, proud of our Maratha identity as legatees of the great Shivaji Maharaj. We are descendants of military commanders, strongly attached to our own unique traditions and ways of living.

Warlike and resolute, the Ranes were ever-ready to defend their land and their way of life. During Portuguese domination, Hindu beliefs were the target of state persecution. But the Ranes fought hard to preserve their faith and often struck terror in the hearts of the Portuguese.

In the fifteenth century, from the West came new visitors to India's west coast—explorers who preceded conquerors, arriving on India's shores to conquer both the material and the sacred world. In 1498, Portuguese explorer Vasco da Gama first arrived in Calicut. In 1510, the Portuguese conquest of Goa began. An uneasy relationship developed between the Ranes in the north and the Portuguese rulers in Panjim, a volatile modus vivendi that lasted over a century. The Ranes initially started out as allies of the adventurous Bhonsle chieftains of Sawantwadi, but later forged their own path.

Troubles began when the Ranes felt that their rights in Sattari were being challenged: taxes were too high, and the Portuguese were interfering in social and religious customs. The famous Rane revolts against the Portuguese began in the late eighteenth century and lasted until 1912. Between 1755 and 1822, there were as many as 14 Rane insurrections. The most powerful of these were the Dipaji Rane Revolt (1852–1855), the Kustoba Rane Revolt (1869–1871), the Dada Rane Revolt (1895–1897) and the Rane revolts of 1901 and 1902. Dipaji Rane, in particular, was, by many accounts, a buccaneering local hero, a stout-hearted leader of his band of guerrilla warriors who used the cover of the Sattari jungles to attack the Portuguese.

In their fierce determination to prevail against a powerful adversary, there are accounts of how Rane fighters would often participate in traditional prayers and worship, as well as certain rituals of war like turning a symbolic stone at the village of Caranzol before setting off on their raids against the Portuguese. Some of the weapons used by the Rane insurgents are displayed on the walls of our ancestral home, including the guns with long muzzles. The long muzzles were necessary since guns in those days did not possess a good range. One of the most priceless items in the Rane collection is a sword offered by the then prince of Portugal to one of the Rane ancestors who entered into a peace treaty with the Portuguese in 1813. Notwithstanding periods of truce, the Ranes kept up their rebellious uprisings against the Portuguese until as late as the first years of the twentieth century.

There were various reasons for regular revolts by the Ranes. The chief reasons were Portuguese taxes and levies, methods of rent collection, bans on wearing Indian clothes, compelling Goans to wear only Western clothes, bans on festivals and palanquin processions, and outlawing wearing the tilak and setting up *tulsi-vrindavan*s in front of houses.

The Portuguese way of subduing the locals was by attacking Hindu beliefs. The Portuguese Inquisition—or forcible imposition of Christianity—began in Goa in 1560 and lasted intermittently until 1812. Particularly brutal methods were used to stamp out and outlaw Hindu and other local religions and cultures. Many Hindu and Islamic practices were labelled as 'witchcraft', and people were brought to trial courts and received sentences like beheading or burning. It was considered a criminal offence to speak Konkani or follow the traditional culture.

The aim was to 'Christianize' the population and undertake a religious as well as a cultural transformation of the people. People were forced to change their name, give up their language and 'become' Portuguese. 'The Portuguese came to Goa with the sword and to spread the message of Christ,' says Pratapsingh. 'Priests would throw holy bread into the small wells of peoples' homes and declare that the people had been baptized. Orthodox Hindus played their part too. They would immediately ostracize those who had drunk this water, unwittingly contributing to the growing numbers of conversions.'

But the Ranes clung tenaciously to their traditional Hindu faith and ways of living. They would not be subdued. They would not give up their religion or their culture. They kept mounting incursions against the Portuguese, not necessarily for any form of sovereignty from Portuguese rule, but to have the right over implementing their own taxation systems, over the use of resources and to their own beliefs and ways of life. The Portuguese may have captured Panjim but deep in the forests, by the calm banks of the Valvanti, among secluded communities where the Portuguese could not reach, little temples were alive with the ancient worship of traditional deities: Vithal, Rakhumai, Dattatreya and Bhumika. The centuries-old Shri Vithal-Rakhumai temple, of which Rane patriarchs have been custodians for generations, is a testament to the determination with which the Rane clans guarded their faith.

There were other reasons for conflict. In the nineteenth century, mass timber construction was on the rise, and timber from the lush Sattari forests was taken away by the Portuguese government. Rights in timber were handed to the British and Americans. Incensed at the systematic depletion of their forest rights, the Ranes hit back. Adept at fighting in the dense Sattari jungles, Rane soldiers unleashed guerrilla warfare on the Portuguese. But the colonialists cracked down brutally, and one of the Rane rebel leaders—Kustoba Rane—was caught. His head was cut off and presented to the Governor General. Many members of Rane clans were imprisoned and even exiled. The last Rane revolt took place in 1912 against the high rents levied on paddy cultivators of Sattari.

The Portuguese conquest of Goa is divided into two phases: Old Conquests and New Conquests. Bardez, Salcette and Ilhas de Goa (or Tiswadi), the island of Panjim (as it was before bridges were built), the islands of Divar and Chorao and other smaller islands were conquered first in the sixteenth century; these were known as the Old Conquests or Velhas Conquistas. Other regions like Sattari, Canacona, Quepem, Sanguem, Ponda and Bicholim were taken over later in the eighteenth century and known as New Conquests or Novas Conquistas. Portuguese religious and cultural imposition was never as strong in the New Conquest areas as in the Old. In the New Conquest areas, particularly Sattari, there was a history of resistance to Portuguese rule. 'The Portuguese were good sailors, but they were bad soldiers,' says Pratapsingh. 'They could never fully overrun the hilly Hindu heartland in Sattari in north Goa. Instead, there used to be a Portuguese *commandante militares* posted there.' In 1910, Portugal became a republic and church was separated from state. But before this, the propagation and imposition of Christianity was a key feature of the Portuguese colonial state.

A Timeless Legacy

In Sanquelim village in Sattari, in a sprawling double-storied mansion—a Maratha haveli or *wada* with pillared halls, interlinked multiple courtyards and long airy corridors—lived the family of Raoji Satroji Rane, landowner and bhatkar of the area. It is a vast rambling yet outwardly simple structure with slope-tiled roofs. Inside, on the walls hang sambar heads, spears, daggers, swords, flintlock guns and guns with unusually long muzzles. Each section of the house leads into open courtyards, and there are almost no windows, so perhaps in the old days, it was designed so that women could not look outside or be seen. The windows are atypical with only narrow vertical openings. The house was, and still remains, a palace-fortress with thick walls and embrasures, designed to protect itself against enemies.

Raoji Satroji Rane, patriarch of a Rane family in Sattari in the early twentieth century, was a popular bhatkar, caring of his tenants with a progressive commitment to education and forward-looking values. His wife Manoramabai Rane, née Bhonsle, who hailed from the small principality of Heyra in Karnataka, was a woman of great beauty. She had chiselled features and smooth, lustrous skin. Dressed in fine nine-yard saris, Manorama was quiet and reserved by nature yet, at the same time, healthy, vigorous, strong and firm. Married to Raoji at the age of 15, she bore him as many as 18 children, of whom eight survived. She was a devoted mother. Orphaned as a child and brought up by an aunt, she delighted in motherhood and dedicated herself to her children's lives and her larger family.

Manoramabai was particularly close to her husband's younger sister, Salu bai. Here I must mention an interesting piece of Rane family history. Spirited and elegant, Salu bai married a Maharaja, the modern-minded degree holder from Cambridge University, Maharaja Madho Rao I of Gwalior. Madho Rao had been married earlier, but his first wife could not have children and the Maharaja was on the lookout for a new, young queen who would give him the heir Gwalior needed. After their wedding, Salu bai was renamed Gajra Raje Scindia and bore Madho Rao a son, 'George' Jivajirao (nicknamed 'George' after the British monarch George V). Years later, Jivajirao's wife Vijaya Raje Scindia and children Madhavrao Scindia, Vasundhara Raje and Yashodhara Raje would go on to become well-known names in Indian politics.

Not only did Gajra Raje marry the Maharaja, but her father

Raoji insisted that if she was to marry Madho Rao, then five of her sisters too should be married to Gwalior noblemen. So, five of Pratapsingh's aunts were married off to Gwalior *Sardar*s, one of them to Sardar Chandroji Angre, another to Sardar Shitole, another to Sardar Mahadik and the rest to other nobles. As it turned out, my own mother, Rajmata Sushiladevi Ghorpade of Sandur, was from the senior Shitole family and, as a girl, often visited both Gajra Raje and Manoramabai saheb in Gwalior.

It wasn't entirely easy for Maharani Gajra Raje, though. Travelling all the way from Goa to Gwalior in Madhya Bharat, she was often lonely and homesick. Manoramabai saheb would regularly visit Gwalior to keep her sister-in-law company. However, when Madho Rao I died while Jivajirao was still a child, Gajra Raje came into her own. She took over as queen regent, proving to be such a competent administrator that the Gwalior noblemen were quite taken aback that a small-town girl from Sanquelim in Goa could govern a large kingdom like Gwalior so efficiently. Thus, there exists a long connection between the Ranes of Goa and today's princely family of Gwalior, who are descendants of the Rane family of Goa and, therefore, bear some Goan blood!

Gajra Raje never forgot Sanquelim. As Maharani of Gwalior, she sent architects and resources back to her home and rebuilt the family's small Shri Vithal-Rakhumai temple, an over 500-year-old temple, into a much larger structure. From Gwalior, she dispatched the Scindia royal gold embroidered insignia and a palanquin for the temple deity. On festival days, the deities of the Shri Vithal temple are taken out in procession in Gajra Raje's richly carved palanquin which bears her royal seal. Gajra Raje maintained the temple in grand style, as if to give thanks to Shri Vithal for her own good fortune.

Today, the Shri Vithal temple, witness to half a millennium of history, occupies pride of place in the Rane's ancestral home, and a Rane family member serves as its custodian. The Ranes have always been rooted in the land of their birth, sharing strong community ties with neighbours and tenants. And so, as CM, Pratapsingh threw open the doors of the temple to all castes and creeds. Every year in the month of 'Chaitra' (end April to early May), the Chaitrotsav festival takes place at the end of April when almost all of Sanquelim gathers together. Festival rituals are presided over by the senior most male Rane who today is Pratapsingh Rane.

Born to Lead

In 1939, on a cool January day, when a light mist hung over the cashew orchards and Raoji Rane's palatial wada was bathed in sunshine, Birju, the village midwife, came hurrying into the house. Birju was of African descent. Her family had first arrived in Goa from the Portuguese colony of Angola, brought in by the Portuguese slave trade. Birju had thrived here, fluent in Konkani, every inch a woman of Goa, in her sari with her hair caught up in a neat bun. Birju now bent over Manoramabai as she went into labour. That day—28 January 1939—a third son was born to Raoji and Manoramabai. His parents named him Pratapsingh. Later that year, World War II would break out across Europe, but he was not a child of war; instead, he would grow up to bring peace and well-being to his land.

Pratapsingh was the fifth of Manoramabai's eight children. The eldest was a sister named Hiradevi. Next came another sister, Sarladevi. Then two older brothers, Satroji alias Vithal Rao and Fatehsingh. Then three years later came Pratapsingh. After him came another sister Indira, then another brother Udaysingh and last, the youngest child, a girl named Jeevanlata. Between Pratapsingh and his eldest sister Hiradevi, there was an age gap of as much as 18 years.

'Life at home was full of people. Lots of children, lots of visitors, my father's tenants, aunts and uncles,' recalls Pratapsingh. 'Sometimes performers, musicians and temple singers who hail from the Gomantak Maratha Samaj would also come.' The huge, elongated kitchens in the house, which form a building complex in themselves, used to, in the old days, feed as many as 1,000 people a day, according to Pratapsingh. Two portraits hang on the walls of the house today: one of Gajra Raje in a rich purple, gold-bordered sari. She has distinctive features, a direct, fearless gaze and is wearing solid gold jewellery with the traditional *nath* (nose ring). There's another portrait of the Rane ancestor who built this house, the 'grandfather of my great grandfather,' says Pratapsingh.

Proud as he was of his Maratha traditions, yet Pratapsingh's father, Raoji Rane was no prisoner of conservatism. He himself had had little opportunities of education. He lost his mother at a young age and remained in Portuguese Goa where schools and colleges of excellence were not available. But he was ambitious for his children and determined to ensure that all his children benefitted from the modern education available in British India. He combed all the schooling options available at the time, even visiting the Doon School in Dehradun to find suitable institutions for his children. His daughters all went to convent schools in Mussoorie and then to Wadia College in Pune, and all became university graduates. Sarladevi was even a talented athlete, a runner and a champion discus thrower. My four sisters-in-law were all modern young women, not trapped in narrow mindsets that would retard their progress. They were not only well educated, but also rather fashionable and hip! Apart from father Raoji, eldest sister Hiradevi also took great pains to see that all her younger siblings were sent to schools and colleges and gained the best possible education to face the challenges of the new era.

Pratapsingh shares a vivid memory: 'We were not allowed to go to the market and spend too much time there,' he recalls. 'I was an extremely naughty child and was often given a good beating. I remember one particular incident: my father used to run a small Marathi school in our family temple to help the children in the surrounding area. One of the teachers at the school was romancing a young female staff member at our house. My mother was outraged by this and used to often loudly reprimand him. I heard the shouts and once joined in to cry out at the teacher to stop his advances. When I did so, the teacher caught hold of me and beat me up. In a rage, I got a kitchen knife from the kitchen and took it to school to try and scare off the teacher. My father was incensed at this. He came striding into the school and gave me a thorough thrashing. Perhaps that's why I was packed off to military school—to get some good discipline.'

After a long search, the Shri Shivaji Preparatory Military School (AISSMS) in Poona was deemed most appropriate for the young Pratapsingh, and in 1944, off went the five-year-old to Poona. It was in this city where for the next decade and a half, through the tumult of India's Independence, he would study in school and, later, at the Nowrosjee Wadia College. He would finally leave Poona only in 1960 at the age of 21. A new India, a brave young republic, was born in this decade, and a new Pratapsingh Rane was born too. In place of Raoji Rane's mischievous son, now emerged a tough, resilient, athletic young man, capable of enormous hard work—a natural leader who led from the front.

The warrior blood of the Ranes stood Pratapsingh in good stead in school. Being a military school, it maintained excellent stables of fine horses and Pratapsingh became an outstanding horseman. Strong, fearless and agile, he could master a horse effortlessly. He rode racehorses at races and in showjumping events. One incident marked his equestrian life: he once mounted a horse that suddenly began to buck and rear dangerously and raced around the ground at speed, out of control. But Pratapsingh held on, refusing to let go, and eventually calmed the stallion down completely. 'After that incident, I knew I could ride any horse, however unruly,' he recalls.

He became such an expert horse-rider that he participated in public racing events as a jockey. These were, as he points out, amateur races for gentleman riders. A news item in the sports page of the Bombay edition of *The Times of India* on 2 January 1953 is headlined: 'Rane steers Excalibur to victory in Bhor stakes.' 'Good riding by Rane on Excalibur in the Bhor Stakes was the highlight of the Second Day of the Kirkee Gymkhana Races here,' the paper reports. 'I won a lot of prizes for horse-riding and often there were write-ups about me in the sports pages of *The Times of India*,' Pratapsingh recalls. Later in life, when he had become an established Congress leader, on some visits to Delhi, Pratapsingh and Rajiv Gandhi would often meet for an early morning ride at the New Delhi Riding Club grounds.

He went foxhunting in Pune too, a very British sport. They would form riding groups with hounds and chase after jackals in the forest. 'Whoever got to the jackal first would get the head, the second got the tail, others got the paws. The parts were hung like trophies. Looking back, I must say it was a very cruel sport,' he recalls.

His spectacular achievements are endorsed by his principal in his school-leaving certificate:

Master Pratapsingh Balasaheb Rane Sir-Desai, studied at the Shri Shivaji Preparatory Military Secondary School from July 1944 to May 1953...During his long stay at the Kindergarten and Secondary school of this institution...he rose from the ranks of the boys to be Head-Prefect. The fact that he held this office creditably and efficiently goes a long way to prove his qualities as a leader, endowed with a keen sense of duty and service. In the class-room as well as on the playing field he impressed me by his keen interest in work. He played Hockey and football. He is a good swimmer and a tough Boxer. He excels in the equestrian art and rode several times in the Kirkee Gymkhana Amateur Races. He can talk and write English well and has studied French too. I understand he is at present taking lessons in German. He is a young man coming from a historical family of Portuguese Goa. He has pleasing manners, has developed a fine physique and an impressive personality. I am confident he will make his mark in work which he is called upon to undertake.

After school, Raoji encouraged Pratapsingh to join university, and he enrolled in Nowrosjee Wadia College for a degree in science, graduating with a BSc. Excelling at all martial sports, he was a good boxer too. He was the undefeated boxing champion in the lightweight category at Wadia College for three years and also won a western India boxing championship for Bombay and Poona. Today, on the Wadia College website, Pratapsingh is listed as one of the college's eminent alumni. College was a whirlwind of activities, sports, visits to Bombay, social events and trips back home to Goa.

Home was Portuguese Goa. In spite of dictatorship and muzzling of liberties, there was much in Portuguese Goa that was pleasurable, particularly for the affluent. A Portuguese sense of enjoying the good life permeated the air. Mercedes Benz cars doubled as taxis, and fine foods and garments from Europe were available. Goan ladies and gentlemen were always impeccably dressed with refined manners and tastes. Portuguese soldiers and captains strolled down the leafy boulevards of Panjim. On narrow tarred roads, small brass-bodied buses called carreras trundled along, bearing suited gentlemen and ladies in lacy mantillas. Piano and violin music rang out from churches and homes. 'Goa was a free port. There was lots of activity and travel. Many things were available. I used to buy chocolates for my college friends and take them back with me to Poona,' recalls Pratapsingh.

This was his home, this place of astonishing beauty with its long beaches, verdant forests and sparkling rivers. Rising skywards, churches stood framed against still waters. Glimpsed through an intricate trellis of trees, earthen lamps in forest temples glowed with sacred light.

Goa was where his heart was, but he was restless to see the

world. He had a successful tenure in school and college, and yearned for new experiences and global adventures. He applied to various US universities and obtained admission at Texas A&M University for a degree in business and industrial management (equivalent to a bachelor's in Business Management or BBM). 'I was inspired by America. America was the first colony to get independence after the 1775–83 American War of Independence, with the Declaration of Independence adopted in 1776. After Independence, America encouraged other colonies too to seek independence and liberation. For providing this example in the world, we need to thank George Washington and the other American leaders,' he says. US President John F. Kennedy was one of the contemporary American politicians who deeply inspired him. 'John Kennedy was the president when I arrived in America. I admired him a lot. His assassination is the saddest memory I have about my stay in that country.'

Why did he choose Texas? 'Many Portuguese officials told my father to send me to Portugal, but I was keen to explore the US. I wanted to go to Texas because I wanted to ride horses there. When I went there, however, I discovered the Texan climate was rather horrible, the summers were very humid.'

New Adventures

He travelled to the US on a Portuguese passport, having obtained a visa from the US consulate in Bombay. The formalities of admission and visa took over a year, so to while away his time, he took admission in law college in Poona, but dropped out as soon as his admission to Texas was confirmed. In the summer of 1960, 21-year-old Pratapsingh Rane arrived in the US.

He cut a fine figure. Well-dressed and good looking, with the manly vitality of the Ranes and the flair and finesse of Goan manners, he soon developed a wide circle of friends. Photos show him with groups of bright, smiling young men and women. Among his friends was a pretty young Indian woman named Leela Parulekar, then studying at Columbia University in New York. Leela was the daughter of the founder editor of the *Sakal* newspapers, Dr N.B Parulekar. In distant America, two young people from western India became friends.

Pratapsingh's friends were not just Indians but came from a variety of backgrounds, including young men from Germany and France who were studying in the US. Christina Figuero from Argentina became a close friend, as did Hans Deiter from Germany. The German indologist Günther-Dietz Sontheimer, who went on to become a specialist of Indian studies at Heidelberg University, has been an old and dear friend since his law college days in Pune. In 1958, the young Sontheimer had come to study in the Law College of Poona University, and Pratapsingh and Sontheimer had struck a lifelong friendship.

His love of riding brought him American admirers. In the company of a group of friends, he visited a Texas ranch and, in photos, is seen in a jaunty Stetson hat, ready to take to the saddle. 'I was surprised to see the cowboys,' Pratapsingh recalls. 'They weren't anything like the glamorous characters we saw in the movies. They were ordinary working men, working long, gruelling hours, weather-beaten by their hard labour.' He thoroughly enjoyed his time on the ranch, (he still says the word ranch as 'rayyanch' with a typical Texan twang) and with his riding and showjumping skills won many local hearts.

There were other influences too. 'I was influenced by the Methodist and Presbyterian churches. I was from Goa and, thus, knew about Christian beliefs. I used to go to church with many of my friends, but I told them that I could never become a Christian as I was too attached to my own religion. They would invite me to Sunday school to talk to them, and I would tell them of my own faith. But I emphasized what I have always believed—that God is one, there are many paths to the same divinity.'

He loved meeting his church friends on Sundays. There would always be a sumptuous turkey lunch, a spread of Texan pies and desserts, and warmth and good cheer would flow. Sometimes, he and his friends would visit the city of Corpus Christi to swim in the clear waters of the Gulf of Mexico off Corpus Christi beach. Friends, sport, hard work in class: life was good. In Goa, Raoji was delighted by his son's achievements and how easily he had adjusted to life in America and the son revelled in his father's pride.

Goa was still under Portuguese rule, but in India it was the age of independence. Led by the first PM Jawaharlal Nehru, the newly born idealistic republic of India, suffused with Gandhian ideals of peace and non-violence, struck out for her own place in the international sun. India opted to be non-aligned, would steer clear of power blocs, would stand for the spirit of international co-operation and commitment to peace. The United Nations (UN), established after the agonizing and catastrophic events of World War II, was created to foster international understanding between nations and prevent future wars.

However, as the tall UN building came up in Manhattan, New York, some sections, particularly among American Republicans, began to protest that the UN's activities would not benefit American national interests. In reaction to this, several non-governmental organizations (NGOs) started to campaign for the UN's charter and to push the cause of the UN in American public opinion. Pratapsingh had been a regular visitor to New York while he was studying in Texas and had been noticed by one of the pro-UN campaigners. On the lookout for bright young people to take up the task of spreading the UN's message of international cooperation, Pratapsingh was recruited by the US Committee for United Nations, an organization that he, by now a young man with a modern global vision, eagerly joined. He worked in New York for a little over a year. Later, he also worked for a few months with The Walt Disney Company.

However, the pull of his home was strong, and he soon decided it was time to come back to his family and to the new nation that had been born. When he decided to return, his boss thought he was being a fool to go back to India when he had a bright future in the US. But he was determined to return.

Liberation!

Pratapsingh's decision to return home coincided with an epochal turning point for Goa: the 1961 Liberation of Goa. After India gained her independence in 1947, freedom fighters in Goa too had begun to yearn for independence from Portuguese colonial rule and the thirst for freedom began to grow strong. Goans had been increasingly coming under the influence of the powerful speeches and writings of figures like Francisco Luis Gomes who, in the nineteenth century, argued for India's freedom and wrote about the impact of Portuguese colonial rule on Goa's economy, and writers like Luís de Menezes Bragança, co-founder of the first Portuguese language daily in Goa *OHeraldo*, who wrote hard hitting pieces in the journal *Pracasha*, calling for freedom and Goan self-determination. Goans were also influenced by articles published in crusading newspapers like *The Hindu* and *Bharat*. But the then dictatorial ruler of Portugal António de Oliveira Salazar (who ruled Portugal from 1932 to 1968) refused to relinquish repressive control over Goa. Salazar dubbed Goa as '*Provincia de ultramar*' or an overseas province of Portugal, thus part of Portugal and not India. Groups of freedom fighters kept up protests in the 1920s and 1930s. These grew more powerful in the 1940s as India inched towards freedom.

In 1928, Goan thinker and activist, the Sorbonne-educated Dr Tristão de Bragança Cunha, today hailed as the father of Goan nationalism, formed the Goa Congress Committee, which linked up with the INC at its All-India Congress Committee (AICC) Calcutta session in 1928. Subsequently, Dr Cunha shifted his base to Bombay, met Congress leaders in 1938 and affiliated the Goa Congress to the INC. After Independence, however, the Congress broke off ties with the Goa Congress.

Throughout the 1930s, 1940s and 1950s, groups of protestors held meetings and protests in Bombay and Goa, with many Maharashtra freedom fighters, particularly, the Socialists actively taking up the Goan cause. On 18 June 1946, at 4.00 p.m., socialist leader Ram Manohar Lohia defied government orders and arrived to address a public meeting and start a satyagraha in Margao with another Goan freedom fighter, Dr Julião Menezes from Assolna. This meeting sparked a civil disobedience movement in many parts of Goa, and today, 18 June is commemorated as Goa Revolution Day in the Goa freedom struggle. In modern Panaji, there is an 18th June Road. The Portuguese cracked down sternly on the freedom protesters, and scores, including Lohia and Menezes, were arrested. Over the years, Goan freedom fighters like Dr T.B. Cunha, José Inácio Candido de Loyola or 'Franchu Loyola', Purushottam Kakodkar, Laxmikant Bhembre and others were deported to Portugal and lodged in the Peniche fortress prison.

Free speech and dissent were strictly muzzled in Goa. 'You had to shout Viva Salazar, Viva Portugal and Viva Goa,' recalls Pratapsingh. 'If you shouted "Jai Hind", you were caught, your head was shaved and you were put behind bars for four or five days.' By the 1950s, almost all Goans wanted independence except perhaps some pockets in the south that remained loyal to the Portuguese.

Freedom was in the air. After Independence, Nehru in his writings repeatedly mentioned that a foreign possession in free India was unacceptable and could not be tolerated. Matters came to a head when, in 1954, a renowned Goa surgeon P.D. Gaitonde, who had nothing to do with politics, innocently cried out *'Eu protesto'* (I protest) at a party when another guest asserted that Goa was part of Portugal. The Portuguese authorities immediately swooped down on the distinguished Gaitonde, and he was arrested, jailed and exiled. Gaitonde's arrest sparked outrage across Goa. Many Goan expatriates and sympathizers for Goa's freedom launched a non-violent agitation. Big satyagrahas were launched in 1954 and 1955, and the Government of India officially protested about denial of free speech to Salazar's repressive regime.

But Nehru would not be pushed to act in a hurry against Portugal, now a NATO (North Atlantic Treaty Organization) member and part of the post-World War II Western alliance of nations. This was the reason why the Congress had, in later years, disaffiliated the Goa Congress from the Congress—because Nehru did not want to be seen fomenting trouble against Portugal. It was in 1955, when the Government of India imposed an economic blockade on Goa to pressurize the Portuguese to leave, that the endgame began.

On 17 December 1961, India launched Operation Vijay. Units of the Indian Army, Air Force and Navy were mobilized. Lieutenant General J.N. Chaudhuri was in overall command with Major General K.P. Candeth (later to become the first military governor of liberated Goa), leading the Infantry division of Indian troops as they entered Goa. India launched a three-pronged armed attack, one on Panjim, the other from the east, and another along the south in Canacona and Margao. The Indian Air Force took to the skies. Fighter aircraft bombarded the Dabolim airport runway and a wireless station in Bambolim. The Navy played its part and enforced a naval blockade.

The Portuguese forces fought back, but within 24 hours, the Portuguese *Estado da India* (Portugal's state of India) fell. Recognizing the futility of attempting to fight the much-larger Indian Army, on 19 December, the Portuguese Governor General of Goa, Manuel António Vassalo e Silva, surrendered at a formal ceremony, bringing an end to 451 years of Portuguese rule. Goa became part of India. Prime Minister Jawaharlal Nehru and his defence minister V.K. Krishna Menon did come in for some international criticism because of the use of force in Goa by peace-loving non-violent India, and the timing of the 1961 action was seen to coincide with general election due in 1962. Yet for generations of Goans, the desire for independence had run deep, as deep as the determination of the Rane warriors who had fought so hard for their homelands in Sattari.

What were Pratapsingh's first thoughts when liberation came? He recalls that he was worried, confused, insecure and anxious. 'I did not know what the future would be. I wrote to my father asking what to do. His first advice was that I should surrender my passport.' He had travelled abroad on a Portuguese passport, as a Portuguese citizen. In his early life when he had travelled to Pune for studies or to any other part of India, he always had to show his *billet idendidad*—or a small identity card with a photo as a citizen of Portuguese Goa. But now, studying in an American university, when he received his new passport, for the first time, Pratapsingh Rane became a citizen of India.

Back Home to Freedom and Love

In 1965, aged 26, Pratapsingh returned to India. 'I could have stayed on in America if I had wanted to, but I did not want to do that. The call of my homeland was strong. I felt a duty to my father. While I was in America, many people, even Portuguese officials, would taunt my father, saying your son has gone off to the US, he will never come back. I wanted to prove these prophecies wrong.'

He came back to a warm homecoming. Raoji and Manoramabai were delighted to have their son home. His older siblings were settled and married by now. Hiradevi had married an army officer, Colonel Hanumant Rao Jagtap. His second sister Sarladevi married into the Chowgule family. Older brother Satroji had joined the army and second brother Fatehsingh had joined a business in Bombay. His parents hoped that Pratapsingh would settle down soon too and were overjoyed when he went on assignment to Telco in Jamshedpur.

And this is where my story, the story of Vijayadevi Ghorpade of Sandur in Karnataka, meets the story of Pratapsingh Rane and the love story of Vijaya and Pratap begins.

I was born on 5 February 1947, in the Sandur House in Bangalore. I was born into the princely family of Sandur, a peaceful, exquisitely beautiful place in Karnataka. It was once surrounded by luxuriant forests and cool, wooded, mist-wreathed hills, and is situated in a deep ancient valley, the Sandur Valley. The valley forms a natural fortress. When Mahatma Gandhi visited Sandur in the early 1930s, he called it an oasis. My family, like Pratapsingh's, is also descended from Maratha warriors, and one of my ancestors from the eighteenth century, Murari Rao, was a general in the Maratha army and said to be a particularly brave leader and skilful horseman. Sandur is close to Hampi, seat of the great Vijayanagar Empire that flourished from the fourteenth to sixteenth centuries.

My parents lived in the Shiv Vilas Palace, our ancestral home, which, today, is a heritage hotel. My mother was Rani Sushiladevi Ghorpade and my father was Raja Srimant Yeshwantrao Hindurrao Ghorpade, the last raja of Sandur. I was one of seven children with four older brothers, an older sister and a younger brother.

The most vivid and awe-inspiring presence in my early years was my mother, Sushiladevi. She was an extraordinary trailblazer. She was born into a Shitole family from Gwalior, and as mentioned before, by serendipitous circumstance, had known my mother-in-law Manoramabai when the latter used to visit Gwalior to meet Gajra Raje. In fact, Manaoramabai used to play with my mother, who was much younger than her.

My mother was a formidable woman. She was sophisticated and extroverted with a reformist bent of mind and a powerful personality. She used to tell me, 'Never say the words "I-don't-have-this" and "I-don't-have-that". Say instead, "I will get it". If you have that determination to get what you want, you will develop the mental capacity to find the resources you need.'

My father, Yeshwantrao Ghorpade, was the adoptive heir of the Sandur Maharaja, Venkata Rao III. Venkata Rao had no sons and it was the British Resident in Sandur, who, after interviewing several candidates from the extended Ghorpade family of *jagirdars*, chose my father, who was very well educated, as the next Sandur ruler after Venkata Rao. As heir apparent, my father was sent to learn statecraft and administrative practices from the bigger and well-governed princely states of Baroda, Mysore and Trivandrum. My father was a keen wildlife conservationist, and later, my eldest brother too came to share his enthusiasm for the natural world. My father was also a committed social and religious reformer who did away with many caste taboos prevalent in the state. Upon his accession, my father, conscious that Venkata Rao's biological daughter must be well looked after when she married, gave away much of the Sandur inheritance to her. He was, thus, forced to build up Sandur virtually from scratch, with my mother by his side to help. My mother, hailing as she did from a Gwalior family, was used to a very affluent and opulent life. Sandur, by contrast, was much smaller, and with my father having given most of his wealth away, circumstances were more straitened than in Gwalior. She was forced to make adjustments very young. When they got married, my mother was only 14 and my father was 20.

The young Sandur couple—both open-minded reformers—got on with the task of rebuilding Sandur, with the guidance of some trusted advisers like the lawyer M.C. Setalvad. Since the earth around Sandur was rich in ores, my father sought mining licenses from then PM Nehru. Nehru, delighted that a young 'royal' was adopting modern industry, immediately granted a 100-year mining lease to my father.

My mother played her part. It was she who, on behalf of the

principality of Sandur, negotiated with Sardar Vallabhbhai Patel on the terms by which the principality would merge with the Indian union. 'We are prepared to merge with India, but what will you give me in return for taking everything from us?' she famously asked Sardar Patel. Sushiladevi was one of the last ruling queens in the subcontinent and reigned as queen consort of Sandur until 1947. Thereafter, my parents built up the mining industry in Sandur and founded The Sandur Manganese & Iron Ores Limited. My mother was director of the company for a few years. She was also a member of the governing council of the Sandur state and in that capacity piloted many reforms.

My progressive-minded parents, who opposed practices that smacked of caste discrimination or social inequalities, prized education above all. All of us were sent to schools and universities. My older brother Murarirao Yeshwantrao (M.Y.) Ghorpade—who would go on to become finance minister of Karnataka—completed his Tripos in Economics from Cambridge University in 1952. I was sent to Good Shepherd Convent school in Bangalore, then to college at Sophia College Bombay. I could not adjust too well to life in Bombay and returned to Bangalore to complete my bachelor's in History from Mount Carmel College. My mother was passionate about the study of History. She authored her memoirs, written in flowing, long-hand Marathi in her stylish handwriting, a book not only about her own life but also about the history of Sandur.

I remember my mother as always full of life and energy, carrying herself with grace and dignity with beautiful bright eyes and a charming smile. She loved people and my parents hosted elegant parties in Bombay and Bangalore for their large circle of friends. Among them was Sumant Moolgaokar, then chief executive of Telco, who mentioned to my mother that since she had a beautiful daughter of marriageable age, he knew of a handsome and bright America-returned young man, who was in Telco in Jamshedpur, who could be a suitable match.

Brought up as I was by my forward-thinking mother, I had my own revolutionary ideas about my future. I had already made it very clear that I would only marry an educated man, preferably Western-educated, and would not accept any union that would push me backwards into stifling conservatism. I was, and still am, of an independent spirit and had absolutely no wish for a marriage where my life would be governed by suffocating and soul-destroying traditionalism. I had emphatically refused to be 'shown' around to eligible men from the right families. Some senior family members like the then Maharaja of Kolhapur despaired of this and said to my father: '*Appasaheb*, at this rate your daughter will never get married.' My mother would clutch her forehead in exasperation at my attitude.

Even before the marriage proposal arrived, my family had other associations with the Ranes. My brother Ranjitsingh Ghorpade studied with Fatehsingh Rane at the College of Agriculture in Poona. My other brother Shivrao Yeshwantrao Ghorpade worked with Pratap when he was briefly in Telco. Recalls Shivrao Ghorpade, today a sprightly 84-year-old and one of Karnataka's leading industrialists, 'We used to have a good time together in Jamshedpur.'

Pratapsingh and I first met in Bombay at his older sister's house, where we were formally introduced. We warmed to each other at once, drawn together by our common values of a modernist approach to tradition. I was very clear about my expectations and told Pratap: if I am expected to remain secluded within the confines of the home, or never come out or be pushed into backward looking practices, or be ordered indoors if visitors come, then let us end it here, say goodbye and part as friends. Either we grow together, or we don't. Fortunately for us both, he was completely in tune with my views.

Pratapsingh was dead against blind beliefs and traditionalism for its own sake. When his sister Sarladevi Chowgule brought the formal marriage proposal to my mother, my mother suggested matching our horoscopes. Immediately my future sister-in-law said, 'Please don't even mention the word horoscope to my brother, because that will be the end of this proposal.' In those days, in tradition-bound princely families, we must have been the rare exception to get married without any idea of whether our stars were favourable or if our horoscopes would bring good luck! However, even without matching our horoscopes, we have had a long and successful marriage.

We hit it off almost at the first meeting. He asked me to come out for a movie, and we went to the Metro theatre to watch the then hit movie, *The Chastity Belt*. After our first meeting, we spent many happy hours watching movies and going out to restaurants. He mentioned that his home in Goa was very old, and I would be going into a traditional rural set up. I did not mind this, as long as we shared the same values: I was a modern, determined and educated woman and expected that my husband would encourage me to play a public part in our marriage. Pratapsingh was with me all the way in my outlook. After getting married, I often did not cover my head with my sari *pallu* as was the custom. Pratap never objected, and I daresay that I set quite a trend. Several women followed my example and stopped covering their heads. We women would walk upright, work hard, and even in our saris, we would stride.

Pratapsingh and I were married in traditional style on 4 December 1969 in my ancestral home, the Shiv Vilas Palace in Sandur. I was 21 and he was 30.

The ceremonies were elaborate and lasted for four days, 2–6 December. They were four glittering days: a Maratha wedding in full glory. The palace was aglow with diyas, marigolds and roses. We started with the *choora* ceremony, then the *haldi* ritual when turmeric paste lathered on *paan* leaves is gently applied on the feet, shoulders and hands of the bride and groom. Then there was a *devak* puja before the wedding, followed by a *mangal snan*. At the mandap, we had the *antar path*, the *varmala* or exchange of garlands, then the *kanyadaan* and, lastly, his sister stepped forward to tie the *mangalsutra* around my neck. I became Mrs Pratapsingh Rane. I wore a bright yellow sari with gold embroidery, accessorized with our ancestral jewellery. All brides are beautiful, and by all accounts, I was too!

The village folk took out a grand procession, and we travelled in an open chariot to the temple as well as to the iron ore and manganese mines owned by my family. There was another puja at the mines for all the workers.

Apa Pandu Majik, who passed away at the splendid age of 105, was one of the tenant farmers on the Ranes' Sattari estate. Wiry and slightly built, he used to often accompany Pratapsingh on his *shikar* trips. Majik was one of the farming folk brought by buses to our wedding and remembered it vividly. He recalled: 'Khashe's [in Sattari, Pratapsingh is known as *khashe* or landlord] older brother came to the Keri well and invited us all for the wedding. We all packed into buses and travelled to the wedding. We went to Hospet and saw the Tungabhadra Dam. The wedding itself was a huge affair; there were so many people from many different parts. The Sandur palace was very grand. We were very well taken care of; we had comfortable quarters, excellent food and even a barber to ourselves to ensure we were well shaved and groomed!'

Yet, there was a poignant tinge to the ceremonies. Pratapsingh's beloved father Raoji, always so proud of his children, a generous benevolent presence to all in Sattari, had passed away a year earlier in 1968. Although she did not show it, I know Raoji's absence at our wedding grieved Manoramabai, who was there alone, the self-contained, bespectacled matriarch in her spotless cream-white sari.

One Door Closes, Another Opens

Three years before Raoji's passing, another sad event had occurred. This incident transformed Pratap's life and completely altered the course of his future. Sometimes a road that looks well mapped out abruptly changes course and runs headlong in uncharted directions. In Pratap's case, the smooth factory floors of Telco, Jamshedpur, gave way suddenly to the rural landscapes of his native Sattari.

In 1965, Pratapsingh's younger brother Udaysingh, the brother who had been given charge of all the family properties and lands in Sattari, contracted infectious hepatitis. 'I was in Jamshedpur at the time, and getting ready to move to Poona as the Tatas were about to set up there. I went to my sister's house in Bombay. She said that our brother was so ill that he should be brought to Bombay for treatment. I rushed to Goa. There were only a few doctors from the Portuguese days still there and the medical treatment available was not the best,' Pratap recalls. Within a few days, the slender and good-looking Udaysingh, a young man in the prime of life and the apple of his father's eye, died. It was a tragic and untimely death.

In Pratapsingh's words, 'My father broke down completely. In fact, I have never seen him so broken down. My youngest brother, who was supposed to look after all the family's lands and properties in Sattari, was gone. I did not know how to console my grief-stricken father. So I stayed in Goa.'

A new life began for Pratapsingh. Educated in Poona and the US and working with the Tatas, where would life ordinarily have led him? Surely living a cushy life, up the corporate ladder in Bombay or Poona, a talented yet unknown senior executive in the wheel of industrializing 1960s India. But no, it did not turn out that way.

Pratapsingh returned to Goa and took up Udaysingh's responsibilities—handling all the estates, lands and farms of the Ranes. Far away from the gleaming Tata factory or the bright lights of Bombay, he took his place, as generations of his ancestors had done before him, as a bhatkar in rural Sattari. When Raoji Rane passed away, Pratapsingh stepped forward as the new bhatkar in Raoji's place. Was it a hard choice? 'I gave my word to my father.

After my brother's death, my father entrusted these vast lands in north Goa to me. I had to do my duty to my father and to my homeland,' he says.

Idealistic and dutiful, he came home to Goa, returning to a relationship with his homeland, which has defined his life. For the Goan is, above all, a man of his village. The place where he was born with its acacia-scented air, its forests, orchards and waters, with egrets picking through the fields and mangoes and jackfruit hanging heavy in the trees; his homeland with its shrines and village squares, its unique food, drink and music: this native land is where the Goan's soul lives and where his spirit finds solace. Turning away from a corporate life with the Tatas was no great loss for Pratapsingh, although his new life in Sattari did bring its own challenges. But in life, when one door closes, another inevitably opens.

A new life and its challenges awaited me too. After my marriage into the Rane family, it was to the ancestral home in Sanquelim that I came to live. Upon my arrival, I set about putting things in order in the huge, unwieldy home, seeing to it that certain changes were made in daily schedules, the rooms were re-designed for more modern amenities and visitors were made as comfortable as possible. With only a few hours of electricity, there was no piped water. Yet I had been well trained for this job by my mother. 'No daughter is ever as comfortable in her husband's home as she has been in her father's', she had told me, 'but it's up to you to create and build your home as you would like it to be.'

The training I had received from my mother contained many stern lessons: she had drilled into me that nothing comes to you on a platter, it's up to you to build it up. There is a Marathi phrase, *Kondyacha Manda*—from the chaff you must create the sweet—and I took up creating a life for myself in Sanquelim as a challenge. I love challenging myself and pushing myself hard, and I am a good organizer. I worked hard and managed things, and soon grew adept at my organizational tasks. I have always liked to keep a well-maintained and efficiently run home, and I like to present a well-laid table at mealtimes. In difficult conditions, with erratic electricity and little water supply, I got on with the task at hand. Goans tend to be a little introverted, even insular, and find it difficult to accept new people in the family or village. By contrast, I love making new friends, and I threw myself into my new life with gusto. I found a friend in Anju Timblo, who came to Goa a couple of years after me, after her marriage to one of Goa's foremost industrialists, Audhut Timblo.

For his part, Pratapsingh would take off every day in his left-hand drive Willys Jeep, trundling over fields and dirt tracks to check on people in the village and make rounds among his tenants. If anybody fell sick, he would simply put them in his Jeep and race off to the nearest clinic or hospital. He travelled tirelessly across Sattari, sometimes gunning his Jeep up steep hills where no road existed, acquainting himself with the people and their problems. He became a familiar figure: the US-returned son of Raoji Rane, driving about in his Willys Jeep, visiting this field here, that hutment there. In many places, he was able to bring real change: he was a passionate agriculturalist and helped start agricultural projects. He worked to create irrigation schemes and small schools. As he traversed across the taluka, his bonds with the people grew ever more intimate.

He created his first piece of public infrastructure at this time. In Sattari, surrounded by thick cashew and coconut forests, nestles the village of Keri in the foothills of the Ghats. The villagers here were terribly short on water, as the village, situated as it was in the far interiors, reachable only through jungle tracks, had no access to potable water. Pratapsingh took it upon himself to bring water to Keri and to improve the Keri well. Until now, the well had produced only a thin trickle of water. Now, Pratapsingh announced that he would enhance the well's capacity: he asked that one man and one woman from every homestead pitch in. They all eagerly came forward.

Work began in full swing as the well was deepened and broadened, and fresh water began to bubble out and flood into the well. Keri village whooped in joy. Whereas earlier they had had to toil to the faraway river with vessels of water, here was life-giving water gushing out in their own village. They carved a date on the well. It was Pratapsingh's well, for which their khashe had rolled up his sleeves and dug along with them, working even through hot afternoons.

The newly minted Sanquelim bhatkar, who was working so hard for his people, now caught the attention of another unusual person. This was someone who Pratapsingh had so far never met. But soon, his life in Goa would change forever.

TWO

STEPPING INTO PUBLIC LIFE: 1969-1977

'I had no background in politics. I was in a corporate job. I came to Goa to look after my ancestral lands. I became a politician by chance.'

Two years after Liberation, the UT of Goa held its first election on 9 December 1963. There was an outpouring of public enthusiasm and excitement. The first ever democratic elections in Goa! National self-determination was in the air. After centuries of repressive rule, a new form of government arrived, full of people's hopes. Democracy had come to Goa.

Everyone had a vote. Now we—all Goans—could vote for our elected representatives who would run an administration based on the principle of 'for the people, by the people and of the people'. A massive and historic change! I must make a mention here of Roque Santana Joao Fernandes of Velim who had played an active role in the freedom struggle in Goa. Fernandes was one of the many idealistic campaigners down the decades who fought for the rights of Goans. In June 1962, Fernandes launched a satyagraha or hunger strike to demand an elected assembly, and not an assembly of nominated members, in Goa. The demand for an elected assembly was granted when elections were announced for December 1963.

There had been lively campaigning for the polls, with advertisements printed in all newspapers. Flags and buntings fluttered from shops and across streets. Four parties were in the fray: the Maharashtrawadi Gomantak Party (MGP) with the symbol of the lion; the United Goans Party (UGP) with the symbol of the hand; the Congress with the symbol of two bullocks carrying a yoke (the Congress symbol from 1952 to 1969); and another party, Frente Popular, with the symbol of the elephant.

'Goans enthuse over first ever election' ran the banner headline of *The Navhind Times* newspaper, with a second headline: 'Women surpass the men in exercising franchise.' On that hot and humid December day, neatly dressed folk stood patiently in orderly queues to cast their vote in the 427 polling booths across the UT. Heavy polling was recorded at Panaji, Margao, Navelim, Ponda, Mormugao and Quepem. The waters of the Mandovi and Zuari twinkled in the sun, bearing witness to this new chapter in Goa's history.

Campaigning on the platform of the party that had brought freedom to Goa, the Congress had been hoping for a big win. But instead, lo and behold, to widespread shock, another leader and another party emerged victorious. In the 30-member assembly (with 28 seats in Goa and one seat each in Daman and Diu) the local Goa-based MGP won 14 seats, while another local party, the UGP won 12 seats and independents won three. The mighty Congress was wiped out. The party of freedom was able to win just one seat, and that too in Diu and not in Goa. Many Congress candidates even lost their deposits. Jawaharlal Nehru's Congress routed in Goa? Shockwaves rippled across Goa and India.

From Goa's Salt of the Earth

The rise of a lively and participative political culture in Goa can be traced back to 1910, when Portugal became a republic. The monarchy was abolished, and the link between church and government was broken. Religion was separated from the state. As a result, a nascent liberal climate developed in Goa. Goan Hindus, no longer stigmatized because of their religion, were set free to participate in public life and numerous groups and associations sprang up. The First Republic of Portugal, however, was short-lived and was overthrown in a bloodless military coup in 1926. In 1932, Antonio de Oliveira Salazar established his dictatorial rule in Portugal. Salazar ruthlessly centralized all power and cracked down on citizen's liberties. As Salazar's biographer Tom Gallagher writes, with Salazar's rise to power, 'The priorities and judgement of one man would come to determine the fate of Portugal and the direction it would take.'[1]

However, in the 16 years of the First Republic in Portugal, Goans tasted some measure of freedom. A taste for politics began among the Goans, although following the repression unleashed by Salazar, public activity was mostly driven underground. Many politically active Goans developed links with the Congress in India. Although these links were snapped after India gained Independence in 1947, yet the stature of the Congress as the party which had won freedom in India was unsurpassed.

After the 1961 Liberation, it was the Congress that was seen as the dominant party in Goa. The Congress was the party of freedom fighters, had fought for Goa's right of self-determination; many Congress leaders had acquired a great deal of prestige because of their dogged struggles and suffering and the long jail terms they endured in Peniche prison in Portugal fighting Salazar's dictatorial rule. Across all India in those days, Nehru's Congress had an overpowering presence, as it did in Goa.

But as the momentum built towards the first election of 1963, the Congress began to lose out. Two undercurrents that had always existed in Goa began to grow stronger—divisions on the basis of religion and division on the basis of caste. This was reflected in the two parties that contested the 1963 polls in addition to the

---

[1] Gallagher, Tom, *Salazar: The Dictator Who Refused to Die*, Hurst & Company, London, 2022, p. 54.

Congress—the MGP (the party largely of non-elite Hindus) and the UGP (the party of mostly non-elite Catholics).

The Congress in Goa began increasingly to be perceived as disconnected from the masses: it came to be seen as dominated by well-educated Goans from both Catholic and Hindu communities. The Congress was perceived to be dominated particularly by the Gaud Saraswat Brahmin community. It, thus, acquired a 'Brahmin' tag in the post-Liberation period. For example, one of the Goan freedom fighters who had been deported and jailed was Purushottam Kakodkar, father of the eminent nuclear physicist Dr Anil Kakodkar. After Liberation, he became leader of the Goa Congress and went on to become a Congress Member of Parliament (MP) in the Lok Sabha and Rajya Sabha. Kakodkar was a Saraswat Brahmin, as were others associated with the Congress in the post-Liberation period like Vaikunthrao Dempo, younger brother of the leading light of Goan industry Vasantrao S. Dempo, founder of the Dempo business group. The royal scion Raghuraj Deshprabhu known as 'Bhausaheb Visconde de Pernem,' the only Hindu viscount in Goa, came from a similar background. Laxmikant Bhembre, another freedom fighter who had been lodged in Peniche prison, was also from a Brahmin background.

'There was a big caste separation in Goa in those days,' recalls Pratapsingh. 'The Saraswats got a bad name because there was a perception that they exploited uneducated people. Kakodkar was a freedom fighter and a very nice person, but he could not get enough support among the common man because of the way the Congress was initially perceived.'

Educated Catholic families also joined the Congress, thus giving the Congress in Goa a 'high-class, upper-caste' profile. In spite of the long struggle of Congress leaders, it was whispered at the time that the Congress was dominated by the upper echelons. In the Congress, among the 28 tickets for the first assembly polls, the majority went to those from the educated and well-established class of Goans.

On the other hand, the MGP was a very different force. It began as a pro-Maharashtra party, campaigning for the merger of Goa with Maharashtra. It was also a people's party, a party of the Goan working class, as against the party of the educated elite that was the Congress.

There are different versions as to how the MGP came to be formed. Some say it was started by a group of Marathi-speaking Goans in Mapusa. But another, more widely held version is that the MGP was first begun in Poona by a group of Maharashtrian politicians who were then in the anti-Congress opposition in Maharashtra. These were well known Maharashtra socialists: Narayan Ganesh (N.G.) Gore, who had participated in satyagrahas for Goa's freedom held on the Maharashtra-Goa border; Shreedhar Mahadev (S.M.) Joshi; trade unionist Peter Augustus Alvares (the first MP from the North Goa or Panaji seat); and barrister Nath Bapu Pai, a committed socialist, regarded as one of India's greatest parliamentarians in the 1950s and 1960s.

The party was founded with an aim to mount a challenge to the Congress, although the merger demand was also supported by some Maharashtra Congressmen. 'The MGP had always been encouraged by some Maharashtra politicians like Yashwantrao Balwantrao (Y.B.) Chavan as a pro-Maharashtra party to try and swallow up Goa and absorb it into Maharashtra,' says Pratapsingh. 'After all, Goa is like the southern tip of the big Maharashtra state. But this was not to the liking of many Goans.'

After 1956, across India, linguistic and regional identity issues had come to the fore as a result of the States Reorganisation Act, 1956, and the redrawing of state boundaries along linguistic lines. In 1960, the colonial Bombay state was dissolved and split into two states along linguistic lines, with the Gujarati-speaking areas becoming the state of Gujarat and Marathi-speaking areas becoming the state of Maharashtra. With sizable Marathi-speaking communities in Goa, Maharashtra leaders were hopeful that linguistic commonality with Goa would draw it into Maharashtra. Sentiments of a merger between Goa and Maharashtra had existed since the 1940s, mostly voiced at *sahitya sammelans* and among writers and intellectuals. The MGP now took it up as an emotive issue to challenge the Congress.

The MGP was drawn from Goa's salt of the earth and was a party that championed the cause of Goa's poor and downtrodden, those who were labouring under the oppression of both wealthy Catholics and Hindus. The banner of merger with Maharashtra was taken up largely on the grounds that such a union would liberate Goa's working folk from the elite oppression. The working folk, fishermen, farmers, *mundkars* (tenant farmers) and small shop owners lived lives that were socially distant from the wealthy, educated bhatkars living in their spacious homes with multiple courtyards or affluent Catholics in their gracious mansions. Some mundkars were trapped in exploitative relationships with bhatkars. They lived in huts and cottages on the landlord's land and eked out a modest living in the underdeveloped Goa of the first half of the twentieth century. There was little electricity or running water, there was no industry except mining and the Portuguese had not built mass-quality schools. The gap between the haves and have-nots in Goa was large.

Into this gap strode the larger-than-life MGP leader who had felled the mighty Congress in the 1963 elections—Dayanand Balkrishna (D.B.) Bandodkar or Bhausaheb, as he was widely called.

Sturdy, physically robust and ruddy complexioned, with a mop of springy hair, Bandodkar was a quintessential man of the people. He hailed from the community known as the Gomantak Maratha Samaj within the larger 'Bahujan Samaj' in Goa. (In Goa, non-brahmin communities are referred to as the Bahujan Samaj.)

Bandodkar was born into a family of modest means in a village in Pernem. But in Portuguese times, he had secured an iron ore license and by the time of Liberation had become a wealthy mine owner. The Portuguese believed that all the earth's wealth that lay under the ground belonged to the state. So, an individual could obtain a manifest or lease or an *aforamento* from the government and make a fortune from mining ore and selling it for export. Mineral-rich Goa has been one of India's top iron ore exporting states. After World War II, as Japan and West Germany sought to rebuild after the devastation of the War, demand for iron ore soared and as the Portuguese colonial state raced to cash in on the high demand for iron ore, mineral production in Goa began to peak. Goa's economy was energized. The 1950s was the decade of Goa's mining boom—the Portuguese handed out mining leases to people giving them proprietary rights over land for an unlimited period. With mining lease in hand, paupers became millionaires overnight, extracting precious iron ore, bauxite and manganese. By acquiring a mining lease, the self-made, up-by-his-bootstraps Bandodkar made himself a fortune.

This made him an ideal leader for the working class-oriented MGP: he was a non-Brahmin but also a wealthy mine owner—a rarity in Goa. Being a person of means, he could also raise resources for the party.

It was said that Bandodkar had fought for his rights against the mestizos (those of mixed Portuguese and Goan ancestry), known to be an influential community. That Bandodkar had held his ground against the powerful mestizos added to his heroic aura. He had a robust and genial manner and the capacity to instantly win hearts. Even though Bandodkar championed the cause of Goa merging with Maharashtra, yet he was rooted in Goa's soil, an enthusiast of shooting and shikar, a friend of the labouring poor, with deep connections among villages and communities, now seen seated with fisherfolk near the sea, now listening to farmers woes deep in the forested hinterland.

The MGP became a party primarily of poor Marathi-speaking migrants from Maharashtra who were settled in Goa and drew its cadres from Goa's less privileged. Bandodkar advocated the merger between Goa and Maharashtra on the grounds that such a merger would enable labouring people to escape the social inequalities of Goa. While some MGP leaders like the fiery P.P. Shirodkar went to the extent of firing up Goan crowds by trenchant speeches against Brahmins, Bandodkar himself always remained an inclusive figure and never spoke against any community. But he unleashed the stirring cry, '*Kasel tyachi zameen, rahel tyache ghar*'—land to the tiller and a home to the mundkar. The MGP campaigned for upliftment of the common folk with the promise of land tenure, right to own homes and the promise to give mass educational facilities to Goa's poor. *Kasel tyachi zameen! Rahel tyache ghar!*

There are some remarkable stories on how Bandodkar set about selecting candidates for the first election of 1963. Kashinath Shetgaonkar, a poor farmer in the Pernem constituency, was once ploughing his fields, toiling under the midday sun. Shetgaonkar was a sinewy villager, often clad only in his loincloth, his skin sunburnt by long hours of labour. Suddenly, Shetgaonkar heard a commotion. He saw a jeep standing at the edge of his field. People were milling around it and calling out to him. 'Kashinath,' his neighbours shouted, 'Come on, they want you in Panjim.' Shetgaonkar was bundled into the jeep to Panaji. There, in a small party office, he was embraced by Bandodkar who declared, 'Kashinath Shetgaonkar, you are my MGP candidate for Pernem.' Off went the weather-beaten farmer on his campaign, often travelling barefoot, wearing his crumpled clothes. The election results were spectacular: the dishevelled farmer Kashinath Shetgaonkar thundered to a mighty win, defeating none other than the Congress's Vaikunthrao Dempo. Ah democracy, you great leveller.

It was a similar story in the constituency of Mandrem. The dhoti-clad Vijay Kamulkar lived in Mandrem and ran a small tea shop. Located outside a temple, Kamulkar supplied tea to devotees from his tiny kettle. He too was given an MGP ticket and roared to a big win, vanquishing his Congress rival. Well-heeled, upper-class candidates were driven to the wall, as the farmers and working men of the MGP emerged dominant. Bandodkar had created a kind of social and political revolution, by bringing all communities into Goa's public life. In this social churning during the 1963 polls, the Congress drew a blank.

Yet no one had given the MGP a chance in 1963. It was universally predicted that the Congress, with its high-profile freedom fighters, enjoying the prestige of being the party that had led the struggle for liberation, would sweep. Perhaps for this reason, Bandodkar had not even contested the elections. It was only after the elections that another MGP candidate, Vasant Velingkar, who had won from Marcaim, resigned, and Bandodkar contested in his place, winning easily.

On 20 December 1963, D.B. Bandodkar was sworn in as Goa's first CM. The MGP would go on to win the next three successive elections in Goa, led by Bandodkar in 1967 and 1972 and, thereafter, by his daughter Shashikala Kakodkar in 1977. Bandodkar remained a grassroots politician all his life, building the MGP's presence in Goa's villages and hamlets, an extremely generous, straight-talking man, with rustic manners but inborn grace.

Goa was still a UT, and important administrative power still rested with the Lieutenant Governor. Yet, the significance of the ascent of Bhausaheb Bandodkar as Goa's plebeian CM was enormous. It was as if the promise of Liberation and democracy had been kept, a son of the soil, a common man, with little education beyond the first few standards of schooling, now occupied the seat where colonial grandees once sat in their imperial grandeur.

As the fresh winds of democracy blew into Goa like a sea breeze, another party—the UGP—became part of the democratic action. While the MGP won the 1963 polls, the UGP came in second and became the Opposition party. Its leader Dr João Hugo

Eduardo de Sequeira, known as 'Jack' de Sequeira and sometimes 'JakSiker', became Goa's first LoP.

Highly educated, with a compelling personality, Dr de Sequeira, with his luxuriant beard and shining eyes, possessed a sharp intellect and powerful oratorical abilities. 'Once I used to play tennis, now I am playing politics...I like it better,' de Sequeira once famously declared. He was a very popular leader, almost a cult figure, winning repeatedly from his constituency, Santa Cruz. He hailed from a Catholic family which owned successful businesses. Just as Bandodkar, being a mine owner, could marshal his wealth for the MGP, so also Dr de Sequeira, with his considerable assets was able to bolster the UGP.

Both the MGP and the UGP were separated chiefly by their differing stances on Goa's relationship with Maharashtra. The MGP advocated the cause of the Marathi language in Goa and wanted Goa to merge with Maharashtra. The Catholic-dominated UGP campaigned on an altogether different plank of a separate and distinct identity for Goa and stood against the principle of merger.

Whether or not Goa should merge with Maharashtra would be the single most potent issue in the years ahead.

Opinion Poll Reaffirms Goan Identity

After storming to power, Bandodkar and the MGP focussed so much attention on merger with Maharashtra and on the politics of identity that administration was somewhat neglected. At this time, there were worries that Goa, having already missed the first two Five-Year Plans of 1951 and 1956, was not catching up fast enough with the rest of India on development because of Bandodkar's focus on Marathi language and merger with Maharashtra. Work on Goa's roads, power supply perhaps did not take off as speedily as it should have. This orientation changed dramatically in Pratapsingh Rane's tenure, when he pulled away from the politics of identity, and politics in general, and launched an all-out developmental leap forward on all fronts. In the first Bandodkar government, such a push was missing.

Bandodkar's ambition of a merger of Goa with Maharashtra and the notion of a separate Goan identity soon became a conflicted issue. As Bandodkar and the MGP stepped up their enthusiasm for the merger, de Sequeira and the Opposition became equally determined to campaign against the merger and demand that Goa be allowed to have her own separate identity as well as language. Dr de Sequeira launched a widespread movement against the merger. Campaigning against Goa's merger with Maharashtra and demanding a Goa status referendum, de Sequeira addressed over a thousand public meetings, crying out his slogan, 'Goa will not become the backyard of Maharashtra.' He called out to 'Niz-Goans' (real Goans) not to support merger with Maharashtra.

Dr de Sequeira took several delegations to Delhi, first to PM Nehru and, after his death in 1964, to Lal Bahadur Shastri. He even went to an AICC session in Bangalore to meet Shastri and present his demand for a referendum on the question of merger. Shastri initially suggested a mid-term poll to sort out the issue. For their part, Bandodkar and the MGP agreed to a referendum, but wanted to hold it in the assembly where they had a majority. However, de Sequeira rejected the idea of holding a referendum in the assembly and kept insisting on a public referendum to be held by secret ballot. After Nehru's death, then Defence Minister Y.B. Chavan, an ardent mergerist, was able to pressurize PM Shastri about merger more strongly than he could Nehru. But the anti-merger cause was being taken forward strongly, not only by de Sequeira, but also by the Goa Congress leader Purushottam Kakodkar, who joined forces with de Sequeira on the Goa referendum issue. Kakodkar recalled in an interview that he journeyed to Delhi to meet Congress leaders and press on them that what Goa needed was not another election or mid-term poll but a referendum on this one single issue of merger.

The merger issue became heated. Shastri had been of the belief that a mid-term poll should be held to decide on the issue, and some others in the Congress like Morarji Desai, former CM of the Bombay state, were of the same view. However, the 1965 India–Pakistan war broke out; Shastri journeyed to Tashkent for peace talks where, on 11 January 1966, he died. Indira Gandhi was sworn in as PM on 24 January 1966. But she was not inclined towards a mid-term poll.

Yet, by now, the Congress leadership in Delhi had become convinced that the issue of Goa's merger with Maharashtra had to be sorted out given the continuing resolutions and statements being moved by the MGP in the Goa Assembly and the fierce opposition to the merger being mounted by the UGP.

Given the pressures from a relentless Opposition, de Sequeira's and Kakodkar's arguments as well as Indira Gandhi's own inclinations against an election, the Congress Parliamentary Board agreed that perhaps a mid-term poll was not the answer. The Board moved a resolution stating that 'some sort of mechanism' (not a mid-term poll but something else) was needed to decide on the single issue of whether Goans wanted to merge with Maharashtra. The resolution came before the cabinet, which approved it, and the Goa status referendum issue was taken up for legislation. But the question was: what would this 'some sort of mechanism' be called? Would it be called a 'referendum'? Or a 'plebiscite'?

The matter landed on the desk of then union home secretary, the distinguished Lallan Prasad (L.P.) Singh, former Indian Civil Service (ICS) officer. Knowing that there is no provision in India's Constitution for a 'referendum' on any single issue, L.P. Singh now proposed a solution: instead of a referendum or plebiscite, how about calling it an 'Opinion Poll'? This was an astute choice of words because the word 'referendum' would uncomfortably focus attention on the tortuous Jammu & Kashmir issue, where a referendum was the demand in many quarters. Also, the word 'plebiscite' could not be used because it is normally used exclusively for international disputes. With both 'referendum' and 'plebiscite' ruled out, in the circumstances, 'Opinion Poll' was considered the best possible phrase. An ingenious solution by a canny civil servant now paved the way for Goans to decide on their future. For relentlessly campaigning, rallying and pushing for this referendum or what became known as the Opinion Poll, Jack de Sequeira is called the 'Father of the Opinion Poll'.

Indira Gandhi gave her approval; the central government passed the Goa, Daman and Diu (Opinion Poll) Act in 1966 and Goa's Opinion Poll was scheduled for 16 January 1967. In tune with the spirit of constitutional democracy of those days, before the Opinion Poll was conducted, Bandodkar and the MGP duly resigned from office. Fresh polls were scheduled for February 1967.

On the day of the Opinion Poll, the atmosphere across Goa was tense yet full of fervour. Both sides had been campaigning hard. The pro-merger side declared that with merger, Goddess Shanta Durga of Goa would meet Goddess Bhavani of Maharashtra, Bhavani being the family deity of Shivaji. The anti-merger side had a more culinary line. They gave the slogan: 'We don't want Maharashtrian Shrikhand. We are happy with curry and rice.' People were excited to take part in this moment of participatory democracy, although they were unsure: what did the future hold? Inside the polling booth, the choice would have to be made for two options: 'yes' for merger by marking the symbol of a single flower, 'no' to merger by marking the symbol of two separate leaves. 'Goa was the only place in India where an opinion poll or a referendum of this kind took place,' points out Pratapsingh. 'The entire exercise passed off peacefully without any major incident whatsoever, a testament to the peace-loving and mature character of the Goans.'

The results were unequivocal: with a high 81.7 per cent turnout, 54.2 per cent Goans voted against merger with Maharashtra. Goa would remain Goa.

Pratapsingh explains it thus: 'Democracy was new to us in Goa. We were tasting freedom. Goans had begun to enjoy power and felt that at last they had their own government and a CM sitting in Panaji who was close by and would listen to them. But now if a merger happened, people were told that the CM would no longer be readily available in Panaji; instead he would be sitting in Bombay, and if we want to get anything done, we will have to go all the way to Bombay. Goans felt that they would lose the power that they had acquired only six years ago.'

Goa did not want to be swallowed. The Goan identity, quietly but determinedly expressed, was growing stronger. The Congress leader Dr Wilfred de Souza worked hard for the cause of separation. 'We worked non-stop. It was real politics—working at the grassroot level to make people conscious of the opportunity to determine their own identity,' Dr de Souza writes in his biography.[2]

What is the Goan identity? It is a distinctive identity, not just the identity of language, although languages, both Konkani and Marathi, are important parts of it. It is instead another, more undefinable thing, located in a land defined by the expanse of limitless waters. It is an identity located in the common shared cultures of villages, an identity born from traditional village shrines that have coexisted for centuries. The Goan is quietly but strongly attached to his traditions. Every family knows which temple or church or *kuladevatha* or *gramadevatha* they belong to and share a kinship with others who worship at the same shrine. With so many crosses, churches and temples dotted across Goa, it's as if the geography itself is sanctified by local beliefs. Even during assaults by the Portuguese, the Goan remained tenaciously attached to his sense of self, adapting from the Portuguese but refusing to fully give up his own ways of life. The Goan spirit is marked by a consciousness of a long history of Goa's own devotional cults, saints, icons, cultural forms, festivals and

---

[2] Alberquerque, Daniel, *Dr. Wilfred De Souza: A Journey with an Exceptional Leader of Goa*, Rajhauns Sankalpana, Panaji, 2015, p. 126.

feasts, each located within a sacred geography that is both physical and psychological. Spirituality and a living history spring from the land. This consciousness is impossible to crush. Every Goan is proud of it and, in 1967, voted to stay true to it.

The merger was rejected. Even within the party of the merger—the MGP—there was a difference in view with some in favour and some against. Perhaps these differences were the reason why, in the February 1967 elections, the MGP won by a wafer-thin majority, winning only 16 seats, with the UGP again coming in with 12 seats. Still the popular face in spite of the merger plank being rejected, Bandodkar was sworn in again as CM on 5 April 1967.

Why did Bandodkar remain popular even though his main campaign of merger was snubbed? The public feeling on Bandodkar was that he was beloved of the people, not so much because of his oratory (he wasn't really an expert orator) but because he was a true philanthropist. Not a single person who came to Bandodkar for help would ever go away empty handed or disappointed; he helped everyone and helped them constantly and would do everything he possibly could to make sure difficulties were sorted out. He had an enormously generous nature.

He was also aware of his great popularity and used to famously joke, 'Even if I smear a stone with *sindoor*, and put up this stone as a candidate, it will win elections.' Bandodkar knew that if he chose even a newcomer, he or she would win.

It turned out that very soon, Bandodkar would choose a candidate who would be noted for never losing an election.

Rise of the Apolitical Politician

'Bandodkar was a true man of the people. He was a self-made common man. He was completely straightforward and totally honest; in fact, he was incorruptible,' recalls Pratapsingh. 'He was not a tricky politician, he genuinely wanted to do something for the people, but because he was often very forthright, some politicians didn't like him.' Was Bandodkar his mentor? 'Well, I came into politics only because of Bandodkar.'

So how did the paths of this US-returned, former corporate executive and now Sattari landholder cross with Bhausaheb Bandodkar, the leader of the ruling MGP?

It was after the 1967 elections that Pratapsingh came in contact with Bhausaheb. 'Bandodkar was the MGP face and the election winner. But he was barely educated, just about enough to sign his name. He needed educated boys to run the administration and ministries. So, his eyes fell on me,' remembers Pratapsingh.

It so happened that a member of the Rane clan, Jaisingrao Rane, had been elected MLA from the Thivim constituency in 1967. Jaisingrao worked closely with Bandodkar. In his mission to build up the MGP and draw in new members, Bandodkar often criss-crossed Goa, meeting as many people as he could. One day, during the course of travelling across north Goa, Bandodkar, accompanied by Jaisingrao, went driving down a leafy country road from Valpoi to Mapusa.

On the way, something unusual caught Bandodkar's attention. He saw a smartly dressed, good-looking young man, driving a tractor across the fields. The stranger was steering the tractor rather adeptly. 'Jaisingrao, who is that young fellow there, driving a tractor?' Bandodkar asked. 'That is Pratapsingh Rane,' replied Jaisingrao. 'He is America returned but now works as a farmer and is doing excellent work among the villages of Sattari.' 'He is America returned and now works on the land in Goa?' mused Bandodkar. 'I would certainly like to meet him.'

Soon, another encounter took place between the two. Freedom fighter Gopal Apa Kamat was a well-known lawyer in Sattari who also happened to be Pratapsingh's lawyer. One day, Pratapsingh went to call on Kamat. Coincidentally, on the same day, Bandodkar, searching for a suitably educated candidate to be a possible Assembly

Speaker and mulling over Kamat's name for the post, visited Kamat's house. As the CM entered, Kamat hurriedly ordered Pratapsingh to leave the room. But Bandodkar had seen Pratapsingh and asked Kamat, '*Toh kosso asa?*' (How is this boy?) 'Oh, he is just a young fellow,' tossed off Kamat airily. But Bandodkar, an excellent judge of men, had made up his mind. The piercing eye of the grassroots leader had fallen on a future asset. Someone who would go on to prove that Bandodkar's choice would not be in vain.

The Canacona-based physician Dr Dhillon Dessai recalls an interaction between his own father and Bandodkar about Pratapsingh. On one occasion, Dr Dessai's father Dr Vithola Naik Dessai happened to be travelling in a car with Bandodkar. 'There is a very talented young man in Sattari, he is foreign educated and holds an MBA degree,' Bandodkar remarked to Dr Dessai, 'but at the moment, he is only occupied in farming and shikar on his own lands.' Bandodkar told Dr Dessai that he was determined to utilize Pratapsingh's talents and had made up his mind to give him a ticket.

Shortly Bandodkar arrived at our ancestral home and was met by a rather bewildered Pratapsingh wondering why the CM was visiting him. 'I want you to contest elections from Sattari,' said Bandodkar, coming directly to the point. 'But sir, I know nothing about politics,' protested Pratapsingh. 'Nonsense,' boomed Bandodkar. 'You must join me.' Elections were six months ahead and Bandodkar had made enough enquiries. Pratapsingh's candidacy had also been strongly endorsed by the local sarpanches.

'When Bandodkar requested me to stand for elections, I said okay right away,' Pratapsingh recalls. 'I had come in contact with him before that. He had actually come to my house and requested me to make a project report for Sattari, which was very backward in those days because the Portuguese considered it hostile territory and there were no facilities. Bandodkar had urged me to work for the development of Sattari. He must have seen in me the ability to do what was needed for the welfare of the people of Sattari.'

Pratapsingh's entry into politics shaped the kind of principled, apolitical politician he became. He did not join out of a desire to play power games or a thirst for power. His goal always remained the public good and using politics as a means to bring progress and change.

When he decided to join the electoral fray, my first thought was, oh my god, here we go again. My older brother Murarirao Yeshwantrao (M.Y.) Ghorpade, whom I called 'Dada', was a long-time Congressman, having joined the Congress in 1954, serving as MLA as well as Rajya Sabha MP. By the end of his political life, he was a seven-time MLA from Sandur. He served as finance minister of Karnataka from 1972 to 1977 under the chief ministerial terms of then Karnataka CM D. Devaraj Urs, and later as rural development and Panchayati Raj minister. My brother was very committed to Panchayati Raj institutions and Pratapsingh too became deeply devoted to strengthening Panchayati Raj in Goa.

A Cambridge-educated economist and an award-winning wildlife photographer, Dada shared a mutually respectful friendship with Pratapsingh. Both of them were educated abroad, and they had many common interests: Pratapsingh in shooting and shikar; my brother in a different kind of shooting—wildlife photography.

The area around Sandur, our home, was endowed with dense forests teeming with all kinds of wildlife like sambars, four-horned antelopes, wild boars and panthers, which inspired my brother. Dada excelled so greatly in wildlife photography that he won several national and international awards, including the Fellowship of the Royal Photographic Society of Great Britain. In 1983, my brother became the first wildlife photographer to be awarded the World Masters of Photography award. Dada was a fervently passionate conservationist and naturalist and once even offered to donate 150 acres of his own inherited land to nature conservation. His book, *Sunlight and Shadows: An Indian Wildlife Photographer's*

Diary, with a foreword by Indira Gandhi, is a collection of some of his remarkable photos.

With Dada already in politics, I knew well the rigours of political life and the restrictions it placed on daily existence. I had been looking forward to a retreat from the public glare, to a quieter life, perhaps occasionally going out to restaurants and outings, unnoticed and enjoying my privacy. But I went along with Pratapsingh's decision because I have always believed that in the end what matters most in 'the bivouac of life' (to use the poet Henry Wadsworth Longfellow's phrase) is the opportunity to do real constructive work.

Dada advised Pratapsingh that since the Congress looked unlikely to win in Goa, it would be better to join a locally dominant party like the MGP to get into the system of public life. Once established in politics, my brother advised, Pratapsingh could later consider joining a national party to become part of the mainstream.

Pratapsingh flung himself into the 1972 election campaign. He says: 'I had given my father my word that I would always work for the people of Sattari and work to improve these lands. My father would have expected me to take care of the family lands and take forward the agricultural development of the areas. To me, entering politics seemed to be a good way to work towards taking Goa out of its backwardness. It was a chance to do something real.'

The people of Sattari needed no introduction to him. He knew their names, knew their families, knew what their children were doing—he was part of their family and they of his. Of course, they would vote for him.

There were challenges, though. The Socialist Party (SP) remained strong in the area and socialist cadres made life difficult for him. 'The party candidate, another man named Jaisingrao Rane, did create problems—they were most hostile. My election symbol was the lion and the socialist symbol was the banyan tree. In those days, the locals used to cut trees to practice shifting cultivation. My rival would tell people that if they elected him, they could freely cut trees. This was of course illegal because there was a law against indiscriminate tree cutting, but this is what he promised.' The SP even attacked his vehicle, but in spite of these early obstacles, he won Sattari by a massive margin in 1972.

Over the next 50 years, he pulled off many records. He contested 11 successive assembly elections from Sattari (the constituency later became Poriem, after being split into two in the 1989 assembly polls) and won triumphantly every time, undefeated to this day. This record places Pratapsingh in the front rank of India's longest serving state assembly stalwarts. Sattari sent him to the Legislative Assembly for every session 1972 onwards. The area had been his family fiefdom for generations; after 1972, it became his electoral fortress. A custom began. Before the start of every campaign, he would first invariably offer prayers at the ancient temple of Bhumika in Poriem. Bhumika, benign and beautiful goddess of the Goan earth, mother goddess rooted in the soil of Sattari, showered her blessings on him.

In later elections, so high did his popularity soar, that all he had to do was stand in the Bhumika temple, announce his candidature and almost instantly sarpanchs would take the word out to voters, the news would spread throughout Sattari—*Khashe is contesting*—and the election would be won on a wave of universal approval. 'Sattari is my stronghold,' he says. 'The people here have stood with me through the ups and downs of life.'

He would go on to be sworn in as CM of Goa six times: in 1980, 1985, 1990, 1994, and twice in 2005. He would be the last CM of the UT of Goa and the first CM of Goa state. He would become Goa's longest serving CM, over five terms.

High Performing Minister from the Start

In 1972, after the thrill of the elections, however, there was a sudden lull. The Indira Gandhi-led central government took its time in allowing the swearing in of the MGP government to go ahead. Indira had just triumphantly won the 1971 Bangladesh war; she was a national phenomenon and the Congress was winning every election. Only in tiny Goa did the Congress lose to the MGP (the MGP won 18 seats while the Congress could manage only one), and an affronted Indira Gandhi took her time in allowing the new MGP government to be sworn in, perhaps hoping for defections from the MGP.

However, Bandodkar kept his flock close, even putting them up in Panaji's Mandovi Hotel to keep them in a good mood and safe from the Congress's poaching. 'Because of the Congress's calculations, suddenly after the hectic round of electioneering, we had nothing to do. We just sat around for almost two weeks. So, Bandodkar used to take us for picnics to Calangute beach to keep us all together.' Pratapsingh and Bandodkar also shared a love for shikar. Did he go on shikar with Bandodkar? 'I used to be a good shikari. I used to trek up the Sattari hills, hunting wild boar. I never hunted sambar though. Bandodkar saw me do it, and was motivated to join in. But since hunting is illegal now, I prefer not to remember those days,' he says.

As soon as permission came, the new government was sworn in. It was a minuscule ministry with just three ministers—Bandodkar, Achyut Kashinath Sinai (A.K.S.) Usgaonkar as deputy minister and Pratapsingh Rane. Pratapsingh, a newbie MLA, immediately became a cabinet minister, remaining so from 24 March 1972 to 11 May 1977. He had no apprenticeship or experience in public life. But so impressed was Bandodkar by the new Sattari MLA that he handed him a slew of crucial portfolios: Law & Judiciary, Labour, Legislative Affairs, Revenue, Local Self Government, Housing, Civil Supplies, Food and Fisheries.

'Bandodkar was not an administrator, although he had a great deal of common sense. Since I was much more educated with a degree in management, I can't really compare myself to him,' he recalls, 'But yes, I was probably a better administrator.' A ministerial berth and charge of crucial ministries was a big responsibility as well as a challenge. Trained as a company manager and always a methodical problem solver, someone who liked to immerse himself in the nuts and bolts of management and administration, he eagerly got down to work.

For the family, Pratapsingh's new life meant, for starters, a shift in residence. From the rambling, centuries-old family home in Sanquelim, where electricity supply was uncertain and water came from wells, we now moved to a smarter minister's residence in Panaji. Our children—Vishwajit, born on 23 March 1971, and Vishwadhara, born on 11 October 1972—started growing up and started school in Panaji.

Pratapsingh's administrative style began to take shape. Methodical, quiet, hard-working and efficient, he would work with the bureaucracy to plan and implement projects. His business management degree from Texas, as well as his excellent grasp of mathematics, science and law stood him in good stead. Some called him risk averse, others called him indecisive, but these are unfair criticisms. He worked painstakingly, with a thorough attention to detail, realizing that governance was not about flashy moves but a daily task of creating and managing changes by which greater amenities would be delivered to the people and economic growth would be achieved slowly but surely.

Bandodkar, in pursuit of his 'Kasel tyachi zameen, rahel tyache ghar' promise, had after the election victory in 1963, already enacted land laws protecting the rights of peasantry and tenants. In 1964, the Agricultural Tenancy Act came into force. In 1968, the Goa Buildings (Lease, Rent and Eviction) Control Act was brought in, as was the Goa, Daman and Diu Land Revenue Code.

The tone of the administration was set, but as a government minister, he also had to set right some of Bandodkar's rather impulsive mistakes. After a meeting with the industrialist Krishna

Kumar (K.K.) Birla, in a flush of enthusiasm, Bandodkar allotted a huge 1,000-acre plot in Sancoale village in Mormugao taluka to the Birlas for a factory. This was Zuari Agro Chemicals Ltd., which was established with the aim of trying to create employment for Goans. But the plant operators at first were negligent on safety, and during production, industrial effluent and arsenic leaked into the sea, the river as well as the soil, polluting the land and waters, resulting in the withering away of crops and causing huge numbers of fish to die. One morning, masses of dead fish lay on Baina and Colva beaches and on riverbanks. Fish-loving Goans, shocked and outraged to see dead fish on the beach and on the banks of the Zuari, erupted in protest, with the Ramponkars or traditional fisherfolk community taking the lead. In 1974, widespread agitations by fisherfolk took place against Zuari Agro Chemicals.

'Goans are very particular about their fish and there was almost a revolution,' recalls Pratapsingh. 'Since I was fisheries minister, the blame came on me.' He hurried to Maharashtra to seek help from the Government of India, which sent experts from the National Environmental Engineering Research Institute (NEERI) in Nagpur to investigate the problem and set it right. The fish disaster of 1973–74 was an example of how Pratapsingh rushed to fight a potential calamity and managed to sort the matter out as soberly and rationally as possible. His work earned him praise.

While work in government started to become his natural forte, as a newbie in the assembly, he occasionally made some gaffes: 'I was excited and nervous when I first entered the assembly. I am of a reserved nature and the quarrels in the assembly were new to me. I remember hearing the LoP Dr de Sequeira refer to Bandodkar as a *"redo"* [buffalo] in the House and was quite shocked. I did not know how politicians expressed themselves. A complete newcomer in politics, I said some things unknowingly. I hardly knew anything at the time.'

In one of his early speeches, while speaking on Goa's unemployment rates, he said that if there were more opportunities in the state, then Goa would not only be known for its 'cooks and butlers'. A firestorm broke out. His comment sparked anger in Goa and beyond. The Opposition was on its feet, angrily denouncing his words as insults and demanding an apology. Expatriate Goans began to phone in their protests and wrote angry letters, furiously stating that as doctors and engineers, they were anguished by Pratapsingh's statement. The issue snowballed, newspapers ran headlines, and it was only after clarifications and pleas about his earnestness in tackling unemployment in Goa that the controversy eventually died down. But it was an important lesson learnt. In public life, we must be very careful about what we say and how we say it. 'I made a very foolish mistake,' he admits today.

Yet there was no doubting his sincerity and capacity for hard work. He won admiration and trust, not just for his work but also because his calm, reliable, corporate demeanour put people at ease. At Shri Shivaji Preparatory Military School in Poona, he had imbibed a great deal of discipline and as an excellent sportsman, he led from the front in setting an example of honest hard work.

His achievements as a MGP minister, however, could not win him the goodwill of someone who in these years became his main detractor—Shashikala Kakodkar, Bandodkar's daughter and political heir.

Battling Politics of Envy and Nepotism

On 12 August 1973, aged only 62, D.B. Bandodkar suffered a massive heart attack and died. He had been Goa's Bhausaheb for a decade, a folk hero both popular and rooted. Some described him as a one man show in his party and government yet he was a genuine leader of people. Since Bandodkar died while holding office, his ministerial and party colleagues were placed in a quandary.

Who could replace the towering personality? After the funeral, then Lieutenant Governor and former ICS officer S.K. Banerji called the ministers in to say that the seat could not be kept vacant and a new CM must be sworn in at once to ensure there was no break in administration.

Goa's politics has often interestingly mirrored national politics. Just as after Shastri's death, the eye of the Congress 'Syndicate' fell on Jawaharlal Nehru's daughter, and Indira Gandhi was sworn in as PM, so also upon Bandodkar's death, with elections four years away, MGP leaders now looked to Bandodkar's daughter. The governor indicated that if a successor to Bandodkar was not found immediately, President's Rule would be imposed. In hasty confabulations (one of these held in the washroom of Bandodkar's residence as his body lay in state downstairs!), the MGP decided on his daughter. Shashikala Kakodkar was sworn in as CM on the same day as her father died. 'Since there was a sympathy wave for her, we were convinced she should lead the government,' Pratapsingh recalls.

There was certainly a huge sympathy wave. In 1974, a year after Bandodkar's death, with Shashikala Kakodkar at the helm, MGP candidates scripted big wins. The young ebullient lawyer Ramakant Khalap won from Bandodkar's constituency, Mandrem. In the high profile Benaulim by-poll of 1974, the MGP, in an act of strategic realpolitik, put up a Catholic candidate Francisco Menino Jesus Ferrao, or 'Luta' Ferrao, thereby splitting the votes against the UGP candidate, Dr Wilfred de Souza, or 'Willy', 'Doctor Wilfred' or 'Doctorbab', as he was sometimes called. The MGP won the by-poll in Benaulim, a constituency considered a UGP stronghold. (Subsequently, Dr de Souza challenged this election result.)

But Shashikala Kakodkar or 'tai' as she was known, proved to be a difficult proposition for Pratapsingh. Kakodkar, Bandodkar's eldest child and an impressive woman leader, had been a political activist from an early age. She held an excellent academic record. She was a graduate from the highly rated Karnatak University in the cultural hub of Dharwad and a post-graduate degree holder from Elphinstone College in Bombay. Kakodkar was an efficient administrator, but she was an introvert and did not possess her father's trusting and genial nature.

Four years older than Pratapsingh, Kakodkar seemed to nurse a sense of a grievance against the younger leader who was becoming well known in such a short time. Pratapsingh, after all, had been made a cabinet minister in 1972, and Bandodkar had given him a raft of heavyweight ministries, while she had remained only a state minister with relatively minor portfolios.

'Shashikala was a very educated person; yet for some reason, she felt a certain jealousy towards me. I continued as a minister in her cabinet but there seems to have been a communication gap between us,' Pratapsingh says candidly. 'Perhaps she resented the fact that her father always had such high regard for me.' Although he remained a minister for the next four years under Mrs Kakodkar with the same portfolios he had held under Bandodkar (in fact both Pratapsingh's and Usgaonkar's portfolios were left untouched by Mrs Kakodkar), his relations with her were never as warm as they had been with her father.

Yet Mrs Kakodkar was no pushover. Goa's first and only woman CM started out as being labelled 'Bandodkar's daughter' but was able to bring a measure of dynamism to the government. She carried forward Bandodkar's work in dam building and infrastructure. A great deal of eventful legislation was brought in. The Goa, Daman and Diu Mundkars (Protection from Eviction) Act, 1975, and Rules, 1977, piloted by Kakodkar, was passed, while Pratapsingh was revenue minister, giving security of homesteads to mundkars or tenant farmers. This was Goa's important Mundkar Act. It was a law that was placed in the Ninth Schedule and, thus, excluded from judicial review.

It was also during Kakodkar's time that Pratapsingh tabled the crucial Goa, Daman and Diu Town and Country Planning Act, 1974 and Rules, 1976. He remains particularly proud of this legislation. 'I could see that what Goa needed was a regional plan. We needed to outline a development plan that provided detailed planning for towns, cities, roads and industrial estates. For example, in the US or Europe, I used to see that some cities like Houston had factories and industries even in residential areas and chimneys would pop out among residential houses, belching fumes. We created industrial estates in Goa, so that industries would not come up in the middle of a town or a village.' Several industrial estates came up in the Kakodkar years.

In politics, under Kakodkar, the pro-Marathi MGP moved towards a more accepting stance towards the Konkani language, although in 1974, her government made Marathi compulsory in all English-medium primary schools to the exclusion of Konkani, a move which was criticized by supporters of the Konkani language. Goa's sensitive language issue, simmering for decades, aroused strong sentiments on both sides and would prove to be one of Pratapsingh's biggest challenges in later years.

After 1975, the personality clash between Mrs Kakodkar and Pratapsingh took a turn for the worse. As the politics of nepotism, intrigue and jealousy took hold in Delhi, the same kind of politics were mirrored in Goa. On 25 June 1975, PM Indira Gandhi imposed the Emergency across India. 'It was a slightly selfish move on Indira Gandhi's part,' says Pratapsingh. 'She was about to lose her government after the Allahabad High Court judgement of 12 June 1975, which unseated her and barred her from contesting elections for six years. Indira was a child of Independence, the daughter of a staunch democrat and was herself educated abroad. In spite of all this, she imposed the Emergency to stay in power.'

There was hardly any impact of the Emergency in Goa. 'We watched what was happening in Delhi, but Goa by and large remained liberal. Yes, some people who overdid things were put behind bars and we would get all the price lists that were to be charged for grain. But we did not have the forced sterilization and coercive practices of the Sanjay Gandhi variety here,' he says.

In fact, Pratapsingh and I organized our own initiatives on family welfare. We did believe in the importance of the need for more awareness, not only on population control but on family management and well-being. I took the lead in organizing family welfare camps across Goa. We brought in the eminent gynaecologist Dr M.R. Narvekar from Bombay to lead teams of doctors. We took care to ensure that there was no coercion or compulsion whatsoever. Instead, doctors were tasked to give women advice not just on birth control but also on infertility, hygiene, welfare of newborns and advice on family nutrition. Our camps were not 'family planning' camps but 'family welfare' camps.

'There was an overwhelming response to these welfare camps,' Pratapsingh recalls. 'Women from all religions—Hindus, Muslims and Catholics—attended these camps. We were both keen on these awareness drives. This is because when forced to bear multiple children, ultimately, it's the women who suffer, particularly if husbands cannot support them.'

But however hard he worked, Pratapsingh could not protect himself from the short-sighted politics of envy and nepotism, which began in Kakodkar's government. There were many allegations of favouritism. Kakodkar's husband Gurudatt Kakodkar, a United Kingdom (UK)-trained chartered accountant, was accused of obtaining transport and cement licenses. His interference in government and party matters also caused deep resentment among old MGP members who were loyalists of Bhausaheb Bandodkar. In a particularly embarrassing incident for the CM, a Marathi publication *Sameer*, edited by Gurudatt Kakodkar, was held up in the assembly by the Opposition's Ananta Narcina (A.N.) Naik or 'Babu' Naik, revealing a lewd centre spread, much to the wrath of the Opposition. Kakodkar was accused of bestowing government advertising to her husband's journal. Bandodkar had been an all-embracing, consensual figure, but Kakodkar ran a highly centralized government and reportedly relied too heavily on the advice of her husband. The unpopularity of Gurudatt Kakodkar took a toll on Shashikala's authority.

Pratapsingh is never critical about anyone and rarely has a harsh word for any political colleague. Yet on Kakodkar, he is unable to restrain himself, clearly still deeply hurt by her treatment of him: 'There was an arrogance to Shashikala that was completely absent in Bandodkar. Although educated, she was a little narrow-minded and cantankerous. These traits did not inspire confidence. It was unfortunate that the person who opposed me was my own CM, only because after the elections of 1972, her father had made me a cabinet minister first while she had remained a state minister.'

Destiny's Child on a New Road

In March 1977, the Emergency came to an end when India went into general elections. The unthinkable happened in these elections: Indira Gandhi was defeated. The Janata Party came to power. Incidentally, in Goa in these general elections, the Congress got a 40 per cent vote share and won one of the two Lok Sabha seats—Eduardo Faleiro from South Goa, or Mormugao, as it was then called.

There were more surprises on Goa's political landscape. Prior to 1977 Goa Assembly polls, Pratapsingh resigned from the government and from the MGP, the party he had joined as a first-time politician. A point to be noted here: Goa is known as the land of defections, with MLAs smoothly switching parties without feeling the need to face fresh elections. But in Pratapsingh's case, he resigned from the government, party as well as the assembly. In that year, several other Bandodkar loyalists in the MGP grew disenchanted and rebelled, and some MGP MLAs like Jaisingrao Rane and Punaji Achrekar left the party, disagreeing with the party line on the merger issue.

But why did Pratapsingh resign from the MGP in which he was once the blue-eyed boy, from a government in which he had once been Bandodkar's trusted lieutenant and a talented minister?

Disagreements kept raising their heads between Pratapsingh and Shashikala Kakodkar. She was uneasy with her father's chosen men and insecure about their capabilities and potential to outshine her. 'In the assembly, the Opposition used to keep praising me,' says Pratapsingh, 'which probably made her even more insecure.'

Pratapsingh carried on with his work, coolly and unflappably, but it was clear that in a government and party led by Shashikala Kakodkar, his future was bleak. 'I had the unmistakable sense that Shashikala Kakodkar was not going to give me a ticket for the 1977 elections. That's the reason I left,' he says simply.

Besides, the advice of my older brother M.Y. Ghorpade echoed in his ears, that sooner or later, he would be better advised to join a national party like the Congress, (whatever be the recent setbacks it had suffered because of the Emergency) and not remain restricted to a regional party like the MGP.

Ramakant Khalap, a close associate of Pratapsingh, tells this story about Pratapsingh's exit from the MGP. 'In 1977, I was a young man about to get married. I went to Mr Rane's official residence in Panaji to invite him for the wedding. I found suitcases and boxes all around. He was all packed up and it looked as if he was ready to leave. What is this, where are you going, I asked. I am not staying here anymore, he replied. I am not getting a ticket for the 1977 polls, so I thought I would go away for a while, maybe I will go to Bangalore. We were all shocked that Rane was thinking of leaving. We rushed to "tai" [Kakodkar] and said, "Tai, you must give Pratapsingh a ticket, he is extremely popular in Sattari and certain to win. If you don't give him a ticket we will lose." People from Sattari also arrived, pleading with Kakodkar to reconsider. But she was adamant,' recalls Khalap.

Khalap was taken aback by Kakodkar's attitude. There had been no hint of any outward tension between Rane and Kakodkar at party meetings, no signs of any bitterness.

The reasons why Mrs Kakodkar denied Pratapsingh a ticket in 1977 remain unknown. Perhaps, being a little arrogant about her birth and inheritance, she lacked the foresight to look after talented party colleagues. Perhaps she also knew that if Pratapsingh remained in the MGP, he was certain to be the foremost candidate for the CM's chair, given his stellar performance as minister and high acceptability among all factions.

With the doors of the MGP closed to Pratapsingh, where would he go? Which direction would he take? He was destiny's child and destiny made sure that a new road opened. A high, broad road that would swoop and circle around Goa, from village school to whitewater dam, from a new bus service to a big city hospital. A road that would take him further than his wildest dreams.

THREE

FACE OF THE CONGRESS IN GOA: 1977–1980

'I have belonged to the Congress party for over 45 years, and I do not think that I would ever leave the Congress party. I belong and will always belong to the Indian National Congress.'

Babu Naik's Announcement

A.N. Naik or 'Babu' Naik, MLA from Margao, was a jolly, bespectacled figure and a rumbustious performer in the Goa Assembly. Once in the UGP, he later joined the Congress—a popular figure who won repeatedly from his constituency, Margao. Naik, also a prominent businessman in Margao, was the LoP against the second Shashikala Kakodkar government which took office on 7 June 1977.

A.N. Naik is important to our story because he played a key role in the career of Pratapsingh Rane and remained Pratapsingh's long-time ally.

In the run up to the Goa Assembly polls of 1977, in the thick of the campaigning, Babu Naik made a prophetic announcement. Campaigning for the Congress on a hot afternoon, Naik addressed a rally at Lohia Maidan in Margao.

The straggling crowd was restless. The sun beat down. Flags and posters fluttered in the hot breeze. Microphones blared out poll slogans. Naik, on stage made an energetic speech about why it was time the Congress was given a chance in Goa. Suddenly, Naik made a surprise announcement: 'Friends,' he shouted, 'If the Congress comes to power, our chief minister will be from the Bahujan Samaj. Our next chief minister will be Pratapsingh Rane.'

If the Congress comes to power our CM will be from the Bahujan Samaj. If the Congress comes to power our CM will be Pratapsingh Rane.

Those fateful words uttered by Babu Naik, that hot 1977 afternoon at an election rally, would prove prophetic.

Life for Pratapsingh changed dramatically in 1977. Refused a ticket for assembly polls that year by the imperious Shashikala Kakodkar and increasingly alienated by her authoritarian and nepotistic way of functioning, he resigned from the MGP and the Kakodkar government.

Almost immediately, Babu Naik reached out to Pratapsingh. In many ways, it was Naik who first brought Pratapsingh into the Congress.

At this time, Dr Wilfred de Souza, the effervescent and dynamic surgeon-politician, also moved to bring Pratapsingh into the Congress. 'Tai Kakodkar refused to give a ticket to Pratapsingh Rane because he was the main contender for the CM's post...I spoke to Pratapsingh and discussions were held. He was also guided by some of his advisors both within and outside the state. He decided to join the Congress. I enrolled him and welcomed him.'[3]

Luizinho Faleiro, former Goa CM and Navelim MLA, who remained a supporter of Pratapsingh through many years, says that although Pratapsingh's political roots may have been in the MGP, which championed merger with Maharashtra and the Marathi language, he was admired in the Congress. 'We admired him

---

[3]Alberquerque, Daniel, *Dr. Wilfred De Souza: A Journey with an Exceptional Leader of Goa*, Rajhauns Sankalpana, Panaji, 2015, p. 157.

because he had had the guts to stand up to the family rule of Shashikala Kakodkar and left the MGP. He had the courage to quit. In Congress, Rane never got involved in any inner party quarrels.'

As Goa MLAs played musical chairs, skipping from one party to the next, Pratapsingh stayed steady in the Congress, a Congress MLA for over four decades. 'During the Emergency, I had been under pressure to join the Janata Party, but I chose to join the Congress. My values had always been close to the foundational principles of the Congress,' Pratapsingh asserts. 'Secularism, modernity, free enterprise mixed with a welfare state and tolerance of all. These were my values which fitted well with the original principles of the Congress. I have remained loyal to those values, although today, the unstable culture of the Congress slightly disturbs me.'

In the early days of his joining, one Congress activist impressed him with her work, and they soon built a relationship of trust and respect. This was Sulochana Katkar. She was an idealistic and diehard Congresswoman, an upholder of Gandhian values, who had participated in the early satyagrahas in the 1940s and 1950s. Sulochana was an indefatigable party worker, working long hours at the grassroots to build the Congress party organization and recruit local leaders. She would go on to become the longest serving president of the Goa Pradesh Congress Committee (GPCC) and would become a nominated MLA in 1985 with the support of Pratapsingh. He brought in three women as nominated members—Sulochana Katkar, Sangeeta Parab and Phyllis Faria—to the assembly of the UT of Goa through a presidential directive. He did this because no women were elected in the 1980 elections, and although nominated members could not vote, Pratapsingh was very keen to ensure that women were represented in the House. 'Mrs Katkar was a committed worker, someone who worked hard for the party and who I could rely on,' he recalls.

Congress Fills a Vacuum

How was the Congress party placed in Goa in 1977? 'When I first joined the Congress, the party had very few active members. It was difficult to hold meetings, hardly any crowds came. There were only a few people, many of them disgruntled elements,' recalls Pratapsingh. 'Only when Indira Gandhi came to Goa would people flock to see her in huge numbers, in spite of the fact that she declared the Emergency.'

The national party had been squeezed out in the 15-year period (1961–76) after Liberation and bipolar politics of two regional parties—MGP vs UGP—had become entrenched in Goa. With the popular Bandodkar as the face of the Goa government and the charismatic de Sequeira as the face of the Opposition, the Congress was consigned to the wilderness.

However, nationally, after 1971, Indira Gandhi became the all-India heroine. Her personality cult as a wartime PM and 'messiah of the poor' spread across the country. Across India, the Congress was a mighty force, undefeatable in elections, with an unchallengeable leader who captivated crowds like no other. Indira Gandhi was a magnetic presence with the added lustre of being Nehru's daughter. Adored at home, dazzling on the international stage, the Congress's popularity soared because of her. National politics has always had an extraordinarily powerful impact on Goa's politics. As a result of the Indira cult, many Goans too began to get attracted to the Congress.

After Bandodkar's death in 1973, the once powerful MGP began to splinter into rebellions and factions, fatally weakening the party. Then, a few years later in 1976, the UGP, divided on the issue of the Opinion Poll, also split eventually, becoming the Naik group and the de Sequeira group, and the faction led by Naik merged with the Congress. Dr de Souza, who was with the Naik faction, became the Congress president. Already in the Lok Sabha polls of 1971, the UGP had lent support to the Congress candidate Purushottam

Kakodkar, who won from North Goa (Panaji) and had become MP. It bears telling here that Purushottam Kakodkar would move a private member's Bill in Parliament demanding statehood for Goa.

Indira Gandhi's rise and fall remains the most striking political trajectory in post-Independent India's history and her changing fortunes had an impact in Goa. In 1971, she was India's elected empress. By 1975, she had become India's dictator who imposed the Emergency. Although its impact was not felt in Goa, the political fallout affected Goa's politics.

With Indira Gandhi's defeat in 1977, the Janata Party came to power at the centre, and the UGP's faction that was led by Dr de Sequeira and his son Erasmo de Sequeira merged with the Janata Party. The UGP thus ceased to exist, its demise corresponding with the rise of the Congress. (In an interesting aside, it may be mentioned here that the UGP may no longer exist, but its election symbol, the open palm, the *haath*, is similar to the hand symbol used today by the Congress Party.) The political vacuum left by the UGP's disappearance was filled by the Congress party, led by Naik and de Souza.

A Political Home

In 1977, the Congress gave Pratapsingh a ticket to contest the assembly polls. He once again threw himself into the election campaign. Many of his constituents were hurt and outraged on his behalf at the way he had been treated by the MGP leadership. Their loyalty to him was steadfast. 'Even while I was minister, I would be in the office in the mornings, but I always made sure that every evening, I would tour my constituency as I had always done, in my jeep, calling on my voters and keeping up my contacts with them,' Pratapsingh points out. It was in this election campaign—Pratapsingh's very first campaign as a Congress candidate—that A.N. 'Babu' Naik made that famous announcement declaring Pratapsingh as a chief ministerial candidate. So why did Naik make that announcement?

Naik knew that Pratapsingh's would be the most acceptable face among all sections in Goa. Pratapsingh was not just a compromise candidate, as many have said, between Dr Wilfred de Souza and Babu Naik. He ticked all the right boxes. As a Kshatriya-Maratha, Pratapsingh is, in Goa, part of the Bahujan Samaj. As a US-educated, English-speaking modernist, a skilful horseman and music lover, he would be a comfortable candidate for Catholics. As a member of a landowning family known to have a gracious lifestyle and be mindful of cultural sensitivities, he would be reassuring to the elites, both Hindu and Catholic. And as a mature administrator, he would provide stability and growth in government and be a steady hand at the wheel. Most importantly, given the simmering rivalry that existed at this time between Babu Naik and Dr Wilfred de Souza, both intent on the top job in government, Pratapsingh would be the ideal universally acceptable choice.

For the time being though, it was the MGP's Shashikala Kakodkar who was sworn-in as CM after the results were declared. In 1977, the Kakodkar-led MGP won 15 seats. The de Souza and Naik-led Congress was not far behind with 10 seats and the Janata Party got just three. When Pratapsingh joined the Congress, he was part of the 10-MLA haul that the Congress netted in 1977, its biggest showing so far in Goa. Pratapsingh won with another record margin. Shashikala Kakodkar formed her second ministry and took office on 7 June 1977. Pratapsingh sat on the Opposition benches with colleagues de Souza and Babu Naik. Naik was LoP and Pratapsingh became deputy leader.

With this began Pratapsingh's lifelong tryst with the Congress. He found his political home. The Congress would be the party he would never leave, even in the face of allurements from others. Soon, he would become the Congress's face in Goa and, through his leadership, put Goa on the national map. Pratapsingh was to become a Congressman of the old style, cut from the same cloth as Congressmen of the same ilk as Y.B. Chavan or Sharad Pawar—a bridge builder, a consensus seeker, with an accommodative rather than confrontational approach. He was called the consensus candidate, the compromise candidate, because even among his rivals he seemed to attract only goodwill. There was hardly anyone whom Pratapsingh ever actively alienated. His secular, non-communal approach enabled him to rise above Goa's parochial identity politics, and bridge the divide between Goan Catholics and Goan Hindus.

Pratapsingh was always a consensus builder, but Mrs Kakodkar seemed to alienate people. In her time, the ruling MGP was hit by a spate of rebellions and resignations. Discontent in party ranks was caused in large part by the interfering ways of the CM's husband.

One of the significant public agitations at this time showed the determination and fighting spirit of Goa's educated youth and considerably damaged the image of the Kakodkar government. A widespread students' movement demanding a 50 per cent reduction in bus fares, the 'half ticket' protests, saw students take to the streets and boycott classes, the agitation taking a toll on Kakodkar's authority.

Babu Naik played a leading role in the fall of the Kakodkar government, constantly challenging the CM on every issue and policy. Naik had vociferously attacked Kakodkar in her first term too, displaying the risqué centrespreads of her husband's publication in the assembly and asking if the government was subsidizing obscenity. By early April 1979, Naik succeeded in luring three MGP MLAs to his side, and Kakodkar's government—with only 15 seats to start with—lost its majority. Fulminated Gurudatt Kakodkar: 'We will break their heads if they try to topple us.' As it turned out, heads nearly did get broken. Kakodkar's government collapsed amid high drama.

On 23 April 1979, the Shashikala Kakodkar government faced a cut motion in the assembly. A cut motion is an Opposition demand to vote against the government on a particular issue, and if the motion is adopted, it becomes a no-confidence motion and the government falls. That day, as MLAs filed into the House after lunch, chaos ensued in the Goa Assembly. As the then Speaker, Narayan Fugro announced that voting would commence to determine the fate of the government, he was shocked to find that four MGP MLAs loyal to Kakodkar were blocking his way to the chair. Another MLA began to bellow loudly, lifted the Speaker's chair and smashed it to pieces. The microphone and Constitution of India on the Speaker's table were thrown to the floor. Shouts and yells rent the air, members hurled paperweights and microphones at each other and pandemonium broke out.

'I was standing in my place [in the Opposition] watching the fun,' Pratapsingh recalls. 'Such was the idiocy of the MLAs that since they had been told that their government would fall because of the actions of the Speaker sitting on the "Chair", they decided they would smash up the said "Chair" so no action by the "Chair" could be taken.' Fugro had been expecting trouble and had kept the police on standby. When steel-helmeted policemen pushed through the melee towards the dais, Kakodkar shouted, 'Get out, get out' and started shoving at them. Shouts and shrieks went on. After 12 minutes of bedlam, the Kakodkar government caved in, losing the cut motion.

Refusing to relinquish office and intent on stalling the formation of an alternate government, Kakodkar rushed to Delhi to plead her case with PM Morarji Desai. The Janata Party PM was sympathetic to this non-Congress CM. Instead of allowing the party with the superior numbers to form the government, Home Minister H.M. Patel clamped President's Rule on Goa. Fresh elections were announced for January and Kakodkar had to finally resign after only a year and 10 months in office. The MGP's dominance in Goa (the party had won four consecutive election victories in 1963, 1967, 1972 and 1977) came to an end. Sixteen years of MGP rule and family rule by Bandodkar and Kakodkar was now history. Babu Naik, as LoP, had claimed a big scalp.

The Congress: Dominant in Every Sense

This period also saw realignments in national politics. Indira Gandhi started to grow more insecure after her defeat in March 1977 and became even more susceptible to the influence of her son Sanjay Gandhi and his rough cronies. Old Indira loyalists like the Karnataka CM D. Devaraj Urs were outraged. Urs increasingly began to forge his own path with his own supporters and hit out against Mrs Gandhi at an AICC session in April 1978, saying, 'Do not mistake me for a sycophant.'

In 1979, Urs was expelled from the Congress (I) and formed the Congress (Urs) or Congress (U) in July 1979. Dr Wilfred de Souza, as head of the Congress in Goa, extended his support to Urs. Dr de Souza's faction became the Congress (U) and he became the president of the Congress (U) in Goa. Congress veteran Purushottam Kakodkar continued to lead the Congress (I). Pratapsingh's old associate and relative Jaisingrao Rane, who had once pointed the tractor-driving Pratapsingh out to Bandodkar, encouraged him to join the Congress (U), which he did.

But Indira Gandhi was a force that could not be stopped. In 1979, flushed with new energy after her re-entry into Parliament through the Chikmagalur by-poll of November 1978 and another crucial Congress victory in the Azamgarh by-poll in 1978, she stepped firmly back onto the comeback trail. By August 1979, the Janata government had collapsed in a welter of ego battles and faction squabbles, Parliament had been dissolved and elections announced for 3 and 6 January 1980.

Indira Gandhi descended on Goa on 12 December 1979. She checked into the Mandovi Hotel in Room 404. Many Goa Congressmen remember this particular venue as it was the site of many deliberations. Indira urged Goa Congressmen to unite to give the party a better chance at coming back to power. A seat-sharing agreement was worked out between the Congress (I) and the Congress (U) in Goa for the assembly polls also due on 3 January 1980, with the latter getting 22 and the former getting only six seats. Indira accepted this seat-sharing formula in return for united Congress's support in the general elections for parliamentary candidates.

Goa has only two MP seats, and the Congress worked unitedly for both candidates. However, in the 1980 polls, the Congress's veteran Purushottam Kakodkar lost to the MGP candidate Sanyogita Rane in Panaji (North Goa), although in South Goa, the Congress's Eduardo Faleiro raced to a win.

Sanyogita Rane was a significant candidate. When she won on an MGP ticket in 1980, she became Goa's first woman parliamentarian. She was married to a Rane of Sattari and was a step-aunt of Pratapsingh, although with Sanyogita being a part of the step-family, relations were not exactly warm. Interestingly, Sanyogita was born in Gwalior and educated at the Gajra Raje High School (the same Gajra Raje nee Salu bai who was Pratapsingh's aunt). Sanyogita had a brave and exemplary son, Vir Chakra-decorated (posthumously) Second Lieutenant Jayendra Rane of the fifth Garhwal Rifles. Jayendra had been killed in the 1971 Indo-Pak war. Throughout her campaign, her supporters dubbed Sanyogita 'Veer Mata' or 'mother of the martyr' and aroused a wave of emotion. Sentiments ran so high for the bereaved mother of the gallant son that Sanyogita won a big victory. 'I was a young MLA at the time,' recalls former MGP leader Ramakant Khalap, 'and I used to campaign full throatedly for Sanyogita, shouting "Vote for the Veer Mata".' Pratapsingh himself would face off against his aunt Sanyogita in another future election.

Pratapsingh began his own 1980 campaign from Sattari, this time as a Congress (U) candidate. But he was no longer just another candidate. By now he was a chief ministerial face and a contender for the CM's chair. His name had already been announced by Naik as a future CM, his achievements as minister in the Bandodkar cabinet were well known and he was by now a well-recognized figure across Goa.

Always walking ramrod straight as a result of his equestrian training, with an aristocratic air, he stood out in a crowd. Pratapsingh was not a politician in the way the word is commonly understood, someone hurling negative epithets at others or making grand promises. Instead, he was always reticent and reserved, making substantive speeches about his own work and urging voters to believe in his development goals for Goa.

The results of the mid-term assembly elections were stupendous for the Congress. The remnants of the UGP supported the Congress (U) making the contest with the MGP a bipolar one. The Congress (U) won a huge mandate—23 seats (with independents). The Congress (I) failed to win a single seat. The MGP won only seven seats, of which five MLAs joined the Congress, leaving behind in the MGP only the feisty Ramakant Khalap elected from Mandrem and Babusso Gaonkar, the MGP MLA from Marcaim. Lo and behold, Shashikala Kakodkar, Pratapsingh's arch detractor, lost her seat and crossed over to join the Congress!

Pratapsingh and the president of his party Dr de Souza scored handsome wins from Sattari and Calangute. Dr de Souza, the Congress's organization man, is often compared to Pratapsingh. Twelve years older than Pratapsingh, de Souza was a politician by passion, while Pratapsingh became a politician by chance. Dr de Souza was a brilliant surgeon, a double Fellow of the Royal College of Surgeons (FRCS) and a political livewire with a broad disarming smile. He was mercurial, shrewd, always darting around Goa, always on the lookout for strategic alliances and moves. He was a forceful and blunt public speaker and not averse to backdoor machinations and intrigue. Pratapsingh was the very opposite. He never said anything injudicious, weighed his words carefully and was cautious, risk averse yet a very reliable chief executive and manager. Pratapsingh would never try to topple an elected government or come to power by backdoor means. Nor was he capable of scheming, plotting and politicking. While Dr de Souza was probably a born politician, Pratapsingh was what Goa, with its multiple problems, needed more—a born administrator.

The Congress's spectacular showing in the polls, the trust that voters reposed in the party even though it had never won before was in large part due to the presence of Pratapsingh Rane. The party had finally managed to shake off the 'elite' tag. As Bhausaheb Bandodkar's chosen candidate, Pratapsingh also carried the mantle of Bandodkar and brought to the Congress votes from groups who would have ordinarily stayed away from the party. He was a Rane from the Hindu heartland of north Goa, as well as a secular unifier who believed in carrying all people along.

Having first detached themselves from the Congress (I), the Congress (U)—the entire splinter group led by Dr de Souza—now simply engaged in a mid-stream switch to merge again with the Congress (I), to form the government for the first time, even though they had all been elected on Congress (U) tickets. 'Goa was the only region in the country which had the Congress (U) and Congress (I) in coalition, one which was blessed by Indira Gandhi,' says Luizinho Faleiro. Then Speaker of the Assembly Froilano Machado told newspersons: 'It was a unique experience.'

For Pratapsingh, this unusual move made perfect sense given the scale of Indira Gandhi's victory and the fact that she was now firmly back as the all-powerful PM. In 1980, Indira Gandhi roared back to power in New Delhi with a two-thirds majority of 353 seats, herself winning from Raebareli in Uttar Pradesh and Medak in Andhra Pradesh. The Congress was back as the juggernaut at the centre and had what can be called a brute majority. Khalap remembers, 'In an assembly of 30, 28 were with the Congress, the Opposition was only two members strong. Imagine what an uphill task it was for me in the Opposition. The Congress was dominant in every sense. Dominant at the centre, dominant in Goa.'

In an interview at the time to *India Today*, Pratapsingh said candidly: 'We would not have lasted three months had we not opted to join the Congress(I).'[4] So, would he describe himself as an Indira loyalist? 'I suppose you could say that I have been an Indira Gandhi loyalist in the Congress. I never left because this is my party and I have always felt that Indira Gandhi put her trust in us to be in this party. It's not in me to change parties. I believe that Jawaharlal Nehru had a broad modern vision. I continue to believe in the original principles of the Congress.' Two great milestones in Goa's history were achieved under Congress PMs—the Opinion Poll of 1967 under Indira Gandhi, and Goa's achievement of statehood in 1987—under Rajiv Gandhi.

A Congressman and Democrat for Life

It is important to understand Pratapsingh's relations with the Congress leadership, which perhaps explains why his ties with the party were so durable. His admiration for Indira Gandhi is undimmed even as he remains critical of her left-of-centre policies. As a believer in free enterprise and open markets, he found some of her policies difficult to stomach. 'She was under a great deal of pressure from the Communists who were eating away at her voter base. Internationally, she was also under pressure from the Russians. These factors could explain her leftward lurch and why she swung towards enacting land reform laws, abolition of privy purses and the like. Yet, although I disagreed with her leftist-oriented economic policies, yes, I did admire her. She was quite a leader.'

When he visited Indira in Delhi at her 1 Safdarjung Road home, he was struck by the way she made it a point to meet

---

[4]'Infighting in Goa Pradesh Congress(I) Reaches Awesome Proportions', *India Today*, 15 July 1982, https://tinyurl.com/ufr3kjfr. Accessed on 6 September 2023.

everyone who was there, talk to them and spend a few minutes with all those who had come. 'When I first got elected, I hardly knew Indira Gandhi. But after I joined the Congress, I would go to Delhi to meet her. You could even turn up without an appointment at her home and she would still meet us and give all of us a hearing.' He remembers being told by some Congressmen that in order to stay in Indira Gandhi's good books, he should come once a week to Delhi to offer her his salaams. He politely refused.

I found myself drawn to Indira Gandhi too. To meet her at first was daunting, as she was a formidable grand dame with a stern air. She wasn't gushy or effusive but had inimitable grace and good manners. In 1983, the CHOGM Summit was to take place in New Delhi. After the summit, a weekend 'Retreat' for CHOGM leaders was planned in Goa. A year before the Retreat in Goa, in 1982, Indira Gandhi came to inspect the Goa situation and arrangements. This was her rehearsal visit and the first time I interacted with her at close quarters.

Indira went to see the Taj Fort Aguada hotel where the Retreat was to be held. She checked all the preparations including the design of the Taj Aguada Hermitage cottages that were being built for the event. During the rehearsals, the then Goa Lieutenant Governor Air Chief Marshal Idris. H. Latif left my name out of various functions. One evening, Indira Gandhi summoned me to ask, 'Mrs Rane, you were not there at the boat ride or at any of the lunches. Why not?' 'Madam, I had no choice,' I replied. 'The governor had not included my name in the Blue Book.' According to protocol, if names are not written in the Blue Book, wives of dignitaries cannot attend functions. Indira Gandhi brushed this aside and said to me: 'Please make sure that if a head of state comes with his wife or if the head of government is a lady, you are always there.'

On one of the evenings of her stay, she invited Pratap and me for a private dinner with her at the Raj Bhavan, where she was staying. Her aide Natwar Singh later informed me that we had been invited so she could form an opinion about us and decide whether we were fit to host such an important event in Goa. We passed the test. I remember being impressed with her attention to detail, such as making sure I went to the Taj Fort Aguada hotel the night before the Retreat to taste all the food that had been prepared, including, to my great delight, the apricot soufflé! She also gave instructions about the Goan guides who were to escort the international VIPs. If, given the recent experience of Liberation, any of the guides said anything critical of India to the international guests, they were to be immediately taken off duty.

Pratapsingh was part of the generation of Congressmen who were loyal to the leadership of Indira Gandhi and later transitioned to Rajiv Gandhi. We formed bonds of mutual respect, bonds which extended to Rajiv as well. I remember Rajiv loved to eat prawns. I once sent him some fresh prawns in a heavy-duty icebox. Subsequently, at a function in Delhi, I found him looking in my direction and gesturing, how about some more prawns. I gestured back that he would need to return the box first. It is rare that a famed national leader bothers to recognize and acknowledge the wife of a state CM and even continue a conversation with her. Rajiv was always very warm, a thorough gentleman. 'I had good relations with Rajiv Gandhi,' recalls Pratapsingh. 'He was very fond of Goa. We shared a common interest in horse-riding.'

The former Indian Administrative Service (IAS) officer Shailaja Chandra was posted as Goa's resident commissioner from 1987 to 1991 and worked closely with Pratapsingh when he was CM. She recalls an incident in Delhi when Goa Day was being celebrated at the Goa state guesthouse on Amrita Shergill Marg. Rajiv, who was no longer PM, arrived unexpectedly early, throwing all the staff into a tizzy. He had turned up unannounced so that he could tuck into the prawns that had been specially flown to Delhi from Goa! Rajiv's down-to-earth informality and unpretentiousness won him the friendship of all of us in Goa.

We had other links with the Congress. Madhavrao Scindia of Gwalior, grandson of Pratapsingh's aunt Gajra Raje Scindia, was a high-profile Congress leader. By relationship, Pratapsingh is Madhavrao's uncle. From my side, my brother had been a long-time Congress member, and I am related to the family of the Maharashtra Congress leader and former CM Prithviraj Chavan. Sharad Pawar, the present-day leader of the Nationalist Congress Party (NCP), has been a close associate and comrade of Pratapsingh for many years. 'I speak to Sharad Pawar on the phone often,' Pratapsingh says. 'He calls me and we talk to each other.'

Even though he is rooted in the Congress, Pratapsingh has always been one of those politicians who has cherished friendships across party lines. This is the mark of the true democrat, one who is able to build bridges even with those who one may not agree with politically. Once, on being asked if he was too friendly with members of the Bharatiya Janata Party (BJP), Pratapsingh said: 'I have so many relatives in the BJP. They come to us; we go to them. I have close family relations with the Scindias. In the Scindia family itself, Madhavrao was in the Congress while his mother was in the BJP. Family relations and friendships should not be mixed with politics.'

During the BJP National Executive in Goa in 2002, Atal Bihari Vajpayee, Lal Krishna Advani and other senior BJP leaders had all come for breakfast to our house. We served them a South Indian vegetarian meal, which Vajpayee greatly relished. 'Vajpayee was a great man,' Pratapsingh recalls, remembering the times when he and Vajpayee had shared a few laughs and greatly enjoyed each other's sense of humour. When PM Vajpayee came to Goa, he was treated with all the ceremonial respect that is due to a state guest.

Today, this spirit of accommodation and ability to form friendships across party lines is sadly disappearing. Leaders like Pratapsingh are part of the 'old' India or 'old' Goa where leaders remained true to their parties but enjoyed warm friendships with those on the opposite side of the political divide. Politics was to be pursued with vim and brio, but not to the extent that it ever damaged the democratic framework that gave elected politicians life.

There is also an unfortunate trend in the Congress today not to give senior leaders their due. Hurtful comments have been made about Pratapsingh, although he had not taken them to heart. 'Certain weaknesses in the Congress have emerged,' he says. 'I am against giving prominence to only one particular family. The beginning of the decay was with Sanjay Gandhi and his foolish acts. Many senior experienced people were pushed aside. Parties are not defined by those who lead them. Parties are ultimately about people. The party belongs to the people. No party should get accustomed to thinking that it belongs to the corridors of power. The Congress cannot always be in power. In fact, being out of power is an equally important part of democracy.' Does he concede that when in power, the Congress, both at the national and in Goa, made serious mistakes? 'Yes, mistakes have been made,' he says, 'We are human beings.'

Best Man for the Job

On 14 January 1980—on a date decided by astrologers—Indira Gandhi was sworn in as PM for the fourth time. How does it feel to again be India's leader, the press asked her. Without batting an eyelid, she replied, 'I have always been India's leader.'

But who would be Goa's leader and CM? The two Congress stalwarts Naik and Dr de Souza, then president of the Goa Pradesh Congress Committee (GPCC), were leaders of different factions and were engaged in a long feud. Both were keen on the CM's post and began their manoeuvres. But there were irreconcilable differences between the two and Naik declared his support for Pratapsingh. The Congress central leadership also realized that a choice between Naik and de Souza could lead to dangerous dissensions, and there

Top: Pratapsingh as an 18-month-old toddler in 1941
Bottom: First row (top right)—Fathesingh R. Rane (Pratapsingh's elder brother); (second row, left to right)—Pratapsingh's sister, Rajmata Indira Devi Mukhne of Jawhar (Maharashtra), Pratapsingh's youngest brother Udaysingh Rane and Pratapsingh

Top: With fellow students at Shri Shivaji Preparatory Military School in Pune. Pratapsingh is seated in the first row, ninth from the right.
Bottom: Pune, 1957—Pratapsingh was an expert horse rider and participated in many public racing events as a jockey.

Competing in public horse racing events in Pune in the 1950s. He won many prizes for horse riding.

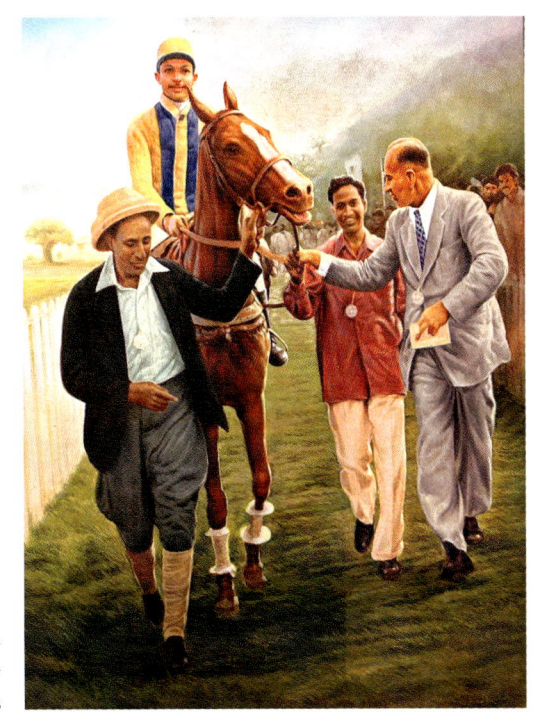

A painting of Pratapsingh, a champion jockey in the Pune horse races, in the 1950s

Top: Receiving a prize at a sports tournament at Nowrosjee Wadia College, Pune, 1959
Bottom: Pratapsingh dressed as a cowboy in Texas, 1963

With close friend Hans Dieter in Paris in the early 1960s

Top: Pratapsingh Rane (extreme left) with two friends from Iran and Indonesia while studying in Texas
Bottom: On a Texas farm with cowboys in 1963. Pratapsingh is in the centre.

Top: Pratapsingh at the United Nations, New York, in 1964
Bottom: On the Sanquelim farm in 1966

Pratapsingh and Vijayadevi at their wedding in Sandur in 1969

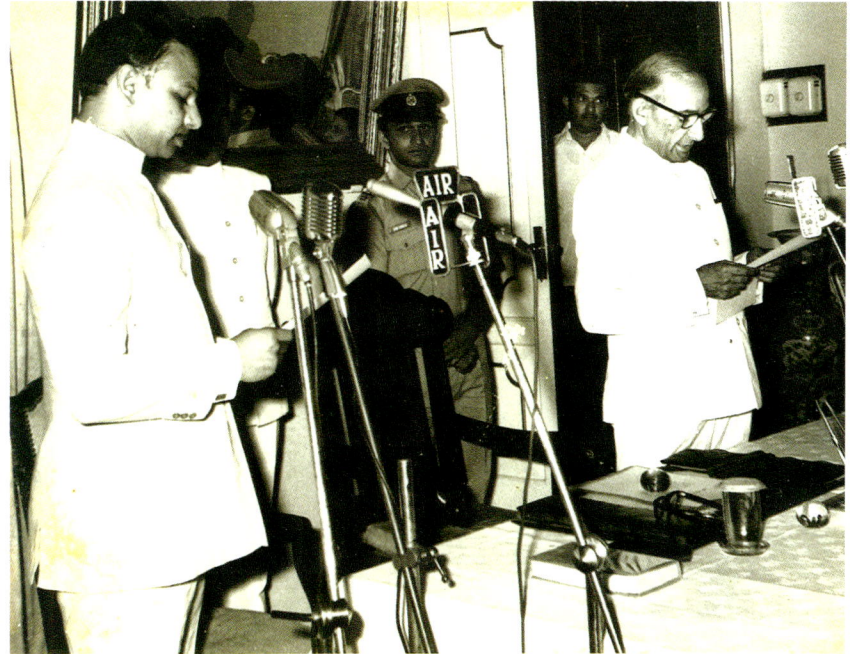

Top: Rajmata Sushila Devi Ghorpade (Vijayadevi's mother) and Manoramabai Rane (Pratapsingh's mother) at Pratapsingh and Vijayadevi's wedding in 1969

Bottom: 1972—Pratapsingh being sworn in as cabinet minister for the first time in D.B. Bandodkar's Maharashtrawadi Gomantak Party (MGP) government by Lieutenant Governor Nakul Sen

Top: Pratapsingh (extreme right) with Shashikala Kakodkar (extreme left) and D.B. Bandodkar (second from left)
Bottom: Introducing Tata 1210 trucks in Goa in 1975

Chief Minister (CM) Pratapsingh Rane and his first cabinet with Goa's Lieutenant Governor, P.S. Gill. Pratapsingh was sworn in as CM for the first time in 1980.

Dr. J. C. Almeida,
Chief Secretary and the Chairman
Kadamba Transport Corporation
Govt. of Goa, Daman and Diu
requests your presence at the Inauguration of
FIRST BUS SERVICE OF THE CORPORATION,
at New Bldg. Panaji Bus Stand
at 9.00 A. M. on 19th October 1980 (A. 27, 1902 Saka)
at the hands of
Col. Partap Singh Gill,
Lt. Governor, Goa, Daman & Diu
Shri Pratapsingh Rane,
Hon'ble Chief Minister
has kindly consented to preside

Top: Invitation to the inauguration of the first bus service of the Kadamba Transport Corporation (KTC)
Bottom: The first bus of the KTC bus service started by CM Pratapsingh Rane in 1980.

With Prime Minister (PM) Indira Gandhi in Goa in 1982

Top: With PM Rajiv Gandhi in 1985 at the centenary celebrations of the Mormugao Port Trust (MPT)
Bottom: Independence Day at the Goa Secretariat in 1985

Top: Inauguration of Goa University, 1985. Governor and Chancellor of Goa University Gopal Singh is speaking. Also seen are Vice Chancellor B. Sheikh Ali (second from right) and dean of Goa Medical College Dr G.J.S. Abraham (extreme right).
Bottom: With President Giani Zail Singh on 25 years of Goa's Liberation, along with artists of the Goan Kunbi dance in 1986

Top: Pope John Paul II visits Goa in 1986
Botom: With St. Teresa (then Mother Teresa) in Goa in 1986

was only one candidate who was universally liked and, in fact, was the best man for the job.

'It was a bit of a surprise for me,' recalls Pratapsingh, 'when Babu Naik, then general secretary of the GPCC and the dominant leader of the Salcette region, came to me to tell me he was going to propose my name for the CM's post. And that's exactly what he did. I have always done what the party wanted me to and so I took up the responsibility.'

As the face of the Congress in Goa from 1980, Pratapsingh became one of the Congress's most high performing CMs who straddled Goa's religious divide. In Texas, he had formed close friendships with Catholics, Presbyterians and Methodists. 'I was influenced to some extent by the Methodists. I was always moored in my own religion, yet struck by how much the Christian communities did for the poor and needy.' The wide vision of the true Goan, born of a harmonious landscape where church and temple have coexisted for centuries, enabled Pratapsingh to reach out to Goa's Catholics, and for the first time perhaps, Goan Hindus and Catholics became united in their common embrace of a CM who belonged to all Goa.

The bountiful waters surrounding Goa call us to this wider vision, where the soul of humankind merges into one and where the divine manifests in every shrine. Beautiful churches, ancient revered temples, Shanta Durga, Francis Xavier, Hindu and Catholic, landlord and mundkar, Goa's identities flourish in peace because the Goan is ultimately rooted in his land and in the local community. It is the beauty all around that gives the Goan a sense of equanimity. Irrespective of caste and religion, the Goan draws his identity from his village, its waters, orchards and forests, the repositories of a village's collective memory. He shares a fellow feeling with others located in a landscape that creates a unique outlook on existence.

Pratapsingh reflects the rooted cosmopolitanism of Goa. This rooted cosmopolitanism enables him to be modern yet grounded, anchored in his own ancestral place yet with the capacity to reach out to all.

Becoming CM would test him severely. He would need to call upon all his inner resources to weather the storms that awaited him.

FOUR

CHIEF MINISTER: 1980–1990

'I followed two mantras as CM. The first: forget about political dissensions and squabbles, just forge ahead with development. The second: however high you reach you must always remain accessible to the people.'

Saturday, 30 May 1987. Pratapsingh had risen early that morning. The previous day, he gave an interview. 'I am highly elated,' he exulted in an uncharacteristic state of excitement. 'It is fortunate that our party has the highest level of national experience to guide and advise us. For the earlier MGP governments, performance did not matter because everything ended here itself. Now, with statehood, quick decisions can be taken. It will be a challenge for the Goans to show their efficiency in being able to run the state in a responsible manner.'

Today—30 May 1987—was the day when Goa would officially become a state and Pratapsingh Rane, the first CM of Goa state.

At 8.00 a.m., he was at the Raj Bhavan. A ravishingly beautiful building with a wood-floored wrap-around verandah, the Raj Bhavan in Goa (earlier the Cabo Palace) is located on the edge of the Arabian Sea. At night, the Cabo Raj Bhavan is bathed in moonlight. By day, the sun glances off the waves into the building, filling it with sunshine.

The Raj Bhavan was all spruced up. The lawns were freshly mowed and watered. The intricately carved wooden furniture had been freshly polished and the tall Cantonese vases set out. Inside the Durbar Hall, the chairs were perfectly arranged and the Bohemian crystal chandeliers were already lit, awaiting the swearing-in of the CM.

The ceremonies began punctually. The new governor of the Goa state, Dr Gopal Singh (who had earlier been the Lieutenant Governor of the Goa UT) was first sworn in by the acting Chief Justice of the Bombay High Court. Pratapsingh and his cabinet had already resigned their posts from the UT of Goa and had been elected leader of the Congress Legislature Party. Now once again in the Raj Bhavan, he was sworn in as CM of Goa state, along with other members of his cabinet who continued to hold the same portfolios they had earlier held. All legislators of the new Goa state too had to take their oath again, since the Goa Assembly had now become a state assembly and they were all ministers of the state of Goa. On the same day, the same man resigned as CM of the UT of Goa and was sworn in as CM of a state. When change came, it came swiftly.

'Welcome, India's Newest State'

30 May 1987: the day when the red earth of Goa throbbed with the footfalls of a new generation. A new Goan was born, a citizen of India's newest state. '*Utt Goykara!*' (Wake up, Goans!) exhorted O*Heraldo* in a front-page editorial that morning. 'The future beckons. The 21st century beckons. Your new destiny as the newest and the brightest state of the Indian Union beckons.'[5]

It was a momentous day. A day of Goa's own tryst with destiny. So many had struggled for this day, had been imprisoned, had

---

[5]Narayan, Rajan, 'A Tryst with Destiny...', O*Heraldo*, 30 May 1987.

fought, lost their lives, campaigned, rallied and marched. Now it seemed as if the spirit of Tristão De Bragança Cunha, who had dreamed of freedom for Goa, and the spirit of the great Rane hero Dipaji Rane who, in the nineteenth century, had fought tenaciously for his rights were present. The spirits of the satyagrahis of the 1940s, of the poets, writers, artists and intellectuals who, through the decades, had kept alive the quest of self-rule for Goa—it seemed as if they were all here too. The freedom fighters who had kept on reminding Goans not to rest until they achieved freedom, those who had kept the lamp of liberty burning during the colonial period, they now could rest easy that this day had dawned. Today, on 30 May 1987, it was as if the spirits of all those valiant men and women who had put their shoulders to the wheel for Goa's long struggle for self-rule hovered over this historic moment.

The name of the Goa Assembly changed. The Goa, Daman and Diu Legislative Assembly was now named, initially, the 'Provisional Legislative Assembly of the State of Goa' (the term 'Provisional' was used until the first session of the new state assembly was constituted). After a long association, Daman and Diu were delinked from Goa and became a separate UT. 'Although we are now politically separate,' Pratapsingh told newspapers, 'Daman and Diu will remain in our hearts.'

Celebrations of Goa's statehood, however, had to wait. Prime Minister Rajiv Gandhi had been scheduled to visit on the evening of 30 May and address a public rally at Panaji's Campal grounds. Campal grounds had already been decorated with flowers and enclosures and a big 'Goa Welcomes You' sign. However, because of the sudden death of former PM Charan Singh on 29 May and India entering a four-day national mourning period, Rajiv was forced to postpone his visit to Goa to 3 June. The public event thus did not take place as planned on Saturday, 30 May, but on Wednesday, 3 June.

On 3 June evening, a gargantuan crowd gathered at Campal

grounds, Panaji's huge park that stretches along the main promenade of the Mandovi river. Parades and sports tournaments are regularly held at Campal, but today it was to witness a more special ceremony. Everyone was here and spirits were high among young and old, male and female, home-maker and officer. It was sweat-dripping hot. But nobody seemed to care because the mood was so jubilant.

There they were on stage. Chief Minister Pratapsingh Rane; Governor Gopal Singh; Union Minister and MP Eduardo Faleiro, an eloquent and talented Goan hailing from the village of Raia. Next to the stage was a giant map of Goa state but, at the start of the function, covered with a ceremonial pink curtain. Soon, a clamorous buzzing in the air began, which grew louder. The crowd craned their necks to see. Prime Minister Rajiv Gandhi was arriving by helicopter from Dabolim airport. A cloud of red dust swirled as the chopper landed in Campal. Out stepped Rajiv, accompanied by Sonia Gandhi in a green sari bordered in gold, and they walked up the flower-bedecked dais, decorated with Goa's fragrant wild florae. Eyes turned towards the curtained mural, hidden from public view. What would it look like?

When Parliament approved statehood for Goa, Rajiv had delivered an evocative message. 'The Goan identity is a composite identity of many languages, religions, customs and traditions. All elements of this identity must be equally respected…Goa has given us patriotism and pride. Goa has given us laughter and music. Goa has given us vitality and verve.'[6]

At the Campal grounds, Rajiv made another encouraging speech. 'I congratulate every Goan on achieving statehood. It has been a long standing demand and it has been achieved through hard work. Your agenda as a state must be to social reform and to cultural continuity. With statehood comes privilege but perhaps more than that comes responsibility. Your primary responsibility is to peace,

---

[6]"Goa: A New State Is Born', *OHeraldo*, 3 June 1987.

to harmony among all the communities and the identification of every Goan in the mainstream of development. At the same time you must increase your contribution to nation building.'[7] The PM spoke both in English and Hindi, aiming to reach all parts of India.

His words were forward looking and spoken in a spirit of outreach, as if he had brought wishes from the whole country. It was as if all of India was saying 'Welcome, Goa; welcome, India's twenty-fifth state.'

A huge cheer went up. Multi-coloured balloons were released. The delighted crowd clapped, shouted and whooped. Uday Bhembre, a veteran campaigner for the Konkani language, writer and intellectual, was in the crowd. 'The sheer joy of the crowd was palpable; thousands of people were all euphoric.' Cultural programmes began: traditional dancers performed vibrant festival dances known as Rath Nach or dancing with a chariot followed by a typically Goan-Portuguese dance, which is part of the folk dance traditions of Goa—the joyful Corridinho. Goa took its place as one of India's most culturally rich and vibrant states, and these dances captured Goa's essence—a state which is a melange of East and West, each enriching the other.

As the finale to the ceremony, Rajiv leant forward and pushed a button, and slowly the pink curtain in front of the mural next to the stage drew back to reveal a huge illuminated map of Goa. The giant map was titled 'State of Goa' with all 11 talukas named and marked. As the curtain drew back, the crowd gasped in wonder: there she was, Goa, that green paradise, *our* paradise, where harmony was a way of life where the people were now getting what we had always longed for—our own identity, our own language and our own state. Above the map, the Goa state emblem was also on display. The emblem was the '*Vrisksha Deep*' or traditional Goan lamp surrounded by symbolic coconut leaves, to reflect Goa's scenic

---

[7]Rajiv Gandhi Foundation, *Facebook*, 30 May 2022, https://tinyurl.com/ypsbd92k. Accessed on 6 September 2022. Also see 'Rajiv Touch to Goa State', *Navhind Times*, 4 June 1987.

loveliness, and crowned by a Sanskrit *subhashita* (auspicious saying) conveying: 'Let everyone enjoy prosperity. Let none suffer any pain.' Addressing the crowd in Konkani, Pratapsingh said: 'Goa is our beautiful state. It should be a model state for the entire country.'

The Mandovi, flowing past the Campal grounds, glittered with evening lights as if lit with a new iridescence. Goa, a Portuguese colony for 450 years, then a UT for 26 years, now at last an independent, self-governing state in the Union of India.

Patrician and Statesmanlike

When Pratapsingh Rane first became CM in 1980 of the then UT of Goa, it wasn't exactly a smooth beginning. His first term as CM ran from 16 January 1980 to 7 January 1985. In this period, he held a large number of portfolios of Home, Transport, Personnel and Administrative Reforms, General Administration, Public Works Department (PWD), including Water Supply, as well as Education and Art and Culture.

He had an enormous number of responsibilities, but politics was afoot and many plotted his downfall. He didn't have his own band of loyalists, nor was he the type to intrigue to keep his faction afloat. He was not a backroom operator who would outsmart rivals through subterfuge. He had no camps or a posse at his command. He was a soft target, someone they thought they could easily bring down. All he would say at the repeated moves against him and demands for his dismissal was: 'These are people motivated by self-interest.' Yet at the same time, his rivals knew—grudgingly admitted—that he was what they could never be: a top rate, calm and steady administrator with no inclination for short-sighted political intrigue. He was patrician and statesmanlike, while many of them were conniving and manipulative. He would build Goa. It was his mission to bring water supply, electricity, town planning, education and jobs to his people. That's all he ever wanted to do, and that's what he would do. And to hell with the petty politicking. *Let's build, with all our heart and soul, a paradise, here, in Goa.*

The centre didn't seem optimistic about his chances, though. Given the volatility of Goa politics, so uncertain were they of the survival of the Rane ministry that they sent Delhi's Lieutenant Governor Jagmohan (governor of Goa from 31 March 1981 to 29 August 1982) out to Goa as the new Lieutenant Governor in such a hurry that the outgoing Lieutenant Governor Colonel Pratap Singh Gill (governor of Goa from 16 November 1977 to 30 March 1981) had not even had the time to properly vacate his official quarters! An unwritten law of gubernatorial norms is that the incoming Lieutenant Governor does not see the outgoing one. But this time for a few days, two governors lived under the same roof at the Cabo Raj Bhavan.

Politics remained factionalized. A familiar tussle was being waged between Dr Wilfred de Souza and A.N. Naik or 'Babu' Naik. For Pratapsingh, the presence in the Congress of Shashikala Kakodkar, his old detractor, was not a source of comfort either. Many aspired to Pratapsingh's job, and there was unfortunate bickering and dissidence in the party. As a news magazine reported, an MLA said rather bitterly at this time: 'We have 28 chief ministers.'[8]

It seemed as if Dr Wilfred de Souza could not forgive Pratapsingh for becoming the CM in 1980. Himself an energetic mobilizer and campaigner, Dr de Souza harboured the notion that the big 1980 Congress win was due to his efforts, and that the Congress had only won because a section of the UGP had merged with it for which de Souza claimed credit. Dr de Souza was of the view that he was the architect of the Congress's victory in Goa and, therefore he, and not Pratapsingh, deserved to be CM.

De Souza was further irked because he was ousted from being

---

[8]'Infighting in Goa Pradesh Congress(I) Reaches Awesome Proportions', *India Today*, 15 July 1982, https://tinyurl.com/ufr3kjfr. Accessed on 6 September 2023.

Congress president by Babu Naik. When corruption allegations hit two of Pratapsingh's ministerial colleagues, the controversial law minister Dayanand Narvekar and agriculture minister Joildo Souza Aguiar, and they quit their posts, their places were taken by Dr de Souza and Babu Naik. The Congress High Command, at this time led by Indira Gandhi, put this balance in place, insisting that the two rivals make their peace and join the government.

Though Dr de Souza reluctantly agreed to become part of the cabinet, he remained somewhat of a dissident against Pratapsingh, even rallying groups of MLAs to his camp to give warning that he could dislodge the CM if he wanted to. To questions about reports of dissension in his party, all Pratapsingh said was: 'It is necessary to allow the heterogeneous elements to settle down and develop at least a working relationship among themselves.'

He remained unflappable. He had a job to do. And he was acutely aware that none of this—state power, a government post or the trappings of the CM's job—belonged to him. There was no personal ownership here. 'Government power,' he says with customary candidness, 'this whole thing, the trappings, the ceremonies and privileges, is not anyone's father's property. It's there only as a service to the people.' He had to get on with providing services to Goans, and that is what he would do. He had promises to keep.

Unmoved while his rivals plotted and schemed, Pratapsingh rapidly began to make his presence felt across Goa. He was a descendant of the warlike Ranes yet at the same time epitomized the cultural sensitivity and *delicadeza* and *decencia* (delicacy and decency) of Goa. He could appreciate Goa's cheerful feni-sipping, music-loving, Latin character, at the same time uphold the Hindu traditions of Sattari. Much to his rivals' dismay, he quickly settled into his groove.

Bhausaheb Bandodkar used to say that development work in Goa should focus on three areas—education, health and transport. It was in these sectors that Pratapsingh began his work. In his campaign, he had promised: 'Interest of commuters could best be served only by nationalization of bus transport.' He knew that the public had suffered due to the 'bus lobbies' of Goa. There had been some unsavoury revelations about the manner in which Shashikala Kakodkar's husband Gurudatt had been trying to interfere in distribution of bus permits for certain routes. Pratapsingh had been witness to the widespread 1979 student protests demanding 'half tickets' on buses and campaigns against the private bus lobbies. He had seen first-hand how in rural Sattari—the area most neglected by the Portuguese because of his rebellious ancestors—people struggled to travel in Goa.

Laced with rivers, covered in thick forests, with the ocean roaring on one side and the Western Ghats marching on the other, journeys in Goa were hazardous and complicated. Travelling from north to south of the tiny state could take up to two days. Rail connectivity was poor too. The only train line out of Goa was a metre-gauge track from Mormugao to Miraj in Maharashtra. A single return flight, IC 163 and IC 164, operated by Indian Airlines, flew between Bombay and Goa.

Efficient and plentiful public transportation was an imperative. 'Connectivity is of utmost importance. There were few roads in Goa. Before I became MLA, I would go into places where there were not even any dirt tracks. I would simply drive my jeep anywhere and everywhere, up a hill, across the fields or through shallow rivers. After becoming CM, I became determined that there would be one proper road in every Panchayat.'

The Pratapsingh government built a network of all-weather roads across Goa. Villages and towns were linked. Former IAS officer Dr Mohammad Modassir was posted as Director, Transport, in Goa at the time. Modassir recalls how determined Pratapsingh was to ensure that travel in Goa and to other states be improved and the monopoly of the private bus contractors be broken. 'Goa desperately needed a state owned bus service, and Mr Rane was very keen on this, given the high fares that private buses were charging and the manner in which the private operators behaved with the travelling public,' says Modassir.

On Dussehra Day, 1980, Pratapsingh launched the State Road Transport Corporation or the Kadamba Transport Corporation Limited (KTCL, commonly known as KTC in Goa), named after the great Kadamba kings of the tenth to early fourteenth centuries who ruled Goa for 400 years and turned the region into a bustling area of trade and commerce, as well as of vibrant culture and art. The Kadambas established thriving universities, built Shiva temples and engaged in brisk trade with Zanzibar and Sri Lanka. The royal emblem of the Kadambas was the lion, and it was this symbol that Pratapsingh adopted for Goa's first public bus service. The first blue and white–painted government-owned buses rolled out bearing the royal emblem of the Kadamba dynasty. The launch of the service on Dussehra day evoked the native cultures of Goa. The colonial rulers were gone; the people of Goa were now the rightful owners of the necessities of their daily lives.

The launch of KTC was not, however, an exercise in nationalization of existing resources. The private bus companies that had existed in Goa since the time of Shashikala Kakodkar were left untouched, although their monopoly was broken. 'I did not nationalize bus services because the idea was to give the public choices and also not to interfere with the supply of buses. The government corporation ran a parallel service with the private players,' Pratapsingh points out. Today, the KTC consists of over 500 buses, runs special services for schools, offers special rates for children and are a familiar part of the daily lives of Goans.

Getting electricity to the villages was his other obsession. In the early days after Liberation, there was barely any electricity in Goa. Some cities had a few generators. In his own ancestral home in Sanquelim, electricity would come on for a few hours. He had seen first-hand the terrible effects of not having access to electric power. Visiting a remote village once, he entered a home to find a woman lying on the floor of the bedroom. Upon enquiry, it emerged that a snake had sprung at her out of the darkness and bitten her to death. The sight of a woman lying prostrate, her dead body riddled with snake bites, haunted him.

He remembered his own experiences as an adolescent in Portuguese Goa, how that smothering, enveloping darkness descended at dusk, with only small dots of illumination provided by lanterns in the ocean of night. He knew how impossible it was to move about at night let alone study or socialize. He was set on his goal. Villages must be electrified. Even if not fully, every home must have at least two bulbs.

He launched the 'electricity to the poor scheme' around the slogan, 'Two points for every house.' The idea was that even small cottages would have access to at least one or two electrical points. Electric poles came up and lines were installed deep in the hinterland. One by one, slowly but surely, dark villages lit up, children ventured to study in the evenings and homemakers found their chores made easier. He says: 'The thought that children could study in the evening gave me a lot of satisfaction.' In the initial phase, a modest 500 huts were selected for electrification, the numbers soon expanding as more areas were added to the scheme.

He took up the task of the best possible utilization of Goa's rivers. Making its way through the hills of the Western Ghats is the river Valvanti. Slender but strong, the river runs through Sattari. Forested hills of the Ghats, garlanded in grey mists in the monsoon, their summits disappearing into rain clouds, rise on either side of the river valley. The jungles here are so deep and so mystical that it is as if ancient spirits dwell in the old trees. Here there is a quiet symphony of mountains, river and forest, birdsong and whispering water, rustling leaves of coconut, cashew, mango and jackfruit trees showering bounty on humankind, both material and spiritual. Earth and sky meet in the water. Blue-eared kingfishers and drongos circle and skim. The tree-clad hills stand sentinel to this undisturbed natural paradise. It is here on the Valvanti that there grew a dam, harnessing the water's power for irrigation and water supply to north Goa. The Anjunem Dam.

Goa's hilly terrain is threaded by rivers, water surrounds every village, defining it and giving it its own unique ecological identity. The profusion of rivers makes Goa into a sort of archipelago by the sea. Yet the hilly land means cultivable land is in short supply and irrigation projects are needed so that agriculture can be developed to its maximum potential. Goa's CMs have all recognized this need, and the early CMs prioritized irrigation projects. The Anjunem irrigation project was initiated in 1972 during the Bandodkar government. It was seen through, supervised and completed by Pratapsingh by 1989. The completion of the Anjunem Dam, located in his constituency, the Sattari taluka, became one of his standout achievements.

In completing the Anjunem Dam project, he also established his own template of development: planned development. 'All development work must go through certain well-defined stages,' he says. First survey the approach to the place. Then establish communication systems and water supply. Next plant trees to prevent deforestation and to hold the soil. Above all, start and maintain dialogue with the people.

His methods were slow because they were methodical. He proceeded by first rehabilitating affected people, offering them land, jobs and remuneration, and moving them to a better location.

He held several rounds of talks with residents, spelling out clearly what he intended to do. He spent days telling those who would be displaced why the dam was in their best interests: water would come flowing into their fields; crops would rise up bringing revenue and security. The villagers were primitive; they did not own land and were unconcerned with modern technology. Many practised *jhum* or slash-and-burn shifting cultivation, meaning cultivating forest land, then setting fire to it and moving on. Pratapsingh convinced them to give up their old ways, making them aware of the advantages of settled agriculture.

His experiences from the Anjunem Dam are worth noting as they provide tips to all administrators trying to build large projects. 'You have to first build trust with the people. Once you communicate sincerely and explain exactly what you are trying to do and how their daily lives will improve from a particular development initiative, they will agree to change. But you have to approach people with respect.'

Unlike volatile protest movements and distrust of big dams in other parts of India, as far as the Anjunem Dam was concerned, people actually volunteered to give up their lands and move out. The CM was sincere and driven. He laid out all the facts and figures about the project. He spoke in an earnest and no-nonsense way, which dignified his listeners.

Once the people had been shifted and settled to their satisfaction, the planners moved in. 'For the development of Goa, I created a Planning Board. I brought in experts, town planners, engineers and industrialists. The Board would discuss projects and try to arrive at the best possible plan.' This is the planned manner in which numerous schools and colleges were built, the way the GIM was established, and the way the Anjunem Dam was seen to completion.

'Pratapsingh Rane was an ace administrator, an administrator to the core,' says Dr Pramod Badami, chief engineer at the Goa Water Resources Department. Badami joined the Goa government as an assistant engineer in his early twenties in 1985 and worked with Pratapsingh on the Anjunem and Selaulim Dam projects. He recalls trekking through forest tracks with the CM visiting irrigation sites. Several schemes for water supply to the villages were worked out: lift irrigation or lifting water from the river to higher ground, and the *vasantbandhara* system or check dams on the river to store water so the river was always full. Wells were dug by getting all villagers to contribute to the digging work. In the interiors, the CM would visit homes and advise farmers on crops and water conservation. In those days, the Government of India was devoting copious resources to developing the Western Ghats, and Goa was able to access electrical lines from the centre's electricity supply as soon as wells were dug and agriculture began. 'Mr Rane had a science background, so he knew the water economy very well,' says Dr Badami. 'He knew about cropping patterns and had the capacity for minute planning. He would observe his officers closely and get reports about how they worked from the locals. He worked so hard all the time that we were motivated to work too.'

Pratapsingh is proud of the Anjunem Dam. Prouder still of the manner in which it was achieved. Today, the dam provides drinking water and irrigates substantial areas of land through its canal system, promoting large scale cultivation. The reservoir created by the dam has created forests in which wild boar can be found. The bison, or the *gaur*, Goa's state animal, can also be seen here. Between the trees, glimpsed occasionally, prowls the leopard. Environmentalists say the dam has played a crucial role in eradicating the drinking water problem and begun a green revolution in the surrounding areas. Crops have sprung up in what had earlier been barren land.

The Selaulim Dam was another focus of Pratapsingh's work. Begun in 1975, work on Selaulim continued during the Shashikala Kakodkar and Pratapsingh Rane years, until it was finally completed in 2000. Shailaja Chandra recalls how Pratapsingh would take off for the Selaulim Dam site in his Ambassador car (without air-conditioning) even in the searing heat of the summer, stopping along the way to inspect schools and primary health centres (PHCs). In those days, PHCs functioned well and were able to offer a range of health services to locals. Sometimes all officers would be taken for overnight picnics at the dam site—a bite to eat and drink at night, then up the next morning early to begin work on the dam. Today, Selaulim Dam provides over 160 million litres per day (MLD) to most talukas in South Goa. The Anjunem and Selaulim dams are spectacular achievements. Water shortages in Goa became a thing of the past. An agricultural boom took place and food production rose exponentially.

P.V. Jayakrishnan, retired IAS officer and former Goa chief secretary from March 1988 to March 1992, says that Pratapsingh was such a gentleman that he immediately put his officers at ease. 'Mr Rane worked closely with his officers and possessed a deep love for the people of Goa,' recalls Jayakrishnan. 'In fact he was so courteous, correct and methodical that he was more a top class bureaucrat than a politician.' Jayakrishnan says that discussions with the CM were always free and totally frank. They had vehement arguments and often disagreed. But once an issue was discussed threadbare, Pratapsingh had no ego in taking his officers' advice on board.

While work was on full speed on the Selaulim Dam, Pratapsingh gave Jayakrishnan a deadline. A water pipe to the city of Margao had to be completed by 2 October 1989. The entire water pipeline was 26 km long. To get the work completed as fast as possible, Jayakrishnan used to walk the full 26 km distance regularly, inspecting the pipeline. One day, Pratapsingh said: 'Jay, I'm coming on the walk with you,' and off they went, CM and chief secretary, trudging the length of the pipeline. 'I don't think any CM today would walk along an open road in the afternoon heat, bending to check on water pipes and waterworks.'

Another time, Pratapsingh presented Jayakrishnan with another task: four swimming pools were to be built in Miramar. One Olympic-sized pool, one for toddlers, one diving pool and the other a regular pool. Officers and workers toiled day and night, and the project was finished on time. The day of the inauguration brought an unusual sight: the CM and the chief secretary were spotted in their swimming trunks in the pool, swimming together. Mrs Jayakrishnan, myself and others watched from the poolside while Pratapsingh and Jayakrishnan swam the length of the pool. This was how the swimming pools and aquatic facilities of Miramar were inaugurated in December 1988!

'Mr Rane had no airs whatever and was completely informal,' says Jayakrishnan. Once on a morning walk in Altinho, Jayakrishnan, his wife and some house guests chanced upon Pratapsingh and myself on our regular walk. We joked and laughed together as we always did and exchanged some humorous stories. The houseguests later asked Jayakrishnan: 'Was that really the CM? He had no security and was so informal.'

Today, as he drives around Goa's villages deep in the interior, over the tarred roads that skirt orchards of cashew, areca nut and coconut, past brooks and rivulets spanned by small bridges, he marvels at the houses he sees. Once there were only huts here, now most homes are modern structures, with well-kept, plant-filled courtyards and with cars or motorbikes parked in the drive. 'Every home here has either a four wheeler or two wheeler parked in front,' he says with visible pride. 'This was unimaginable when I first started work.'

Availability of water supply, irrigation and the reservoir created by dams is a godsend for biodiversity and wildlife. Always an ardent environmentalist, Pratapsingh developed and upgraded the Cotigao Wildlife Sanctuary, established the Salim Ali Bird Sanctuary and improved the Bondla Wildlife Sanctuary. In 1984, the Pratapsingh Rane government passed the Goa, Daman and Diu Preservation of Trees Act. 'To cut down a tree, particularly a tree of a certain girth, you have to get the permission of the forest department. I set up a Tree Authority. I felt it was my duty to do this else the greenery of Goa would vanish,' he says. Today, in Goa, although there has been an unfortunate rise in construction activity, we still see every shade of green as layers of trees blend into each other in forests that are full of mystery and magic. An intricate latticework of trees—emerald, olive, moss and bright green—is draped on Goa's hillsides.

In November 1982, violence broke out in the port town of Vasco as tensions developed between locals and non-Goan workers, mostly from Karnataka. Hutments were set on fire and migrant families fled the area. Pratapsingh immediately dispatched his best officers to Vasco, among them Rajeev Talwar, then a young sub-divisional magistrate (SDM) in north Goa, given magisterial powers in the south as well. The army was called in, but in Goa, they possessed no weaponry. Wooden batons were supplied. One clear instruction came from the CM: 'Stay awake all night.' Since riots were taking place at night, officers and armed personnel stayed on duty through the night hours and the violence eventually petered out.

Rehabilitation was begun. All the houses that had been burnt were rebuilt. Those who didn't find habitation were accommodated in tiled roof homes. Pratapsingh told the press: 'I have taken a vow to protect the interests of everyone residing in Goa, and I will not hesitate to do all that is in my hands to fulfil this vow.' He has always placed great faith in government rehabilitation efforts to win public trust. 'I rehabilitated all of them [those affected by the Vasco violence], gave all of them houses and plots of land,' he recalls. This was his way of facing challenges—to listen and rehabilitate as best as he could.

In pursuance of his aims of creating a law-abiding government and enabling Goa's citizens to have access to justice and law courts, Pratapsingh went all out to ensure that the Bombay High Court bench was established in Goa in 1982.

Boosting Goa's Arts

Pratapsingh had other important promises to keep, and he kept them. Hadn't he heard the music of the Goan air? Yes, he had listened to the *mando* sung in concerts and homes, the *bhajans* and kirtans in the temples and the hymns in the churches.

'Music is in our [Goa's] water, I think it is in our mud,' the great singer Kishori Amonkar once said. Legendary vocal maestros Kesarbai Kerkar and Kishori Amonkar are both originally from Goa, and India's nightingale Lata Mangeshkar too comes from a family of Goan origin. No surprises that, for Pratapsingh, music and the arts are precious. He learnt to play the piano, and when he was in the mood, he would play his favourite concertos.

In Goa, each village is its own universe surrounded by water and forest, focussed on its own temple or church and its own unique artistic traditions. As a result there is a dizzying profusion of song and dance forms and variety of cultural styles in Goa. 'There is rich local culture everywhere in Goa,' says Pratapsingh. Hindu communities in temples play the *pakhawaj* and *mridangam*, *shamel* (drum) and the *ghumot* (the pot drum, declared a heritage instrument in Goa). In temple courtyards, Dashavtara dance dramas are held. A rousing and energetic symphony of *tashe* (vertical drums) and *shehnai* is played during chariot or palanquin processions in temples. The *chowgudo* drums are typical to Goa, consisting of two drums called the *dobe* and *zil*. Across Goa's temples, the *chowgudo* are often played four times a day.

At harvest time, women sing the *dhalo* or invocations to the *Vanadevata*, divine sprite of the forests. During the *Shigmo* or spring festival, celebrated at the time of Holi, many forms of music and dance are presented. These days the Goan Shigmotsav is celebrated with much fanfare. Goa is known for *dekhni* (folk dance and song) and *dulpod* tunes with their flirtatious lyrics and joyful melodies that make everyone clap and dance. '*Hanv saiba poltodi vethan*' (Please sir, I want to cross the river) is one such popular dekhni dance accompanied by song.

Hindustani classical music traditions were also kept alive in Goa by the Gomantak Maratha Samaj or traditional temple performers. Temples nurtured classical music. Festivals in Goa begin with the Ganesha Vandana. In Gramadevatha festivals, or Dashavtari Kaloutsav, the Raat Kalo is performed. *Kalo* means a mix of dance, music, drama and dialogue and Raat Kalo are all-night concerts in the kalo form featuring themes from the Ramayana and the Mahabharata.

To this palette of music has been added the Portuguese influence: Catholic communities performed the yearning soulful tunes of the *fado*. There are the heartful expressive melodies of the mando as well as the stylized mando dances. Catholic communities play the piano and violin. There are also *natak, zatra, tiatr* and *khel-tiatr* traditions in Goa.

Marathi theatre groups, with their intensely dramatic plays, would often come to Goa in the early days after Liberation. Lacking proper stage facilities, these plays were sometimes staged under a canopy of coconut leaves and also in spaces enclosed by coconut leaves. After the monsoon, when Goa's green environment is bathed in new luminescence, feast days are celebrated in every village in honour of patron deities and saints of chapels. Fairs and concerts take place in the village in which all communities join in. These village feasts, such as Our Lady of Milagres feast in Mapusa, in honour of a deity from a group of seven sisters who, it is believed, were once Hindu, are celebrated by Hindus and Catholics.

The performing arts are complemented by the visual arts. 'Goa has produced some of the best artists in the country,' Pratapsingh says proudly. It has indeed. Master painters Francis Newton (F.N.) Souza and Vasudeo S. (V.S.) Gaitonde hail from Goan families. There are many forms of art here—folk paintings and temple drawings, rosewood carved furniture in homes, *kaavi* art on residential and temple walls. There are Portuguese-style indigo tiles and painted tiles—the *azulejos*. Behind the outwardly plain facades of Hindu homes, interlinked courtyards and pillars open up revealing a hidden world of design. Goa's famous mother of pearl windows and delicate stained glass can be seen in church windows and Catholic mansions, with their ornamental railings, slope-tiled roofs, deep verandahs or *balcaos* and delicately decorated *salas* or living rooms.

Kala Academy: Jewel in Goa's Crown

Goa's multi-layered, rich and complex culture needed its own shrine. During Bandodkar's chief ministership, the Kala Academy had been started in 1972. Now, under Pratapsingh Rane, a new iconic structure for the Kala Academy came up on Panaji's broad Dayanand Bandodkar Marg, which was completed in 1983.

The Kala Academy was Pratapsingh's dream project. He served as its longest-serving chairman, from 1983 to 2012. It was, in every sense, his baby. It was designed by Goa's master architect, Charles Correa, and the building reflects the spirit of modern Goa. On the banks of the Mandovi River, made of the red laterite stone that is native to Goa, the building is an example of the architecture known as 'tropical modern', breaking the barrier between 'outside' and 'inside' and creating a relationship between the building and its surroundings. Trees and lawns merge with the structure and the building is open to the sun and sky. It is a building full of the presence of the river running next to it and the trees that surround it. Its main auditorium, the air-conditioned Dinanath Mangeshkar Kala Mandir indoor auditorium, was inaugurated by then President

Giani Zail Singh. Its open-air auditorium was inaugurated a year later by then PM Rajiv Gandhi.

Govind Kale, curator of the Kala Academy library for over three decades, who also looked after the State Art Exhibition, says that the kind of importance that Pratapsingh gave to the Kala Academy was no less than to matters of governance as CM. 'The Kala Academy enjoyed enormous prestige in Pratapsingh Rane's time because he gave it the same primacy as all the other development work being carried out. The Academy was his flagship project.' Kale says that one of Pratapsingh's great interests was to popularize the bhajans of Goa. Traditionally sung in temples, Goa's bhajans are sung in the classical style and are high art forms. The Kala Academy would organize annual bhajan competitions. Awards would be given for bhajan singing, and the best bhajan singers would be taken to perform in Pandharpur and Belgaum. The devotional bhajan *'Kannada vo Vithalu, Karnataku yene maza lavayila vedhu'*, sung in praise of Shri Vithal, was sung by Goan singers in concerts in Belgaum.

Kale also helped to organize annual artists camps at the Kala Academy where the works of Gaitonde, Souza, Prabhakar Kolte and Ravi Paranjape would be displayed, and sometimes the painters themselves would participate. The vivid blues and greens of Goa's waters and forests and the rich red of its earth have lent themselves to scores of canvases by local artists on the Kala Academy campus. Awards were also given in photography so young Goans would become aesthetically sensitive and open their eyes (and lens) to the spectacular and abundant natural world around them. In Pratapsingh's time, the academy became a showpiece for Goa's traditions as well as a fountainhead of cultural and artistic innovations.

Noted academic Dr Pandurang R. Phaldesai, authority on Goa's folk traditions, was member secretary of the Kala Academy and worked there for 35 years. He recalls how, as chairman of the Kala Academy, Pratapsingh strove to make it a centre of international excellence. The Kala Academy offered courses on Indian classical music, western classical music, creative drama and also had its own drama repertory company. Later, the academy helped to start the Goa College of Music and the Goa College of Fine Arts. 'Every time we had a visit from a foreign VIP or a function, Mr Rane would ask the Kala Academy to produce a show. If he liked it, he wouldn't compliment us, he would simply say, this small thing could have been better. This meant that 99 per cent of it was fine.'

The CM procured a grand piano for the Kala Academy from Germany so that international maestros could be invited to play in Goa. Doyens of Hindustani classical music like Pandit Jasraj were invited to perform at the Kala Academy. Dr Phaldesai says the CM had an expert eye for art, picking out paintings from exhibitions for the Kala Academy's walls. The Goan artist Shridhar Kamat Bambolkar remembers Pratapsingh's love of paintings and how, when we wanted to present a gift to any of our friends or relatives, we would often purchase one of Kamat's vivid watercolours. 'He had a passion for art,' says Kamat. 'He gave me opportunities to visit art melas in Bangalore.' Our favourite artist in Goa was Prafulla Dahanukar, the aunt of our son-in-law Vishwajit Dahanukar. Prafulla Dahanukar's subtle abstract landscapes hang on our walls at home.

Dr Phaldesai says Pratapsingh encouraged the Kala Academy to learn from international theatre. 'He would watch Broadway plays in New York and come back to Kala Academy and tell us what he had seen and how we could stage similar enactments. He would make it a point to come for performances, and when he came, would stay until the end. If for some reason he could not stay, he would approach us Kala Academy staff members, at the beginning of the concert to convey his apologies and inform us that he would be leaving at interval.'

Pratapsingh was possessive about the Kala Academy and determined that it should be insulated from all politics or political activity. Politics was to be kept completely out. Once when P.V. Narasimha Rao, then a minister in the Rajiv Gandhi government, wanted to hold a meeting of political workers at the Kala Academy, Pratapsingh said a firm no. He made sure an alternative venue was provided to Rao. He would refer to the Kala Academy as 'my Kala Academy'. For him, it was the jewel in Goa's crown.

On the twenty-fifth anniversary of Goa's liberation, a grand celebration was held at the Kala Academy. President Giani Zail Singh arrived to flag off the proceedings. It was a mark of the determination of the Pratapsingh Rane government that silver jubilee celebrations went ahead, even though the language agitation was roiling some places at the time.

Even as Goa's cultural achievements were being recognized, a piquant incident on this occasion revealed how once upon a distant time, one of Goa's most talented performing communities, the Gomantak Maratha Samaj, had experienced exploitation and ostracism. At one of the functions at the Kala Academy, CM Pratapsingh Rane sat flanked by President Zail Singh on one side and India's greatest singer Lata Mangeshkar on the other. Mangeshkar's family originally came from the village of Mangeshi, and her family belonged to the Gomantak Maratha Samaj attached to the Shree Mangeshi temple. At the function, Zail Singh asked Mangeshkar to sing, and she answered, 'I am sorry Rashtrapatiji, I will never sing in Goa.' An outraged Zail Singh rose to his feet and stomped out of the auditorium, leaving Pratapsingh to rush after him and see him off as politely as possible. Mangeshkar remained deeply hurt by the sufferings of her community. So much so that she never performed in her ancestral state.

The Kala Academy in Panjim was not the only centre for the arts which was created. In order to decentralize the movement to revive Goa's arts, the Pratapsingh Rane government set up five Ravindra Bhavans at Ponda, Curchorem, Margao, Vasco and Sanquelim. Each was designed as a cultural hub, with state-of-the-art auditoriums complete with modern acoustics, exhibition halls and outdoor performance spaces. The idea was to encourage local talents by providing them with well-equipped facilities and a platform to present their performances.

CHOGM Retreat: Pulled Off to Perfection

In 1982, Pratapsingh took an astute decision. In 1983, it was India's turn to host the CHOGM in New Delhi. While the summit was being planned Pratapsingh decided to write to PM Indira Gandhi suggesting: why not hold the summit's weekend Retreat in Goa? As a UT, the centre would have full control, and the international VIPs would see a different India from New Delhi. They would see an India of white sand beaches and palm forests and also catch glimpses of what a smooth transition Goa had made from Portuguese rule. Importantly, the event would provide a big boost to Goa and enable a massive infrastructure upgrade. Indira Gandhi agreed to consider it, arrived for an inspection in 1982 and gave her approval.

Arrangements began in full swing. The Zuari Bridge from the airport was completed. Roads were widened. Street lights were installed; in fact, street lighting in Goa improved considerably after the CHOGM Retreat. The Hermitage Villas were constructed at the Taj Fort Aguada hotel. Long-distance phone lines were installed and arrangements were made for golf, waterskiing, windsurfing, parasailing, sailing, rowing, fishing, squash and billiards. The Taj built a sports complex for tennis, volleyball and a health club. The hotel also stocked up on smoked oysters, salmon, caviar and T-boned steaks. The cellars were replenished with fine wines.

'The CHOGM Retreat transformed Goa forever,' recalls Rajeev Talwar, former IAS officer who served in Goa from 1980 to 1984. 'It changed the roads, the bridges, the flights, the tourism, in fact the entire infrastructure. Sleepy-friendly Goa was transformed to action packed Goa. We prepared meticulously for it. From 1982, reports would go every day to Delhi on the state of roads, flight connectivity, building of the Taj Hermitage and city repairs.'

Yet, even as hectic preparations were on, on the eve of the CHOGM Retreat, a political crisis blew up. Dr Wilfred de Souza, increasingly frustrated that his efforts to displace the CM were not succeeding and that the party High Command was refusing to dismiss the Rane government, walked out of the Congress. Dr de Souza, who seemed to have become Pratapsingh's arch adversary, kept on demanding that the Rane government be sacked, claiming that Pratapsingh did not have the support of all MLAs. In 1983, a group of MLAs broke away with de Souza and formed a group named Goa Congress. The Goa Congress built its platform on two main demands—statehood for Goa and official language status to Konkani. After leaving the Congress, Dr de Souza brought several no-confidence motions against the Pratapsingh Rane government all of which were defeated. The departure of Dr de Souza's group was no loss to Pratapsingh, who still had a majority in the House and carried on with the work at hand. Furthermore, the plaudits Pratapsingh received for his expert management of the CHOGM Retreat bolstered his position against his attackers.

The day of the Summit Retreat dawned on 25 November 1983. Planeloads of VIPs—39 world leaders and their entourages—arrived. They were to spend the weekend in Goa from the evening of Friday, 25 November, through Saturday, 26, and Sunday, 27. Upon arrival at the Taj, Canadian PM Pierre Trudeau, elated at the warm weather and the sight of the sea, immediately cast off most of his clothes and dashed into the waves. Margaret Thatcher wore a wide smile and made quite an entry to the formal dinner that evening at the Raj Bhavan in a stunning plum-red gown. Indira Gandhi, too, shed her formal saris and opted for an elegant kurta. The arrangements were immaculate, rehearsed to a T. Timings were perfectly maintained. The food was delectable. Taking no risks whatsoever, the sea was patrolled by frogmen, making sure it was safe for the international visitors to swim.

After a perfect weekend of sun and sea, the Commonwealth

heads of government departed in a very good mood. A triumphant Indira Gandhi had warm words of praise for CM Pratapsingh Rane. At a press conference at the airport, the PM said she was very happy that the Retreat event had gone off so well and the choice of holding it in Goa had been perfect. Armed with a ringing endorsement from the High Command, his name in national newspaper headlines, his rivals temporarily silenced, infrastructure development work speeded up and Goa placed firmly on the national map, he was on a high.

Talwar insists Delhi recognized that Goa could have stable governance only when Pratapsingh was at the helm as he stood head and shoulders above his political colleagues in delivering calm, sound administration. What was his secret? 'Mr Rane abided scrupulously by the law and was highly disciplined in his habits. Because he stuck to the letter of the law, the entire government became law abiding and disciplined. He set that tone.' Talwar says Pratapsingh had an 'ever-ready smile' and 'no temper'.

Uday Bhembre, Konkani writer and journalist who joined the assembly for the first time as an independent MLA in 1984 after pulling off a giant killer feat by defeating Babu Naik in Margao, used to meet Pratapsingh regularly. 'Mr Rane was a very well-mannered man and a disciplined man,' recalls Bhembre. 'He maintained great discipline in his own personal life, and in government and administration in a manner in which even Mr Manohar Parrikar, who was dubbed a so-called "strong leader", was not able to do. Rane maintained high standards quietly and without making a fuss.'

Remembering Indira Gandhi

Just a year after the high of the 1983 Retreat came the despondent low of Indira Gandhi's assassination on 31 October 1984. We were shocked at her death. She had been in Goa just a year before, relaxed and smiling in her tasteful kurtas and kaftans, and her gorgeous formal saris. 'I was in Delhi the day of her assassination and due to meet her. I could never have imagined that not only would I not see her that day, but that I would never see her again,' Pratapsingh recalls.

Indira Gandhi played a significant role in Pratapsingh's life. She had given him her unstinting support and had been a source of strength and encouragement. She guided him, built him up and, when he took over the reins of government, gently supervised this rather raw, young CM. She never let him feel he had to keep running to Delhi to seek her support, and he never did. She would say: 'Is there anything specific you want to see me about, Mr Rane? If not, please just carry on with your work.' The press made a big deal of this, as if to suggest Indira Gandhi was deliberately not meeting Pratapsingh, but actually the opposite was the case. She trusted him so much that she did not feel she had to monitor him in any way. 'There will be a lot of pressure on you from all kinds of vested interests,' she told him, 'Ignore them all and focus on your development work.' When delegations of malcontents would go to Indira Gandhi to rail against Pratapsingh and to complain that he was 'indecisive', Indira Gandhi would ask them, 'Is he corrupt, is he inefficient? If not, then why are you complaining?' 'Indira Gandhi trusted me fully,' Pratapsingh recalls.

In general elections later that year, the Congress would win over 400 seats in a tsunami of public sympathy. Pratapsingh went into the assembly elections of December 1984 with confidence that Goa, always mirroring national politics, would win too. Dr de Souza's breakaway faction—the Goa Congress—launched a high-voltage campaign centred around demanding statehood for Goa and official language status for Konkani. But the Goa Congress lost all the seats it contested except one. Only one Goa Congress candidate, Luizinho Faleiro, won from Navelim. The Congress (I), with Pratapsingh as its chief ministerial face, won again with 18 seats. Pratapsingh single-handedly led the Congress to victory.

The Second Term

On 7 January 1985, at the age of 46, Pratapsingh was sworn in again as CM. This was his second term, which was to run from 7 January 1985 to 28 November 1989. He once again held a raft of portfolios of Home, Transport, Personnel, General Administration, Vigilance, Finance, Town & Country Planning, PWD, Education and Art and Culture.

The new CM would now have to call upon all his inner strength for what lay ahead. There would be a violent agitation for language, there would be bitter political manoeuvrings, but a crowning glory would come his way too, when Goa would become India's twenty-fifth state. From a CM with only limited powers, constantly answerable to a Delhi-appointed Lieutenant Governor, he would become a state CM answerable only to his own people. In his second tenure, he would work not with Indira Gandhi but instead with her son, his 'good friend' PM Rajiv Gandhi. Rajiv would prove to be as supportive a friend as Indira Gandhi was.

After his election win in 1984, Pratapsingh's rivals were chafing at the bit. They were desperate to puncture holes in the CM's statesmanlike aura. Pratapsingh was in his prime as a leader. In the House, he led from the front, confident, composed and thoroughly well-prepared with all facts and figures. As CM, he was firm, informed and so steeped in domain knowledge that it was universally acknowledged that in his cabinet, the CM was the highest performer.

The cheerful, ever-smiling Congressman Luizinho Faleiro had been an ally of Pratapsingh. But in Pratapsingh's second term, the actions of Luizinho were to have a big impact. Luizinho had been a student activist, then a trade union leader in Zuari Agro Chemicals, as well as in other unions, before joining the Congress. In 1983, when Dr de Souza left the Congress and formed the Goa Congress, Luizinho joined Dr de Souza's breakaway faction. At this time, he was the MLA from Navelim. I recall in 1983, before leaving the party, Luizinho came to our house with his resignation letter. 'I had close relations with the Ranes, and I felt I must inform them that I was leaving the Congress,' recalls Luizinho. 'My reasons for leaving were that I wanted to campaign strongly for the cause of the Konkani language in Goa as well as statehood for Goa, issues which I felt were not getting their due.'

The demand for the Konkani language and statehood had been gathering force over the years. In July 1983, in Pratapsingh's first term, Luizinho had moved a private member's resolution on statehood for Goa. Now in Pratapsingh's second term, on 19 July 1985, Luizinho, the lone Goa Congress MLA, moved a private member's Bill to make Konkani Goa's sole official language. 'The sentiments and demands around the Konkani language were genuine and had grown over time, but the manner in which Luizinho brought the Bill was nothing but a political gimmick to create trouble and weaken me,' says Pratapsingh.

Some argued at this time that Luizinho was perhaps motivated by the desire to embarrass the Pratapsingh Rane government. Some misrepresented Pratapsingh as a pro-Marathi Maratha who had made derogatory remarks about Konkani and looked down upon the language. Nothing could be further from the truth. Pratapsingh may have himself been Marathi-speaking and a proud Maratha, but he knew well the peoples' love for Konkani, a sweet, lilting, rhythmic language that chimes with the playful beauty of the Goan landscape. Pratapsingh himself speaks fluent Konkani.

Driven primarily by the desire to give proper and lengthy consideration to a decision on such a sensitive issue as language, Pratapsingh promised to introduce an official language Bill at 'a more appropriate time'. However, two months after Luizinho Faleiro's Bill, the Congress Party Executive passed a resolution, with the backing of then MP Eduardo Faleiro, supporting the demand to make Konkani the sole official language of Goa.

Luizinho's Bill and Pratapsingh's perceived 'stalling' became what Luizinho himself describes as something that 'sparked the powder keg'. Luizinho today is at pains to point out that the reason why he brought this Bill was not to weaken Rane but because, on a visit to meet Indira Gandhi in Delhi in January 1980, when he had blurted out to her that the people of Goa craved their own state, Mrs Gandhi responded with the words, 'First you decide your language, then we will give you statehood.' If Goa wanted to be a state, she needed her own language.

A few words here about the long demand for the Konkani language (and by extension statehood) in Goa. The cultural and literary ferment around Konkani began around 1910, when intellectuals and writers from the Konkan region began to increasingly write and speak in Konkani to build up its cultural and linguistic traditions. When the Portuguese arrived and embarked on the religious and cultural transformation of Goa, Konkani was driven underground as the colonial rulers tried to stamp it out entirely. However, Konkani continued to be spoken in households and communities.

In the 1950s, when the linguistic organization of states was being undertaken and language agitations were at the forefront of public debate, groups of students from Konkan—mainly Mangaloreans and Goans—began to form Konkani *mandal*s just as other language groups were forming Gujarati mandals and Kannada mandals. 'It was a quest for identity,' recalls Bhembre, who joined a Konkani mandal in Bombay where he was then a student. 'Konkani became for us the language of the Goa identity,' Bhembre says.

The Marathi speakers, however, insisted that Konkani was only a dialect of Marathi. For years, this literary and cultural movement for Konkani went on, confined mainly to writers, scholars, littérateurs and poets. In 1963, the Marathi newspaper *Rashtramat* was founded to campaign for the Konkani language and to campaign against merger with Maharashtra. 'We were trying to mount an intellectual, social, historical argument for Konkani and for a separate identity for Goa,' says Bhembre, who was assistant editor of *Rashtramat*.

Sentiments around Konkani were linked to the demand for statehood because a separate language also implied the need for a separate state. Demands for statehood had been asserting themselves since the Opinion Poll of 1967. Ever since the issue of Goa's merger with Maharashtra had been settled with the 1967 Opinion Poll, Konkani as a language for Goa received a fillip. After the 1961 Liberation, India's central government moved to make English the medium of instruction. Although by the end of the nineteenth century, many parishes in Portuguese Goa had introduced English education, the standards were not as high, nor was English as widespread as in British India. After Liberation, therefore, it was English that became a much sought after language and Goa soon became an almost completely English-speaking state. But after Liberation, for the first time, Konkani became the medium of instruction in a small number of schools.

When Luizinho introduced the Bill for Konkani as Goa's official language, initially this was seen as a diversionary tactic and not allowed in the assembly. Generally, governments across legislatures do not accept private members' Bills when they are moved by Opposition members. But Luizinho's Bill became a catalyst. A powerful movement took off. The demands were twofold: official status for Konkani and statehood for Goa. The feeling was that although the white colonial masters had gone, now ministers and bureaucrats from Delhi had become the new masters of Goa. Thus, the demand for Konkani was linked with strong statehood sentiments, sentiments which soon spread from thinkers and activists to the people at large.

Matters came to a head when the Konkani Porjecho Avaz (KPA) or voice of the Konkani people, an organization of Konkani writers and intellectuals championing the Konkani cause, fixed 19 December 1986, the twenty-fifth silver jubilee anniversary of Goa's

Liberation, as the deadline for making Konkani the official language. The KPA simultaneously announced a boycott of government-organized silver jubilee festivities and even demanded CM Pratapsingh Rane's resignation. The KPA organized a massive rally at Panaji's Azad Maidan, which unfortunately went out of control. The agitators had three demands: statehood for Goa, official status to Konkani and that Konkani be placed in the Eighth Schedule of the Constitution, which lists India's official languages.

Pressures grew on Pratapsingh as people came out on the street across South Goa and in Panaji. 'We tried to keep our movement as peaceful as possible, confined to holding meetings, morchas and rallies. Some, however, like Churchill Alemao, betrayed us and did things of which none of us approved,' recalls Bhembre, then a leader of the KPA. Churchill's supporters were accused of planting hundreds of iron spikes on the road as roadblocks and stoning government buses. Eight people lost their lives because some hotheads in the agitation turned violent. Life in South Goa came to a standstill with tourists stranded in hotels and public transport and train services paralysed. The agitation continued to gather momentum at the tail end of 1986, becoming what some have called 'the fiercest protest movement in Goa's post liberation history'.

The KPA issued an ultimatum on Konkani. On the other side, Marathiwadis took up cudgels. 'Marathi has taught the Goans patriotism, it can't get cowed by goondas,' declared Ramakant Khalap of the pro-Marathi MGP. Said Pundalik Naik, convenor of the KPA: 'Konkani is the language of the Goans, whether Hindu or Catholic. How does one say *"mhojem xet bangarachem koshem dista"* (how golden is my land) in Marathi and still convey an authentic feeling?'

Riding Out the Language Storm

Pratapsingh Rane showed his true mettle in this agitation. He dealt with it in a balanced yet firm manner. The police were quick to take action. Companies of the Central Reserve Police Force (CRPF) were deployed. The army staged flag marches. The CM's resolve in the face of the protests never faltered. He stayed calm, collected and courageous. Six years earlier, in 1980, in response to accusations about one of his ministers, he had declared, 'I have the blood of Chhatrapati Shivaji Maharaj in my veins,' showing his iron resolve in crisis situations. The Pratapsingh Rane government controlled the protests with firmness, without any form of brutality on protesters.

Yet, once peace had been achieved on the streets, the battle now shifted to the political arena. The Congress party was divided on the language issue, with one section vociferously demanding Konkani as sole official language. There is no doubt that many in the party wanted to use the language issue to bring about Pratapsingh's downfall. There were several reports in fact that the hand of some Congress (I) leaders was behind the KPA. The persistent demand for Pratapsingh's resignation is proof of this hidden hand from within the Congress itself.

However, Pratapsingh was convinced of the strength of the pro-Konkani sentiments among the people, and his government introduced a Bill proposing a dual language formula in July 1986. But this Bill did not pass because eight MLAs rebelled, including two from Gujarati-speaking Daman and Diu, and the session had to be prorogued. Votaries of Konkani held Rane squarely responsible for the last-minute abortion of this official Bill. A group of ministers—Power Minister Harish Zantye (who aspired to Pratapsingh's job), Law and Revenue Minister Sheikh Hassan Haroon, Tourism Minister Luis Proto Barbosa, and Panchayati Raj Minister Francisco Sardinha—rushed to Delhi to meet Rajiv

Gandhi, demanding that Pratapsingh be dismissed. But Rajiv refused to even see these ministers, leaving them no option but to resign in a bit of a huff.

Pratapsingh was on the horns of the dilemma: the Hindu-dominated north Goa might explode in protests if Konkani was given official status, and the Catholic-dominated south would erupt if it wasn't. It was as if the old MGP vs UGP rivalry of a Hindu north Goa vs a Catholic south Goa was opening up again in the political sphere. He himself was determined that every language of Goa, be it Marathi or Konkani be respected. As a strong champion of statehood for Goa, he was also convinced of the need for an official language of the state, distinct from Marathi, and thus accepted the need for Konkani. He was acutely aware that Goa's language question would have to be resolved if the UT of Goa was to become a state. Visiting Goa at the height of the agitation, Rajiv Gandhi, echoing his mother's words, had repeated to protestors: 'Decide on your language issue and you'll get statehood.' However, supportive as he was on the need for a distinct language for Goa, at the same time, Pratapsingh thoroughly disapproved of the manner in which Konkani agitators had allowed the movement to go out of control.

With the language issue now splitting the party and with the four rebel ministers having resigned, the Congress High Command began to worry about party unity. Mediators were dispatched from Delhi and arrived in Goa—Congress General Secretary Raghunandan Lal (R.L.) Bhatia and Minister of State for Home Chintamani Panigrahi. The message to the Congress in Goa was unequivocal: patch up at once. Delhi's emissaries were in no mood to listen to the rebel ministers' demand for the dismissal of Pratapsingh Rane. In fact, the moment Bhatia got off the plane at Dabolim airport, he greeted a flummoxed Zantye with the mocking words: 'How are you, Chief Minister?' showing that the national leadership was well aware of the games being played. By nightfall, Zantye and others withdrew their resignations and patched up with Pratapsingh. The visitors suggested a formula to the language imbroglio: the Hindus should not insist that Marathi should be the official language and Catholics should not insist on using roman script for Konkani.

The Goa, Daman and Diu Official Language Bill, was presented to the Legislative Assembly in 1986, and the Goa, Daman and Diu Official Language Act was passed on 4 February 1987. The law read: 'Konkani language shall…be the official language for all or any of the official purposes of the Union territory…*Provided that*… in case of the Goa District the Marathi language, and in the case of Daman and Diu Districts, the Gujarati language, shall also be used for all or any of the official purposes and different dates may be appointed for different official purposes….'[9] So Konkani shall be the official language, *provided that* Marathi shall also be used. With that sentence ended Goa's language conflict.

The long struggle for Konkani and Goa's long drawn out language battle had been brought to a peaceful conclusion and all sides were satisfied. Since then Konkani writers like Ravindra Kelekar and Damodar Mauzo have gone on to win Sahitya Akademi and Jnanpith awards, bringing pride to all Goans. Today, official invitations in Goa come in four languages: Konkani, Marathi, English and Hindi.

Chief Minister Pratapsingh Rane had ridden out the storm—both street agitations and political manoeuvring to bring him down—to emerge on the other side, the unwavering captain steady at the wheel. He had reached out to reconcile different factions with his customary calm: 'When the people's demands are strong for a certain policy, no elected government can afford to ignore it,' he recalls. 'We tried our best to keep all sections happy and I think we succeeded.'

---

[9]The Goa, Daman and Diu Official Language Act, 1987, 14 April 1987, https://tinyurl.com/y3bu97hy. Accessed on 1 August 2023.

New State, New Challenges

Once Goa had its official language, statehood for Goa could not be delayed any longer. Milestones followed in quick succession. Two months after the Official Language Act was passed, the Lieutenant Governor gave his assent to the Act on 14 April 1987. On 28 April 1987, Pratapsingh along with Eduardo Faleiro, union minister and MP from South Goa; Shantaram Naik, MP from North Goa; and other members of the Pratapsingh Rane cabinet met Rajiv Gandhi to urge statehood for Goa. As CM of the UT of Goa, Pratapsingh had always made the strongest possible case for statehood. 'We have one of the highest per capita incomes, our tax collections have soared and our claims to statehood are much higher than others,' he told newspersons in 1985 when preparations were being made to celebrate 25 years of Goa's Liberation.[10] The Statehood for Goa or Goa, Daman and Diu Reorganisation Bill was introduced in the Lok Sabha on 6 May, it was passed on 11 May to thunderous applause, with a total majority of all 315 members of Parliament present voting for it. On 30 May, statehood was conferred on Goa, with Pratapsingh Rane as the first CM of the Goa state.

Statehood for Goa! What a thrilling challenge for an administrator who thoroughly enjoyed the hard work of governance, the CEO-CM for whom executive action that produced concrete results was a lifelong calling. After statehood, to accelerate planned development and administrative efficiency, one of the first steps taken by the Rane government was to split Goa into two districts, north and south, with their headquarters in Panaji and Margao, respectively. Goa was divided into four subdivisions—Mapusa, Ponda, Vasco and Quepem—with all talukas divided among them.

Now that he was fully in charge, the remaining work on the Anjunem and Selaulim dams were taken up on a war footing.

---

[10] 'Rane's Strong Case for Statehood', *OHeraldo*, 4 October 1985.

Work was speeded up in infrastructure projects. The agricultural achievements of Pratapsingh's government must be specially noted. Systematic efforts were made to ensure that farmers adopted the latest technologies for cultivation. New technologies were brought into Goa, including new soil nutrients, weedicides, battery powered fencing, scientific animal husbandry, procedures for cross-bred milch animals and veterinary sciences. Fisheries, horticulture, scientific management of forests and multiple cropping patterns for paddy fields were developed. The national watershed development project for rainfed areas was started to conserve rainwater. Farmers were incentivized to cultivate a variety of cash crops, including sugarcane coconuts, bananas, mangoes, cashews, spices, vegetables, pulses and areca nuts.

After the Goa, Daman and Diu Public Health Act, 1985, was passed making provisions for health and sanitary facilities for Goans; for the first time, Goans got some form of health insurance. In the early stages, it was not a formalized scheme as it is today but involved a guarantee from the government for reimbursement of healthcare costs.

Tourism was recognized as an industry by the Goa government in 1987. Goa's Regional Plan, prepared under the Town and Country Planning Act, was approved in 1986, and greatly expanded Goa's tourism industry by providing for tourism development in many areas.

'Shiksha Samrat'

'I had always believed that Goa should have its own independent university. Without it, students would have to sit for examination papers that were set in Bombay,' he says. The Goa University Act had been passed in 1984 and the Goa University was set up, commencing work shortly thereafter. The university campus, spread over 175 hectares (430 acres) and located in Taleigao plateau, began to come up. The artist Satish Gujral designed the university buildings—an imaginative design of peach-coloured walls, brick-coloured sloping roofs and arched windows and entrances in the Goan-Portuguese style. The structure has been much remarked upon. Goa University offered honours courses in Arts, Science and Commerce, and in 1987, the Rane government also helped establish the department of Portuguese and Lusophone studies, given Goa's Portuguese background.

For Pratapsingh, Goa's distinctive Portuguese heritage needed to be studied and not forgotten. For example, in 1980 when miscreants attacked a statue of sixteenth century Portuguese poet Luís Vaz de Camões whose epic poem 'The Lusiads' praised Vasco da Gama's voyage to India, the statue was moved into the Archaeological Museum of Goa for safety. Pratapsingh also made a concerted effort to learn official-level Portuguese. He knew a bit of Portuguese from his childhood but not enough to be able to read early administrative and property records of Goa, which were all in Portuguese. The academic Dr Maria do Ceu Barreto recalls how she was approached with a request from the CM to teach him the Portuguese language. 'I met Mr Rane at his official residence in Altinho. His charming wife welcomed me. A well-groomed, cordial and serious gentleman came in and introduced himself as Pratapsingh Rane. I asked him why he wanted to learn Portuguese. He said his wish to learn the language was not to engage himself with something other than politics but to be able to understand his property documents, which were all in Portuguese. A fair motive.'

Dr Barreto was pleasantly surprised to see how hard Pratapsingh worked at learning Portuguese, did his homework regularly and, in spite of his busy schedule, rarely missed a class. By the end of the course, he could read and translate Portuguese documents and even converse, although haltingly, in Portuguese. 'The serious gentleman I had first met disappeared and was replaced by someone who loved to talk, who would laugh at the various funny incidents that happened during his political life, who loved to narrate about his stay abroad when he was a student. I came to know that what he cherished most was to promote education. The school he patronized in his constituency in Poriem had all the facilities of any other school in any Goan city,' recalls Dr Barreto. She has become our family friend and a regular at our annual Ganesh Chaturthi lunch functions.

Pratapsingh also started on plans to expand the GIM. The GIM had originally started from a small room in the V.M. Salgaocar College of Law. Later, when an old building fell vacant in Ribandar, the GIM was shifted there. Unmindful of his political rivalries with Wilfred de Souza, Pratapsingh brought in Dr de Souza's brother, the distinguished educationist Romuald de Souza, a Jesuit priest who had served as director of the XLRI in Jamshedpur, to work as founder-director of the GIM. In 2010, Dr Romuald de Souza was awarded the Padma Shri for his contribution to education. The GIM found its permanent home when Pratapsingh shifted it to Sattari and ensured the institute got as much land as required. The GIM is now a nationally ranked and recognized management college. It has a spanking futuristic campus in ochre and white, situated on a Sattari hill top surrounded by green slopes. This new GIM opened its doors to students in 1993. In 1987, the International Centre Goa (ICG) was founded, aiming to create a global centre of excellence for ideas, debates and research from India and around the world. Once complete, the ICG was formally inaugurated by then President Shankar Dayal Sharma in 1996.

Establishing government schools was another priority. Private proprietors like the Chowgules and Dempos had their own schools and colleges, such as the well-regarded Dhempe College of Arts & Science, but government schools were lacking. A network of primary schools had existed since the days of Bandodkar. Building on Bandodkar's plans, Pratapsingh began to set up government higher secondary schools and government colleges. Primary, middle, secondary and higher secondary schools were given funds to upgrade facilities. Sattari got its first government college. The sprawling Government College of Arts, Science and Commerce in Sanquelim opened in 1988. A year later, the Government College of Arts, Science and Commerce was established in Quepem, and in 1989–90, the Government College of Arts, Science and Commerce was established in Khandola, Marcela. The Goa Medical College was upgraded and the government colleges of dentistry and architecture were opened. The Fatorda sports stadium was completed in 1989 and opened to the public.

'Pratapsingh Rane is Goa's Shiksha Samrat,' says writer Shashikant Punaji, who has been our close associate and worked with us at the Goa Bal Bhavan. 'It is his deep and abiding love of Goa and Goa's people that lies behind all the policies which he planned and implemented.'

He not only loved Goa's people, he loved Goa's fragile beauty. In 1988, the Goa Prevention of Defacement of Property Act was passed to protect Goa's picturesque skyline from being disfigured by posters and banners.

Finding My Calling

After Pratapsingh became CM for the first time, I had initially busied myself with setting about settling into our new home. We had moved into the CM's residence in Altinho. Altinho is an exclusive enclave on a hill, with tree-shaded official bungalows, lush green parks set amidst sloping shrub-lined roads. At the top of the hill sits the grand archbishop's palace. The CM's house is a stately home, with red sloping roofs, patterned balustrades and railings, just down the hill from the Archbishop's palace. In pursuance of his goal of never losing touch with the people, Pratapsingh would meet scores of people at this house every morning before leaving for his office at the Old Secretariat in Panaji. The morning meetings gave him an opportunity to assess peoples' needs and work on them in his own methodical way.

In 1956, the National Bal Bhavan movement was started from New Delhi. The Bal Bhavan was an all-India programme to encourage children across India to excel in the creative arts. In his second term, CM Pratapsingh Rane brought the Bal Bhavan scheme to Goa. He arranged for two rooms at the Lyceum Complex in Altinho to start Goa's first Bal Bhavan in 1986. And this is where I found my calling.

The Bal Bhavan was to become an integral part of my life. I had always been interested in public service. I'm not one for occupying myself with only ladies' kitty parties. To try and make a difference, to provide a space for children to discover their talents makes my heart sing with joy. When the Bal Bhavan was started, I took over first as vice chairman and then as chairperson and remained at this post until 2012. By the time I left, Goa had 42 Bal Bhavans, and the Panaji Bal Bhavan moved to two marvellous new buildings in the city centre. We became an institution with full autonomy and threw ourselves into our work with passion. The concept of the Bal Bhavan movement was for the child to discover his or her latent talents outside the school walls. In a free atmosphere, it was amazing to see how the child discovers herself or himself and excels in her or his inborn talent with confidence.

Rupesh Kashinath Gawas was a little boy from the village of Keri. His father was the village carpenter, but Rupesh showed a talent for vocals from an early age, singing kirtans and bhajans in his local Hanuman temple. The Bal Bhavan volunteers found Rupesh, heard his melodious voice and began to train him. He was so talented that when it came to selecting candidates for the National Bal Shree Awards, the committee decided on Rupesh. But we thought, he's such a tiny, slight child; will he be able to compete for an all-India award? Not only was Rupesh able to compete, but he won. One of the first ever winners of the National Bal Shree

Award—instituted in 1995—presented in a ceremony at Rashtrapati Bhavan in the presence of the then president Shankar Dayal Sharma, was 14-year-old Rupesh Gawas of Keri village from Goa.

Returning to Goa, Rupesh was felicitated by us in Panaji in 1996 when then PM P.V. Narasimha Rao came for the function. We gave a VIP invitation to Rupesh's father. One of the ministers, Harish Zantye, in whose firm Rupesh's father worked, saw Rupesh's father enter the VIP enclosure, and, recognizing him, asked what he was doing there. 'As the father of India's first Bal Shree winner, there is no more important guest than him,' I told Zantye with pride.

Today, Rupesh Gawas is a lecturer of vocal music at the Kala Academy. 'Without the rural Bal Bhavans, I would not be there today,' he says. 'After winning the award, I often visited Rashtrapati Bhavan and met many presidents including APJ Abdul Kalam. Kalam told me that the real talent of India is in the rural areas.' Rupesh has a photograph of Pratapsingh and myself presenting him with a sitar. The boy is very small and the instrument dwarfs him, in the same way that tiny Goa has still created an efflorescence of artistic work that dwarfs the state's small size.

My work at the Bal Bhavan also allowed me to develop my own administrative skills. Our first director Ramachandra Bhimanna Jirage guided me. I learnt how to manage people and sort out matters with understanding, care and attention to detail. Indira Gandhi had been the founder-chairperson of the first National Bal Bhavan, and she was followed by extremely capable successors like Pupul Jayakar, Mekhla Jha and others. Mekhla Jha visited us in Goa, and I received a great deal of guidance from her.

We also started the process to set up the Sanjay School or Sanjay Centre for Special Education. This school for children with disabilities was established in 1983. I brought in Tessie Rebello, who was the wife of the then Captain of the Port Trust authority and a trained special educator, to help us. Initially, we had just a small room; later, when the Sanjay School began to expand, we became much bigger and relocated to Porvorim. I brought in specialists like Dr R. Marthanda Varma, founder-director of National Institute of Mental Health and Neurosciences (NIMHANS) from Bangalore, and Rukmini Krishnaswamy, who was an authority on special education, to guide and help us. We started an outreach programme to get parents to bring their children to the Sanjay School as there was so much stigma just to bring in children with disabilities. Later, in 1988, the Sanjeevani section was added for slow learners, then higher secondary schools were set up.

Today, the Sanjay School system in Goa has bounded forward, expanding by leaps and bounds with immense work being done in the field of research, outreach and training for children with disabilities. Both initiatives—Sanjay School and Bal Bhavans—brought many new opportunities to the children of Goa. I like to think that we broke an important mental barrier in Goa when we brought in vulnerable children into the schooling system. In an interview with Oprah Winfrey on her book *The Light We Carry*, former US First Lady Michelle Obama once shared an important insight on parenting. She said: parent the child you have, not the child you wish you had.[11] In our own way, I think we too imparted valuable lessons on parenting.

Sunset on Goa's Golden Decade

Pratapsingh had miles to go and many promises to keep. He was a man in a hurry. Only the best would do for Goa. Goa must develop on all fronts, must develop fast and develop to global standards. How he loved Goa, the people here in this green archipelago. He had weathered storms and strife, factionalism and protests, bloody street violence and cunning intrigue. He had presided over a UT

---

[11]'The Light We Carry: Michelle Obama and Oprah Winfrey', *Netflix*, 25 April 2023

that had blossomed under his watch into a full-fledged state. But through these ten years he never lost focus: *Let's build, with all our heart and soul, a paradise, here, in Goa.* This red earth, these waters, this green archipelago of such infinite variety, this Goa whose invisible music rang in his ears. He had taken every opportunity to bring modernity, change and international standards of industry and town planning, leisure and tourism, and he was eager to see the changes through, to ensure the work got done. But it was not to be.

By the 1989 assembly elections, the sun set on Goa's golden decade. The Congress got 20 seats in the polls, with the MGP as a close second with 18 seats. On 9 January 1990, Pratapsingh was sworn in as CM for the third time. But 40-year-old Churchill Braz Alemao, Congress MLA from Benaulim, someone who was alleged to have brought in violent elements during the language agitation, broke away from the Congress with his supporters, and the Pratapsingh Rane government's majority collapsed. Thus, Alemao brought down Pratapsingh's three-month-old government. On 27 March, his government fell and Pratapsingh resigned. In Pratapsingh's place, Alemao was sworn in as CM.

This misguided act by Alemao began Goa's dreadful decade—the 1990s. This was a 10-year period that would see as many as 13 CMs come in and be rapidly despatched, when governments fell like ninepins, and other governments were sworn in at regular intervals, each administration failing to complete a full term. Coming on the heels of the 1980s, a decade when development had truly taken off, when institutions had been built, when plans had been laid for even better opportunities, it was as if the steadily burning candle of continuous growth was suddenly snuffed out. Without her ablest captain at the wheel, Goa dived headlong into turmoil and turbulence. The best of times gave way to the worst of times.

FIVE

THE TURBULENT DECADE: 1990-2000

'It is the greed for power among certain politicians which causes instability.'

We could never have imagined what lay ahead of us in those happy days of the 1980s. We were always busy. Our children were growing up, Pratapsingh had his all-consuming passion for Goa's development driving him forward, I had my work at the Bal Bhavan. We could not have imagined that we would be betrayed and people would be short-sighted enough to pull down a CM who was straining every nerve to bring the best to Goa. Only the best would do for Goa: artist Satish Gujral to design the Goa University; master architect Charles Correa for the Kala Academy; experts and economists on the Goa planning board. 'Short-sighted people became resentful of my long tenure,' says Pratapsingh. 'People were ambitious. They thought, he is doing all of this, maybe I can do better. But perhaps they had certain shortcomings because their governments could not last.'

Pratapsingh's close friend Shahu Chhatrapati, Maharaja of Kolhapur, provides insights on why Pratapsingh was such a misfit in Goa's unstable decade of the 1990s. A direct thirteenth descendant of Shivaji, Shahu Chhatrapati is a true Maratha doyen. A well-read and knowledgeable person, he is an authority on Maratha history and traditions and today lives in the richly designed Kolhapur Palace, which he maintains with painstaking care.

Shahu Chhatrapati is our family friend. He attended our wedding in Sandur. He believes Pratapsingh was, unlike others, focussed on a delivery-oriented government because of his disciplined approach. 'Pratapsingh Rane went to the Shri Shivaji Preparatory Military School, which is a school designed to train boys to join the army. That is why, from an early age, he became highly disciplined and was able to bring in a great deal of discipline into his administration as well as in his personal life. Whatever the provocation, he always remains cool and composed. Even if he gets angry, he never shows it. He is always approachable to the public. But although he does not play petty politics, it is a mistake to think that Pratapsingh Rane is politically simple. No one can stay CM for so long unless he can gauge the political situation well. Pratapsingh is not Julius Caesar. I would say he is Mark Antony.' (Caesar was a supremo of ruthless ambition, but Mark Antony was known to be decent and loyal.)

Shahu Chhatrapati points out that before 1987, when Goa was a UT, the centre lavished resources upon Goa hoping to bring the UT up to speed with the rest of India. Pratapsingh made the best use of these resources in using them to provide what Goa needed the most. Tarred roads, irrigation and healthcare and education were his priorities. Always very comfortable with high performing bureaucrats, Pratapsingh was able to give off his best.

With the coming of statehood in 1987, the administrative structure of Goa was transformed. Now Goa was no longer under the centre's supervision but run by its own politicians. In this sense, there was a power shift from bureaucrats to politicians, from a politically passive, New Delhi-controlled enclave run by administrators to a tumultuous full democracy where politicians had full sway. Statehood was a boon for Goa, but in some ways, it also spurred vaulting political ambitions.

In the decade between 1990 and 2000, the first decade after

statehood, Goa was in a state of turmoil, punctuated only with the periods of calm when Pratapsingh was in power. Since the achievement of statehood, Goa has had as many as 18 CMs. Chief ministers in the 1990–2000 decade rose and fell at breakneck speed. Most of these politicians seemed to have no loyalty to any party; they all seemed to be motivated by the feeling of why-should-Pratapsingh-Rane-be-CM-every-time-and-why-not-me. They could not recognize that every time he took the CM's chair, he outdid them in effective and disciplined governance. 'Democracy is in a nascent stage in Goa, as well as in the rest of India. As generations become more educated, the quality of democracy is bound to improve,' Pratapsingh believes.

It all began with the assembly polls of 1989, which were tantalizingly close. The Congress won by a wafer-thin margin of two seats, winning 20, while the MGP won 18. At one point, both the Congress and MGP were 18, but the Congress got two extra seats because two seats were countermanded. With the MGP and the Congress neck and neck, Ramakant Khalap of the MGP staked a claim to form the government.

In Khalap's words: 'Look, I had the highest swing in my favour. The Congress had fallen from a final tally of 28 (in 1980) to 18. But I had risen from two to 18. It's perfectly obvious that I had the people's mandate. Mr Rane only won because two seats had been countermanded in the elections, and they later went in the Congress's favour. But they did not allow me to form the government, and I had a sense of indignation at this unfairness. Rane continued as CM until the two seats were filled, and so the Congress became 20. With such a close difference between the Congress and the MGP, anything could happen. Members of Legislative Assembly were anxious for ministerships. There was pressure from both sides. Myself as LoP and Mr Rane as CM were trying to control our people. The Congress was trying to pressurize my group. In the middle of all this tension, I suddenly got a call from Mr Rane. "Ramakant," he said jokingly in colloquial Marathi, "your 'bull' [referring to an MLA] is harassing me for a cabinet berth, how can I give him this, it's impossible." "Maybe the 'bull' is infatuated with power," I said in a risqué joke. We both laughed. I later found out that this "bull" was Pandurang Raut, a newly elected MLA from Bicholim, who had become a little swollen-headed after defeating veteran Congressman and former minister Harish Zantye. I told Raut: "Cool it, we don't have the numbers and the governor will not call us." But Raut kept calling and pestering me. The next thing I know is that he had joined up with Churchill Alemao, who was angry that Rane had not made him sports minister. Together, they formed a splinter group called the "Group of 7". A faction from the Congress also broke away and we became 18+7.'

This group, with Churchill Alemao as its frontman, got ready to pull down the Pratapsingh Rane government. Churchill, the big, brusque, tough-talking MLA from Benaulim, was regarded as a controversial individual who was briefly jailed in an alleged smuggling case but played Robin Hood to his supporters. The reckless Churchill, who had a great passion for football, was demanding that he be made sports minister. But Pratapsingh, ever the meritocrat, aloof to political pressures, insisted that the sports ministry go to Francisco Monte Cruz, who had overseen the building of the Pandit Jawaharlal Nehru Stadium (locally known as the Fatorda multipurpose sports stadium) in record time of six months, so that the international Nehru Gold Cup Football Tournament could be held there before a packed crowd of Goa's football fans. Pratapsingh was of the view that Churchill was still too much of a greenhorn to be a minister. Furious, Churchill defected from the Congress. The Pratapsingh Rane government, which only had a precarious two-seat majority, collapsed.

Some reports said the idea of pulling down the Pratapsingh government in 1990 had actually originated from the veteran leader Dr Luis Proto Barbosa who wanted to be CM. Barbosa was a distinguished figure, a Congressman widely known as 'Proto Barboz', who had played an important role during the 1967 Opinion Poll. In 1990, however, Barbosa played a wily game. Barbosa was the Speaker at this time, and he, along with six other Congress (I) MLAs, including Churchill Alemao, walked out of the Congress. The 18-MLA-strong Opposition MGP offered support to the defectors, with the aim to form a government.

But Barbosa did not immediately become CM. He could not resign from Speakership for fear that Deputy Speaker Simon D'Souza would disqualify all those who defected. So, a new party—Goan People's Party—was hurriedly formed, which was backed by the MGP. One of the defectors, Churchill Alemao, was chosen as CM. Churchill was propped up to keep the seat warm for Proto Barboz. All these machinations were extremely shocking for Goans who now saw that Congress MLAs defected to make common cause with the arch-rivals MGP only because certain individuals seemed to desperately want Pratapsingh's job.

A no-confidence motion against the Pratapsingh Rane government was passed by 25 votes to zero. The Congress (I) boycotted the assembly and instead decided to take the matter to court. Under the Anti-Defection Law, disqualification can be pre-empted if one-third of the legislators of a party defect. With seven defectors—(six MLAs plus Speaker Barbosa) out of the 20-MLA-strong Congress (I)—the Barbosa-led group got around the disqualification clause. Interestingly, all the six Congress MLAs who defected were Catholics.

In fact, the defectors all seemed to be motivated by a certain identity-politics mindset. Perhaps they defected because they felt it was time Goa had a Catholic CM.

This was evident from Barbosa's statement to the media: 'We acted in the interest of Catholic–Hindu unity.' It was ironical indeed that the MGP, originally the party strongest among the Hindus of north Goa, made common cause with the Congress defectors who seemed to be motivated by the desire to make someone of a Catholic background the CM. The Barbosa-led Goan People's Party and the MGP now created an alliance named Progressive Democratic Front (PDF) and formed the government.

Crazy Game of Thrones Hurts Governance

From March to April 1990, Churchill stayed as CM for a month—at the time, the shortest spell for a CM ever in Goa. Ramakant Khalap of the MGP, with his trademark thick, wavy hair and bright, intelligent eyes, became deputy CM. Khalap is an outstanding intellectual and lawyer, and for him to share power with a figure like Churchill was disturbing for all to see. Goa's descent into an extended period of political chaos had begun.

In April 1990, Luis Proto Barbosa, true to the plan, became CM. But Barbosa's Goan People's Party and Khalap's MGP could not pull along. Both groups kept squabbling over allocation of ministerial portfolios and the loaves and fishes of office. By the end of 1990, Khalap withdrew support from Barbosa and Barbosa's PDF government fell on 13 December 1990 without completing even a year in office.

The political musical chairs game was so preposterous that even seasoned observers were bewildered. After withdrawing support from Barbosa, Khalap tried to reach out to Pratapsingh and seek the support of the Congress (I). For his part, Barbosa tried frantically to patch up with Khalap. Khalap then won over three of Barbosa's aides. Subsequently, Barbosa's group jumped onto the Congress (I) bandwagon with two MGP legislators, who suddenly surfaced after a disappearing act. 'In politics it seems rats can marry snakes and bulls can chase lizards,' commented the newspaper *OHeraldo*, in picturesque imagery from Goa's wildlife.[12] With all this frenzied instability, President's Rule (which all parties had been desperately trying to avoid) was clamped in Goa from 14 December 1990 to 24 January 1991.

The irrepressible Dr de Souza now became set on hoisting the Congress (I) back to power. Dr de Souza succeeded in persuading the relatively unknown Ravi Naik, once the second-in-command to Khalap in the MGP, to join the Congress along with a group of other MGP MLAs. Naik left the MGP and joined Dr de Souza. Dr de Souza approached Governor Khurshid Alam Khan and demanded that his party be invited to form the government. President's Rule was lifted, and Ravi Naik became Goa CM on 25 January 1991.

In the midst of this political turbulence, tragedy struck. While campaigning for the general elections of 1991, Rajiv Gandhi was assassinated on 21 May in Sriperumbudur in Tamil Nadu. Ironically, three days before the assassination, Rajiv had held a public meeting at Azad Maidan in Panaji. His assassination was devastating news for us. Perhaps Rajiv Gandhi's government in New Delhi had, on occasion, been ill-advised on certain policies, but to Pratapsingh and myself, he was always ever supportive and kind, the soul of charm. Rajiv was not only our friend but he was a true friend of Goa. We mourned his passing.

Rajiv's untimely death created a leadership vacuum and deepened the instability in the Congress and in Goa politics as a whole. Rajiv was slain while Naik was Goa CM, and after the assassination, Naik's government began to look shaky. Reports began to emerge that according to a secret 'leadership contract', Naik was supposed to step down as CM in favour of Dr de Souza but refused to do so. A tug of war ensued between the Naik group and Dr de Souza's supporters with an angry de Souza increasingly eager to oust Naik. The crazy game of thrones continued to rage

---

[12]'Luis Proto Barbosa's Exit Signals Instability in Goa', *India Today*, 31 December 1990.

in Goa. In these years, our state unfortunately becoming known for 'perennial professional habitual defectors'.

After 28 months in office, the Ravi Naik government fell after the Goa bench of the Bombay High Court on 14 May 1993 upheld the disqualification of Naik under the Anti-Defection Act. Khalap and the MGP had challenged Naik's defection to the Congress and filed disqualification petitions against him. The court struck Naik's defection down, and he was forced to resign in May 1993. Naik's loss was Dr de Souza's gain. Our old friend, the exuberant, incorrigibly adversarial Dr de Souza became CM in May 1993 and stayed as CM until April 1994, a period of 11 months. Dr de Souza, a highly intelligent and dynamic person, was not without his own plans for Goa's development. In this period, construction was begun on the Goa State Legislative Assembly complex in Porvorim. Dr de Souza also built the nursing home of the Goa Medical College.

However, CM Dr de Souza soon found himself in the cross hairs of the then Goa governor, Bhanu Prakash Singh, who prided himself on his 'royal' lineage, hailing as he did from the principality of Narsinghgarh in Madhya Pradesh. On one occasion, Dr de Souza failed to make an appearance at the governor's Holi party because it happened to be the same day as Good Friday. In another incident, it was reported that Dr de Souza had been publicly heard making intemperate remarks against the governor. These remarks outraged Bhanu Prakash Singh. In a highly unusual move, which at the time had never happened before in post-Independence India, the governor (without any such orders from Delhi) unilaterally made an announcement that he was 'withdrawing his pleasure' from the de Souza government and unceremoniously sacked Dr de Souza. New Delhi was outraged. How dare the governor act on his own in this manner?

At this time, 1 April 1994, Bhanu Prakash Singh was in a quandary. He heartily disliked Dr de Souza, but the High Command was forcing Dr de Souza back. Bhanu Prakash Singh dialled Pratapsingh.

'Please become the CM,' he pleaded with Pratapsingh. 'Certainly not,' immediately replied Pratapsingh. Why did he refuse? 'There was no question of my becoming CM in these circumstances,' he says. 'I had not been elected by the Congress Legislature Party (CLP). No proper procedure or processes were followed. I could not just be a party to the governor's bizarre game.' In fact, since Bhanu Prakash Singh had called on 1 April, Pratapsingh at first thought the governor was playing an April Fool's joke!

The adamant governor disregarded the Congress High Command, and, on 2 April, swore in Ravi Naik. But just a few short days later, the governor was forced to dismiss Naik on the High Command's insistence. Naik's tenure of *less than a week* reveals the truly small-minded, indeed burlesque politics being played out at this time. After Naik's departure, once again, in came the governor's *bête noire* Dr de Souza, who remained as CM until assembly polls in November 1994.

For daring to sack him by 'withdrawing his pleasure', Dr de Souza now turned the tables on the governor and promptly had the high-handed Bhanu Prakash Singh sacked and put on a plane back to Delhi. Given the widely held perception that Bhanu Prakash Singh was pursuing a personal rather than a constitutional agenda, the centre recalled the governor. This became the first instance in post-Independence India where a CM had a governor removed. In Bhanu Prakash Singh's place came the mild-mannered Karnataka Congressman B. Rachaiah as the new Goa governor.

A colourful range of dramatis personae indeed. A brilliant surgeon yet a perpetually manoeuvring political livewire, Dr Wilfred de Souza—stout, bespectacled and energetic. The lumbering misguided missile Churchill Alemao. The grave and respected Dr Luis Proto Barbosa, yet someone not above the politics of short-termism. The ever-ready Ravi Naik. The outstanding lawyer-intellectual Ramakant Khalap, yet perhaps nursing a sense of injury that so talented a man as he could not become CM. And thrown into the mix a feudal chieftain, the Raja of Narsinghgarh, the easily offended and rather thin-skinned Bhanu Prakash Singh.

The revolving-door governments of Goa in the 1990s took a toll on governance. In these years, the Konkan Railway project ran into obstacles. Running for over 750 km along the western coast and aiming to link Bombay with Mangalore, the Konkan Railway was a high-profile and flagship railway project. Beginning in 1993, protest movements flared up against the Konkan Railway, some of them acquiring a communal colour and feeding into the age-old divide that has existed in Goa between the Hindu-majority north and the Catholic-dominated south. Chief ministers during this time, Naik and Dr de Souza, were unable to control the agitations, and the centre had to step in to try and find a solution. When he returned as CM in 1994, Pratapsingh pushed forward the Konkan Railway Project as far as possible, inaugurating one leg of the railway with then Railway Minister Ram Vilas Paswan in 1997.

Instability in the administration brought disappointments such as the manner in which the Nylon 6,6 project in Ponda—a Thapar DuPont nylon manufacturing industry—was initiated. This project resulted in a tragic stand-off with local residents. But the Pratapsingh government that came to power in December 1994 acted quickly to ensure that the unpopular project was speedily wound up. The development of the information technology (IT) sector in Goa, an industry to which Goa is uniquely well suited, also did not receive the sort of attention it should have because of the short-tenured governments of the 1990s.

During this period when there was so much petty and debilitating intrigue about him, Pratapsingh was content living in Golden Acres, our farmhouse in Karapur village in Sanquelim, with his orchards of mangoes, cashews and coconuts. The events of these years disappointed us, but we are both descended from Maratha warriors and our spirits were strong. As he likes to quote, 'Tough times don't last; tough people do.' In 1991, Pratapsingh had travelled to the US for an angioplasty procedure performed by Dr Fayaz Shawl at the Washington Adventist Hospital in Washington, D.C.

To be away from the daily stresses of government was, in many ways, a relief. Jason Abraham, an IT specialist, was born and brought up in Goa. He is one of our friends and now lives in the US. He recalls how carefree Pratapsingh used to be even when his governments were toppled. 'I was the leader for National Service Scheme (NSS) at Dhempe College of Arts & Science, and due to unforeseen events, I was unable to secure a reasonable venue for our annual field camp,' recalls Abraham. 'At the advice of my father, I approached Mr Rane to ask if he could help. His government was toppled and he was just an MLA. He immediately invited me and my colleague to join him and Mrs Rane at their farm in Sanquelim and spend the day with them. They drove us from Panaji in their car, and what a fun ride that was—ferry crossing and all! The Ranes graciously hosted us at their home.' Being out of the hot seat meant there was more time for the simple joys of life.

Back in the Saddle as the Builder of Modern Goa

But soon, Pratapsingh returned to the job that he loved doing—building and developing Goa. Assembly elections were held in November 1994. Pratapsingh started his campaign as always from the Bhumika temple in Poriem. The word again went out: *Khashe* is contesting. Expectedly, he won hands down. The Congress won these elections with 18 seats, edging past an MGP–BJP alliance. The 1994 polls brought a new party to Goa. For the first time the Bharatiya Janata Party got four MLAs: Digambar Kamat from Margao, Shripad Naik from Marcaim, Narahari Haldankar from Valpoi, and another young MLA who would go on to play a stellar role in Goa. He was elected for the first time from Panaji. He was youthful, Indian Institute of Technology (IIT)-educated and a good organizer of his party. His name was Manohar Parrikar.

After the polls, four observers from the centre—G.K. Moopanar, Ghulam Nabi Azad, S.S. Ahluwalia (then in the Congress) and Janardhan Poojary—arrived in Goa to sort out the factional tussles with Dr de Souza's supporters, and the so-called 'stalemate' between two chief ministerial contenders, Pratapsingh and Dr de Souza. At the CLP meet, Pratapsingh was unanimously elected as the party's candidate, much to the chagrin of Dr de Souza. Pratapsingh was again appointed CM.

This started Pratapsingh's fourth term as CM, which ran from 16 December 1994 to 29 July 1998, almost a full term. During this tenure, he held the portfolios of Personnel, General Administration, Vigilance, Finance, Town & Country Planning, PWD, Education, Art & Culture, Home, Transport, Forests and Mines. He also took charge of the *provedoria*s or Institutes of Public Assistance.

Pratapsingh's tenure from 1994 to 1998 was the longest any CM lasted in that mad world of 1990s Goa. Why did he choose to return as CM in this rocky time when every government was in danger of being toppled? Shahu Chhatrapati has this analysis: 'Pratapsingh's heart was in his development projects. It pained him to see so many projects that he had begun neglected and falling by the wayside. He wanted to hold the reins again to get the projects going again. That's why he wanted to be CM.' Pratapsingh agrees. 'Yes, I was asked to take on the responsibility of being CM again, and I did so. I did not want to become CM for the sake of the post but because I wanted to see that the work got done. Chief ministers are there to work for Goa, not for themselves.' Our daughter Vishwadhara recalls a telling incident: 'One evening, I saw my father sitting in his study until late at night. I asked why he was working so late. He said, look at this file, the last time it was read and signed was when I had done so ten years ago! Since then, the file has not even been looked at.'

R. Mihir Vardhan, the former IAS officer, was working in Goa at this time. He had previously met Pratapsingh in 1988 as a member of the Goa Civil Service. In 1994, Mihir Vardhan was working in Goa as managing director (MD) of the Sanjivani Sahakari Sakhar Karkhana Ltd. Pratapsingh's enthusiasm for farming was great; he was used to tilling his lands by driving the tractor himself and, in the past, had even supplied sugarcane to this particular factory. Since company management was his forte, Pratapsingh took charge as chairman of the karkhana to try and improve its fortunes. 'Whenever I visited other states and mentioned that the Goa CM was the chairman of the factory, it would draw expressions of disbelief,' remembers Mihir Vardhan. Pratapsingh's first-hand farming experience as well as experience in the corporate sector came in handy. The Sanjivani sugar factory did very well and had good crushing seasons in 1995–96 and 1996–97. 'He was determined to see that the factory did well...In spite of his busy schedule he used to make surprise visits...He would encourage me to go to other states to get sugarcane...One season, there was too much surplus from Karnataka and he sent me as an envoy to then Karnataka CM H.D. Deve Gowda in a conciliatory move between two states.' After more than two decades of continuous losses, the sugar factory made a profit continuously in the two years that Pratapsingh ran it. Mihir Vardhan adds that working with Pratapsingh was a challenge. It took a lot of work to earn the CM's trust.

In 1996, Pratapsingh, quick to recognize talent and dynamism, inducted the young industrialist Shrinivas Dempo as chairman of the North Goa Planning and Development Authority. 'I was only 25 years old,' recalls Dempo. 'I was worried that I would be considered too young for the job, but Rane expressly told me that he wanted to bring in honest young people into decision-making. He told me I was to do what I thought was best and not give in to any pulls and pressures, however powerful the parties may be. There were some very powerful MLAs working under the guidance of the board, including then MLA Manohar Parrikar. But Mr Rane believed in encouraging and bringing in youthful energy into Goa and gave me full support in taking decisions purely on merit. It is very rare for CMs to provide this kind of support.' Pratapsingh brought Dempo into other administrative bodies as well, such as the Economic Development Corporation (EDC) Board and the Goa University Executive Council.

This strict insulation of government from politics has meant that even today, although standards are perhaps not as high as they were in Pratapsingh's time, officials in authority in Goa hesitate to give out undue favours or recklessly practise favouritism, as they often do in other states. This administrative hesitation to step outside the law, a sense of caution on unreasonable 'V.I.P requests' and a certain tug of the official conscience (however faint) when asked for out-of-turn privileges, still exists within Goa's governments.

Dark Clouds, Silver Linings

The year 1998 began on a happy note for us. Here in the CM's house in Altinho, our daughter Vishwadhara married Vishwajit Dahanukar on 8 February and our son Vishwajit married Deviya on 17 May. We celebrated both weddings with joy. There were functions in Panaji as well as in the ancestral home in Sanquelim. Our friends and family gathered together for both occasions. There were emotional moments when Vishwadhara stood as a bride in our family temple of Shri Vithal to be blessed by the benign and ancient deity standing witness. Her wedding was celebrated in the same spot where so many past generations of Ranes had wed.

With our children married and settled, my work at the Bal Bhavan and the Sanjay School was keeping me occupied. It was tremendously rewarding work, watching children explore their talents and rise to new heights. The new green-and-white Bal Bhavan building on Dayanand Bandodkar Marg in Panaji buzzed with activity and was alive with the spirits of the talented children gathered there.

Pratapsingh was brimming with new plans for Goa. It was at this time that plans were first drawn up for a new airport, the Mopa airport in north Goa. 'The existing airport at Dabolim was a naval airport and there were certain times during the day when aircraft could not land or take off due to movement of navy aircraft,' recalls Pratapsingh. 'I was looking for another site.' However, the Mopa airport project would take years to get off the ground and would not properly start before 2005. It was in 2000 when Pratapsingh was no longer in power that the International Civil Aviation Organization came to inspect the airport site.

The Pratapsingh government took various other initiatives, including passing the Goa RTI Act in 1997 predating by eight years the centre's RTI Act, which only came into force in 2005. Goa became the second state, after Tamil Nadu, to establish a legal RTI.

Former IAS officer G.C. Srivastava served as chief secretary in Goa from 1995 to 1998. 'Mr Rane was a highly capable administrator, head and shoulders above others,' Srivastava recalls. 'His informal manner with officers delivered results, because he would work alongside us.' Srivastava recalls how, during meetings, Pratapsingh would suddenly say, 'Come on, let's go for a round.' They would jump into a car, with the CM driving and the chief secretary seated next to him, and inspect places around Panaji and further afield. If, on these drives, Pratapsingh ever noticed anyone relieving himself in public, he would make sure that the person was caught. If he saw anyone cutting a tree or damaging a hillside, he would make sure to note it down and report it to the forest department.

The legendary tiatrist M. Boyer, a renowned figure of the Konkani stage, even composed a rollicking *cantar* (song) about how the CM has brought in a law forbidding Goans to do their business, so that they must now carry around a bottle! In 1997, the Pratapsingh Rane government brought in the Goa Prohibition of Smoking and Spitting Act, 1997, prohibiting chewing and spitting of tobacco, *pan* masala and *gutka* in public places or public vehicles. The reason why the public environment in Goa is relatively clean and why public hygiene is high is not only because of the strict laws that exist for it but also because there was once a CM who went driving around in his car, personally checking if anyone was making the mistake of urinating in public or cutting trees or spitting in public places.

'Mr Rane was a hands-on CM,' recalls Srivastava. 'He just rolled up his sleeves and did things himself. He never minded any kind of dissent. I used to have many arguments with him, but he took all of these on board, and often acted on what I told him.'

Srivastava enumerates the following as Pratapsingh's big achievements: establishing the Goa University, upgradation of the Goa Medical College, setting up the GIM, establishing the International Centre Goa (ICG), building the Kala Academy and Ravindra Bhavans, introducing the Bal Bhavan movement in Goa and taking it forward successfully, starting the Kadamba Bus Transport Corporation, building all-weather roads across Goa, laying down plans for the Mopa airport and pushing through a slew of environment-protecting legislations that were rigorously planned and worked on. Srivastava says that it is the building of these institutions that makes Pratapsingh a CM who laid the foundations of a modern Goa. 'Rane is Goa's foremost institution builder; no one else comes close,' says Srivastava.

He wanted to forge ahead towards building modern Goa, but others only wanted to put roadblocks in his way. July is Goa's monsoon month. The monsoon brings a sort of other-worldly beauty to Goa. Dark clouds pile up in the sky like towering grey peaks. As sheets of rain slant down from grey-black skies, rivers and forests, brooks and streams, lakes and fields are filled with fresh energy. Deep green trees are clad in glittering raindrops like bursts of shining jewels on sheets of turquoise satin. Nights are infused with enchantment: as the rain pours down on rooftops and orchards, it's as if all of Goa is given over to visiting spirits which fill the landscape and waterways with new life.

The monsoon is also the time of hardship. Roads become impassable, there are repeated power shutdowns, and homes and buildings spring leaks and cracks. The Pratapsingh Rane government was hard at work at this time, repairing bridges, draining flooded roads and seeing to power lines. But as dark clouds circled Goa, those clouds spilled into the government as well.

Dr de Souza, always Pratapsingh's detractor, seemingly ever ready to pull him down at every available opportunity, never did rest easy when Pratapsingh was at the helm. He had been uneasy with Pratapsingh since 1980, uneasy that Pratapsingh became CM in an election that Dr de Souza believed he had won by getting the UGP to join the Congress. When Goa became a state in 1987 and Pratapsingh transitioned smoothly from CM of a UT to CM of a state, Dr de Souza called Pratapsingh and his administration 'an illegal government headed by an illegal CM' because, according to Dr de Souza, once Goa became a state, fresh elections should have been called and a new CM should have been 'chosen by the people'. In 1987, Dr de Souza also demanded to know why the Goa Assembly was given only 40 seats. He saw this as a mark of Goans being treated as 'second-class citizens'. In 1994, he was again enraged that the Delhi High Command chose Pratapsingh and not him as CM, although de Souza seemed to have forgotten that Pratapsingh Rane had been unanimously elected by the CLP.

Dr de Souza seemed always perturbed by Pratapsingh. The latter was generally not disliked by anyone; he is a consensual and reconciling figure, a gentlemanly, super-efficient administrator and statesman. Yet these qualities of Pratapsingh perhaps made Dr de Souza a little insecure, more so because Pratapsingh was popular even among Catholics, Dr de Souza's vote bank. Pratapsingh was able to reach out beyond community walls and appeal to both Hindus and Catholics. I have always believed that although highly educated, Dr de Souza possessed a slightly communal mindset and seemed always rather threatened by Pratapsingh. Nonetheless, Dr de Souza was a bold and confident man as well as a clever political strategist, yet someone who always seemed to be plotting Pratapsingh's downfall. 'Dr Willy's problem with me was that he wanted to be CM and I was the one who was,' recalls Pratapsingh.

In July 1998, a group of ministers and MLAs split from the Congress and formed the Goa Rajiv Congress under Dr de Souza's (Dr de Souza was then revenue minister) leadership. This group now approached the then Goa governor Lieutenant General (retd) J.F.R. Jacob seeking the dismissal of the Pratapsingh government. Dr de Souza told newspersons that he was motivated by the deteriorating law-and-order situation and failing power supply. In reality, seeing Pratapsingh settled into his groove, ably handling the administration and looking set for another uninterrupted spell of stable governance, Dr de Souza had become nervous. He paraded his supporters before the governor. Wonder of wonders, Dr de Souza, in his feverish bid to pull Pratapsingh down, even made common cause with his political antagonists. He announced to the governor that the Goa Rajiv Congress had the support of eight MGP MLAs, one independent MLA and, lo and behold, four BJP MLAs. The governor ordered that the Pratapsingh government face a floor test and prove its majority.

A monsoon force storm broke out in the assembly on 28 July. The Congress demanded the removal of those who had quit the party and weakened the Congress at a critical time when government stability was so urgently needed. Amidst shouts, Pratapsingh read out the confidence motion, which was quickly passed since the Congress still had a majority.

What followed was absurd drama. After the confidence motion was passed, the Speaker Tomazinho Cardozo departed from the House. Immediately, irresponsible Opposition members announced that the Speaker had 'abandoned the House' and that Deputy

Speaker Deu Mandrekar was now in charge. The 10-member Goa Rajiv Congress and 13 Opposition members passed a no-confidence motion against the Pratapsingh government. The farcical nature of this move was that assembly staff was not even present in the House to record these proceedings. Dr de Souza persisted with his fiction that the government had lost its majority.

Governor J.F.R. Jacob dismissed the almost four-year-old Pratapsingh Rane government which was doing such good work. 'With the Rane ministry losing the confidence of the people, I had no option but to dismiss it,' Governor Jacob declared to the press. Dr de Souza was installed as CM. The controversial Dayanand Narvekar, MLA from Thivim, became his deputy.

But many questions arise about the events of July 1998: how did the governor conclude that the Pratapsingh Rane government had fallen when it had, in fact, survived the confidence motion taken by the Speaker while he was in the Chair? How could the Rane government be dismissed considering that it had won the vote of confidence, simply on the basis of a sham, a farcical no-confidence motion brought in when the Speaker and assembly staff were absent? And what of the so-called 'secular' principles of Dr de Souza, who took the support of his avowed ideological adversaries, the MGP and the Hindutva-leaning BJP, to form a rickety coalition? Blinded by ambition and apparently disturbed by Pratapsingh's success, Dr de Souza seemed to have lost some perspective.

As the monsoon tore into Goa, another stable and delivery-oriented Pratapsingh government was unfortunately pulled down. Industry leader Shrinivas Dempo, who was working in an advisory role in the government, was disappointed. When the Pratapsingh government fell in 1998, Dempo too handed in his resignation. 'I believed in Pratapsingh Rane's vision,' says Dempo. 'He laid down a governance code. He was always ahead of his times. He believed in young people; he had a commitment to education and he was always forward looking. I had been appointed by him, so when he resigned his post, I did so too.'

Dr de Souza installed himself in the CM's chair in July, but he did not succeed in keeping it. He lasted only four months. Luizinho Faleiro, MLA from Navelim, determined to bring the Congress back to power, decided that it was time he took a shot at becoming CM. Luizinho brought down Dr de Souza's government and was sworn in as CM on 26 November. Luizinho stayed as CM for less than three months. In the chaos and disruption, President's Rule was clamped from February to June. A new round of assembly polls was ordered for June 1999.

Non, je ne regrette rien

In the elections of 1999, the Congress won 21 seats. Dr de Souza's Goa Rajiv Congress was able to win only two measly seats, one of which was Dr de Souza himself from his long-time constituency of Saligao.

After the big Congress victory, it was widely expected that Pratapsingh would once again become CM. As the face of the Congress in Goa for decades, as the best performing CM, surely Pratapsingh was the man Goan voters wanted when they voted the Congress in with a big victory.

But the Congress High Command in Delhi did not serve Pratapsingh well. Instead of clearing the way for him to be the CM as the people had clearly chosen him to be, the High Command plumped again for Luizinho, perhaps in an attempt to win over the Catholic vote bank. This was the time when the Atal Bihari Vajpayee-led BJP was ruling at the centre. It was the time of Mrs Sonia Gandhi as Congress president, and it is possible the High Command felt that a Catholic CM in Goa would be an assertion of the Congress's 'secular' ideology at a time when the BJP government held sway in New Delhi. In a move that was both unfair to Pratapsingh and to the people of Goa, Pratapsingh was denied the chief ministership. If Pratapsingh had been made CM in 1999, the history of the Congress in Goa may have been very different to what it is today.

Luizinho Faleiro was sworn in as CM on 9 June, while Pratapsingh was appointed Speaker of the Goa Assembly on 15 June 1999 and would remain Speaker until 11 June 2002.

Did he regret not having a shot at chief ministership in 1999? 'Not at all,' he replies immediately. 'I abide by the decisions of the leadership. Mrs Sonia Gandhi told me that I should be Speaker and so I did.' Édith Piaf was an acclaimed French singer who sang soulful and expressive songs of love and loss. In the 1960s, she sang her great song 'Non, je ne regrette rien' (No, I have no regrets). Whenever he is asked if he has any regrets, Pratapsingh quotes from this Piaf song: *Non, je ne regrette rien.* No, I have no regrets.

Parrikar Makes a Splash

Luizinho lasted five months. It was now the turn of the bespectacled Francisco Sardinha to take his turn in the Goa spotlight. Encouraged by BJP's Manohar Parrikar, now LoP, Sardinha walked out, split from the Congress and, on 24 November, was sworn in as CM. Sardinha remained CM for only 11 months as Parrikar now scented blood. It was he who had offered to support Sardinha to topple Luizinho Faleiro, Sardinha thus becoming the Trojan horse who first brought the BJP to power in Goa. At this time, in another sign of the BJP's growing clout in Goa, in the Lok Sabha polls of September–October 1999, the BJP won both of Goa's parliamentary seats. Sensing the intense factionalism in the Congress and quick to take the opportunity to seize power, Parrikar (leading a 10-member BJP band) lured in eight MLAs from the Congress and secured the backing of eight others, including independents. With 26 MLAs supporting him, Parrikar toppled the Francisco Sardinha government and became CM of Goa on 24 October 2000.

Seeking a fresh mandate and confident of a bigger win on its own, the Parrikar-led Goa Cabinet recommended a premature dissolution of the Goa Assembly in 2002. 'We can do much better if we get a full mandate,' Parrikar declared. Assembly polls were held in May 2002. But the BJP did not get the 'full mandate' that Parrikar had hoped for. Instead, the assembly was hung. The BJP did better than its 1999 10-seat tally, but came in at 17 seats, just one seat ahead of the Congress, which won 16. At this stage, Parrikar obtained the support of five other MLAs—two from the MGP, two from Churchill Alemao's United Goans Democratic Party (UGDP) and one independent—and formed the government. Manohar Parrikar was sworn in as CM on 3 June 2002, but this government would not last a full term either.

Parrikar, at 45, was young, highly educated and projected a modern vision for Goa. As CM of Goa, he made quite a media splash. 'I had good relations with Parrikar although I did not find him to be very friendly or sociable,' says Pratapsingh. 'He seemed rather taciturn. He didn't seem to believe in much social interaction. But he was a young man educated at the IIT, and I had high expectations of him. However, he did not quite fulfil these expectations.' Parrikar would soon emerge into the spotlight not only in Goa but on the national stage.

Manohar Parrikar was projected as a new age, dynamic face of Goa, the IIT-educated CM with a modern vision. But long before Parrikar, there was Pratapsingh Rane. Pratapsingh, who became CM at 41, was younger than Parrikar was when the latter became CM at 45. Pratapsingh, the US-educated former corporate executive, the horse-riding, boxing champion who had worked at the US Committee for the United Nations in New York and the Walt Disney Company, and had a promising career with the Tatas before he joined politics, was surely even more of an attractive, young CM than Parrikar. Pratapsingh excelled in his academic career as well as in sports and quit his assignment in Telco to return to Goa. All these achievements would make him a media hero by today's standards. But in Pratapsingh's heyday, there was no TV media or social media to project his persona as well as today's leaders manage to do.

The Extraordinary Politician

In these years, when CMs were sworn in and toppled with alarming regularity—13 CMs in 10 years—there were moments when Pratapsingh was only an MLA, watching from the sidelines. Perhaps this may be the place to explore Pratapsingh's relationship with politics in general. He never considered himself a politician in the usual definition of the term. He was not the usual type of 'party leader'. He brought the discipline of the sportsman, the professionalism and meritocracy of the corporate sector and the openness and transparency of a well-travelled, foreign-educated person to politics. This made him a rather unusual, even extraordinary, 'politician'. Our daughter Vishwadhara describes him perfectly when she calls him 'the CEO of Goa'.

He had never been a typical political animal, who intrigued or plotted or built coteries. When elections came round, he did not specifically promote a single group; instead he believed in working with those who won. This was a uniquely meritocratic way of doing politics. He would say, 'I have no candidates here and there who I am putting up or supporting. I will work with those who win.' Himself always sure of winning from Sattari because of his dedicated work in his constituency and his family ties with the people, he was never motivated to practice any kind of manipulative politics. He was even a little indifferent to it. 'I never had any favourites, nor did I practise any favouritism. I was not interested in any dirty tricks or in manipulating transfers and postings or any kind of appointments. I always made it a point to be scrupulously fair and to make sure that only merit matters.'

Some have said that Pratapsingh was perhaps not political enough, that he did not take too much of an interest in party political matters, did not devote his energies to party work and remained largely indifferent to inner party issues. This is because building Goa and not necessarily engaging in party work was his priority. His duty was to the people of Goa and not only to partymen. The lack of discipline and commitment of some of Goa's politicians deeply disturbed him and was perhaps a reason he did not like to cultivate any favourites or camps. The inability of the Congress's central leadership to enforce discipline and ideological commitment in the Goa party unit created a pattern of wayward behaviour that became common among many politicians; their loyalties were fickle. Pratapsingh himself never wavered from the Congress path.

Perhaps because he never played favourites or had his own 'lobby', some thought of him as fair game. In the early years of his chief ministership, the erratic and rough Dilkhush Desai, the MGP, later Congress, MLA from Rivona, used to attack him regularly. 'Dilkhush was a ruffian and a bully, and the Opposition used to encourage him to attack me,' Pratapsingh recalls. Dilkhush, who had the odd habit of holding an unlit cigarette between his fingers, was a rather obstreperous character. When journalists once asked him why he kept on holding an unlit cigarette in his hands as if he was smoking, particularly in front of then CM Shashikala Kakodkar, Dilkhush replied: 'I never smoke, but this is only to give courage to my other colleagues who, despite being chain-smokers, would shudder at the thought of smoking in the presence of Tai.' Such was the comical eccentricity and misconduct of Dilkhush. When Pratapsingh became CM, Dilkhush would hurl abuse at him, calling him '*nalayak*' and an 'incompetent CM'.

In the early 1980s, Dilkhush became entangled with some unsavoury people and was even accused of sexual assault. One evening when Dilkhush was sitting at home, someone took aim with a pellet gun and shot Dilkhush in the head. 'I got a call saying Dilkhush had been shot in the head and we needed to shift him to hospital in Bombay,' Pratapsingh recalls. 'I had good relations with the navy, which had a big base in Goa, and arranged for him to be transported by a naval aircraft to Jaslok Hospital in Bombay where he was treated and eventually recovered. Those were days of trunk calls, and I used to get daily trunk calls on Dilkhush's progress.' On returning to Goa, a hysterical Dilkhush kept hugging Pratapsingh and calling him 'my chief minister, my chief minister'. But Dilkhush soon returned to his outlandish ways, constantly raising slogans and harangues against Pratapsingh.

One day, many years later, Dilkhush behaved in an unexpectedly appalling manner with Pratapsingh. Every year, 9 January is marked as Goa Legislators Day as it's the day in 1964 that the first Goa Assembly was convened. On Legislators Day in 2007, when Pratapsingh was CM for what would be his last term, the usual formalities were taking place at Goa's assembly and secretarial complex in Porvorim. That afternoon, Pratapsingh was coming out of the lunch hall when Dilkhush, who was no longer an MLA and had by now become mentally unstable, rushed towards Pratapsingh, extracted a packet of cow dung from his pocket and flung it in Pratapsingh's face. Security personnel were taken aback by the sudden act of dung-throwing and hurried to overpower Dilkhush and drag him away. Shocked but unfazed, Pratapsingh quickly wiped the filth off his face and clothes and drove back home to Altinho to shower and change. He then appeared for his evening function, where the media asked him if he would press charges against Dilkhush. 'Of course not,' Pratapsingh told the media, 'This is democracy; it's nothing; these things happen.' He also advised the media to ignore it. Veteran journalist Gurudas Sawal was present at that meeting. Sawal says: 'It was most unusual to see how Pratapsingh easily forgave Dilkhush and did not make an issue out of it. It showed that he was a democrat.' Today, Sawal says, 'Speaking as an objective newsman, Goa's best days were when Pratapsingh was CM.'

Another MLA who kept attacking and abusing Pratapsingh was Dayanand Narvekar. It was these two—Dilkhush Desai and Dayanand Narvekar—who had once voted with the Opposition in a no-confidence motion against Shashikala Kakodkar in 1978, which she survived. 'Dilkhush Desai and Dayanand Narvekar were so unruly and naughty that they were called Billa and Ranga,' Pratapsingh recalls. 'They kept creating problems for me.' 'Billa' and 'Ranga' were the nicknames of two notorious and infamous Delhi murderers who brutally killed a brother and sister in 1978, and it was telling that these two Goa MLAs were called by such names.

The politicians Pratapsingh admires the most—Bhausaheb Bandodkar, Indira Gandhi and Dr Jack de Sequeira—were all exceptional leaders. Pratapsingh admires Bandodkar for his earthy rootedness and man-of-the-masses popularity, Indira Gandhi for her charisma and force of personality and de Sequeira for his intellectual capacity and terrific powers of oratory in the assembly. 'We used to all listen in awe when Dr Jack de Sequeira spoke in the house,' he recalls. Pratapsingh saw these three as working for a higher ideal, driven by a loftier goal other than simply bickering and squabbling for the spoils of power.

Perhaps this rather noble, governance-oriented approach to politics was the reason why Pratapsingh Rane, a lifelong Congressman, received an unexpected and unasked for tribute from Goa's BJP government.

SIX

THE LATER YEARS: 2000-2022

'It's the love of the people that drives me on.'

A Sense of Pride

Close to our farmhouse Golden Acres, where we currently reside, is the Sanquelim Ravindra Bhavan. The Pratapsingh Rane government had set up five Ravindra Bhavans, or cultural hubs, across Goa, and today, more are being established. In our retired life, whenever we have an evening free, Pratapsingh and I often visit the Sanquelim Ravindra Bhavan to see if there are shows that interest us, and if there are, we always try and find seats. In April 2023, we went on one of our evening visits to the Ravindra Bhavan, peeked into the auditorium and saw, much to our delight, that Bharatanatyam *arangetram* (debut performance of a young dancer) recitals were going on. Two well-trained young women were dancing with such grace and skill that we were enthralled. We crept into the auditorium through a side door and, unnoticed, took our place quietly in the audience. I glanced at Pratapsingh as he looked on, one among the audience, watching two young, fully trained classical dancers of Goa in a state-of-the-art auditorium equipped with modern acoustics. I noticed a proud, slightly bemused smile on Pratapsingh's usually impassive face and immediately knew that his mind had gone back to an earlier time. To a time when, in this place where the Sanquelim Ravindra Bhavan today stands, there was only jungle and rock. A young CM had arrived here with his team, all wearing their construction helmets. They had inspected the site, drawn up plans for its future and supervised the construction of what is now a glass-fronted gleaming structure set amidst lawns. Today, decades later, local performers have an ultramodern stage to show off their talents and the former CM sits in the audience, a paterfamilias looking on in rapt attention. *Let's build with all our heart and soul a paradise here in Goa.*

In 2002, the Manohar Parrikar government was sworn in after assembly polls the same year. However, this government did not last and was toppled in 2005 by a group of rebels. Among them were Benaulim MLA Francisco 'Mickky' Pacheco, Taleigao MLA Atanasio 'Babush' Monserrate and Margao MLA Digambar Kamat. In a severe jolt to the BJP, the popular Kamat left the party and joined the Congress. On 2 February 2005, Parrikar resigned. As leader of the second largest force in the assembly, Pratapsingh came in as CM but only for 32 days, from 2 February to 4 March. A period of President's Rule followed in unpredictable and volatile Goa where governments ebb and flow like the ocean tide.

In June, five by-polls were held in Goa because five BJP MLAs resigned when they toppled Parrikar. The Congress won three of these by-polls and its ally, the NCP, won one, thus boosting the Congress's tally in the assembly. President's Rule came to an end. Pratapsingh was unanimously elected leader of the CLP and sworn in as CM on 7 June. This time, Pratapsingh returned as CM for his sixth and final term, which ran for two years till 5 June 2007.

However, in the post-2000 period, he also held other public posts almost continuously. He was Assembly Speaker from 15 June 1999 to 11 June 2002. He was LoP from 13 June 2002 to 2

February 2005. He was again Speaker from 15 June 2007 to 19 March 2012. He was once again LoP from 19 March 2012 to 14 March 2017. He was able to hold these posts because he was a permanent fixture in the assembly, winning every single election he contested from Sattari, later Poriem. In 2001, he was awarded the honour of 'Legislator of the Millennium' for his unbroken three decades in the assembly. The motion was adopted in the assembly on 23 March 2001. Even his most recalcitrant detractors stood to make speeches in his praise. The incorrigible Churchill Alemao went to the extent of declaring: 'I realized my mistake in overthrowing a good leader like you. [In 1989,] some instigated me, and being new, I was lured.'

The Final Term

Returning to the CM's chair in 2005, Pratapsingh's first task was to take the Greenfield Mopa airport project towards completion. At this time, R. Mihir Vardhan was in Goa as director of transport and in charge of Mopa airport. A site for the airport had been finalized in Pernem taluka in north Goa. 'One day, Mr Rane said he wanted to visit the site and we went together in his car,' recalls Mihir Vardhan. 'At that time, the area was still all barren land. As we walked across the length and breadth of those fields, he looked at it from every angle and shared his vision of the airport with me. I was amazed at his imaginative skills.' The progress on Mopa was slow due to Opposition protests and some feet-dragging by the centre, but today, Mopa is fully functional and is regarded as a top-class facility. 'The airport owes a lot to Mr Rane's visionary leadership in those days,' says Mihir Vardhan. Pratapsingh says with a touch of pride: 'I identified the place for the Mopa airport and created plans in its early stages, and feel happy to see it functioning so well today.' He did not stay as CM long enough to see it through. The airport finally opened in 2022.

His tenure from 2005 to 2007 may have been short, but it saw another important initiative. This was the Goa Rural Employment Guarantee Scheme of 2006, unveiled on 6 September, providing for guaranteed employment for the rural poor. The Mahatma Gandhi National Rural Employment Guarantee Act (MGNREGA) had already been launched on 2 February 2006 at the central level by the Manmohan Singh-led United Progressive Alliance (UPA) government. In Goa, in an innovative move, Pratapsingh encouraged a group of law students to organize a seminar on the Panchayati Raj system with participation from all of Goa's village sarpanches on the very same day as the Goa Rural Employment Guarantee Scheme was launched.

Goa-based lawyer Yatish A. Naik, then a student at V.M. Salgaocar College of Law, who organized the Panchayati Raj seminar, recalls how excited Pratapsingh was about local democracy at the village level. Naik is a gold medallist from Goa University and regarded as one of Goa's brightest young legal minds. 'When we went to meet the CM to suggest the idea of a Panchayati Raj seminar, he was delighted. He kept telling us how important it was that local panchayats acted according to the Goa Panchayati Raj Act and that sarpanches were made aware of their responsibilities,' recalls Naik. As a devoted farmer with a close understanding of village life, for Pratapsingh, making self-governance work in villages was essential not only for democracy as a whole but also for ensuring that government welfare measures like employment guarantees actually reached those who needed them. The bright and well-informed Yatish and Pratapsingh formed such a fond friendship at this time that today, Yatish has become a close friend of us all, almost like a family member.

In 2007, assembly polls were scheduled for the month of June. Being the CM, Pratapsingh led the party into elections. This assembly election was to be our son 36-year-old Vishwajit Pratapsingh Rane's first election. At first, Pratapsingh was unsure about Vishwajit joining politics. He said to him, 'It is better to be independent and stand on your own feet before taking the plunge.' But Vishwajit pointed out that if he did not join fully, he would not be able to help Pratapsingh in future with the needs of the constituency. However, when the Congress decided not to give more than one ticket per family, Vishwajit resigned from the party and stood and won as an independent from Valpoi.

Pratapsingh was happy that Vishwajit contested as an independent as he firmly believes that members of the same family should not be in politics and that, too, in the same party. Many years ago, some Congressmen had attempted to get me to contest, but Pratapsingh was not in favour of this. He would tell me, 'Don't neglect our children, and let's always try, above all, to keep the family together.' Even if I was campaigning, he would insist that I return home to be there when the children returned from school. It was only after Vishwadhara went to college that I devoted myself to my public welfare work. To keep the family together was always a non-negotiable priority for Pratapsingh. He was determined never to let the ravages of politics touch our precious family life.

The assembly polls gave the Congress a slender victory. Unfortunate manoeuvrings broke out in the party after the results. Several people threw their hat into the ring, and the party leadership in New Delhi directed Congress veterans Sushil Kumar Shinde, Margaret Alva and R.K. Dhawan to oversee developments in Goa.

Malojiraje Chhatrapati, the younger son of our friend the Maharaja of Kolhapur Shahu Chhatrapati, was at this time a Congress MLA in Maharashtra. He was sent to Goa to assist the party in the elections. Malojiraje had also been the Congress party observer for Valpoi and Poriem constituencies and had accompanied Pratapsingh on the election campaign. In 2007, when it came to government formation, Malojiraje was still in Panaji. 'It was a tense time,' recalls Malojiraje. 'The Rane family were in their residence in Altinho and the observers from Delhi were staying at the Cidade de Goa hotel. Communications were taking place between the CM and the Delhi leaders, with myself often the messenger. I remember Pratapsingh Rane being perfectly calm and composed throughout this time. He would say that he would abide by whatever decision the party takes,' recounts Malojiraje.

Pratapsingh remains a politician of the old school. He is upright in his dealings, plays strictly by the rule book and adheres to constitutional discipline. He was and is completely averse to playing any form of petty politics. But at this time, the High Command seemed to be in the mood to appoint someone who would not only abide by the High Command's directions but also be a good fit for the kind of politics that the Delhi leadership wished to pursue in Goa. The High Command chose Digambar Kamat from Margao.

It is intriguing that Pratapsingh, the loyal Congressman, lost the chief ministership to someone who is today in the BJP. It had been Kamat who, along with Monserrate and Pacheco, had brought Parrikar down in 2005. Kamat subsequently joined the Congress and became minister for power, mines, art and culture in the two-year Pratapsingh government. In deciding on Kamat, the central leadership in Delhi opted for someone who was perhaps more of a political activist than Pratapsingh could ever be.

However, Pratapsingh bears no ill will towards anyone for the fallout of those days. 'I did my best towards all my responsibilities. If certain responsibilities were taken away, I expected others to fulfil them to the same high standards I tried to uphold,' he says philosophically. Kamat, a canny political strategist and a well-liked person, has connections across parties, and we have always shared a cordial association. As far as their personal relationship is concerned, Pratapsingh had always trusted Kamat immensely and counted him as a supportive colleague.

I must confess I was annoyed by the manner in which the Congress behaved towards Pratapsingh by appointing Kamat as CM ahead of Pratapsingh. The party leadership acted rather intriguingly by making Pratapsingh work hard for the elections, saying they could not win without him, and when victory came, they ignored the very man who led them to the win. Since the elections had been fought with Pratapsingh at the helm, it was logical, and indeed the constitutional convention, for Pratapsingh to continue to lead the government in the interests of stability and continuity. But Pratapsingh was denied the chief ministership and instead requested to take up the position of Speaker. This instance proved how the Congress High Command has failed to look after its senior leaders, a failing which has resulted in the current sorry state of the party.

Olympian Stature to Speaker's Post

Pratapsingh became Speaker in 2007 for the second time and remained as Speaker for five years until 2012. He brought the same discipline and hard work to his tenure as Assembly Speaker as he had to the post of CM. When he first became Speaker in 1999, he had been an MLA for close to three decades. Totally *au fait* with assembly rules, he functioned according to the letter of the law, abiding strictly by constitutional procedures and ensuring that discipline was maintained. He enjoyed his stint as Speaker. The post resonated with his non-partisan and constitutional way of functioning and of ensuring that governments functioned according to the laid down norms and processes of democracy.

The Goa Assembly was infamous for its defections, unruly scenes, erratic behaviour and an idiosyncratic approach to party politics. But he brought to the Speaker's post the Olympian stature of someone who had never switched parties. He was like a steady lighthouse presiding over a churning sea of MLAs. How did he manage to control members who behaved so differently from himself? 'I knew all the rules and laws of the assembly,' he says, 'So they did not take liberties with me.'

Namrata Ulman, Goa Legislative Assembly secretary, recalls

Pratapsingh's knowledge on rules and norms. 'As a Speaker, Mr Rane had mastery over the Rules of Procedure and parliamentary practices; his brilliance over the rules of procedure was often displayed in the form of rulings that he delivered in the assembly,' says Ulman. 'His command when he was presiding as Speaker was so majestic that decorum was followed in House proceedings and members were motivated to follow constitutional principles.'

Pratapsingh says, 'When Bills are being brought, a Speaker should study the Bills thoroughly, not simply be a thumb man [that is, simply giving his assent to Bills without reading them]. The Speaker should not focus on popularity; instead he should do his job to the best of his ability.' In 2019, when Rajesh Patnekar, BJP MLA from Bicholim, became Speaker, Pratapsingh had these words of advice for him: 'The Speaker is there to judge many of the decisions of the House. To be a good Speaker, you must do justice to both the ruling and opposition sides.' This is the level of meticulous neutrality Pratapsingh maintained throughout his tenure.

It is a testament to Pratapsingh's commitment to the strictly impartial constitutional responsibilities of Speaker that although he first became Speaker when the Congress's Luizinho Faleiro was CM in 1999, he was retained as Speaker by the BJP's Manohar Parrikar in 2000 when Parrikar formed the government. It is rare that a CM belonging to one party would accept a Speaker from a rival party, and the fact that Parrikar kept Pratapsingh on as head of the House speaks volumes for Pratapsingh's scrupulous impartiality.

Ulman says that Pratapsingh as Speaker was also highly enthusiastic about e-governance and using technology to deliver welfare to the poor. Our friend Jason Abraham helped Pratapsingh upgrade the technological features of the assembly. An assembly website was created. Desktops replaced typewriters for staff and ministers. The process of digitizing assembly records began. Pratapsingh oversaw the building of a new assembly library, complete with computer equipment.

As Speaker, he not only maintained high democratic standards but also enforced similarly high standards when it came to the physical upkeep of the Goa Assembly. Abraham recalls how particular Pratapsingh was about maintaining the assembly building in spick-and-span condition. When it comes to cleanliness, Pratapsingh is a bit of a fanatic. Artist Shridhar Kamat Bambolkar says, 'Saheb [Pratapsingh] loved cleanliness. He has the same cleanliness in his heart.'

While working on the digital upgrade of assembly records, Abraham noticed that the catering service running the cafeteria was cooking and serving food in an extremely unhygienic manner. He informed Pratapsingh of this, who immediately strode over to the cafeteria to check. Lunch hour was over, and as they entered, Abraham and Pratapsingh were shocked to see a clothes line running across the cafeteria with clothes belonging to the catering contractor hung up to dry. The floors were mucky. Pratapsingh tried to inspect the washroom, but it was locked as the caterer was taking his bath inside. 'The very next day, the contract of this particular caterer was cancelled, and a much better vendor was hired,' recalls Abraham. Once the slovenly caterer was sacked, the catering was transformed. The Goa Assembly complex in Porvorim as a whole was modernized, fibre-optic cables were laid and the assembly building—as was Pratapsingh's dream—took its first steps into the twenty-first century.

Uday Bhembre too recalls how Pratapsingh maintained both the assembly complex and the Kala Academy in top class condition and what a stickler he was for cleanliness. Pratapsingh made a strict rule that in the assembly complex, no minister could take their teacups into their chambers. Tea was to be drunk only in the canteen so that the assembly premises were kept as hygienic as possible.

Pratapsingh's drive for the highest standards in cleanliness is shared by me. I too always ensure that our homes and offices are as clean as they can possibly be. At home, our washroom taps are always dry and shining, and our counters are always scrubbed and bone dry. I must confess, I cannot abide an unclean, untidy or slushy bathroom!

'During my time as Speaker, I greatly enjoyed the travel to many different countries,' Pratapsingh recalls. Him being Speaker, we got opportunities to witness the best parliamentary practices across the world. Travelling to many different countries, from Australia to Tanzania to the Bahamas, where the annual Commonwealth Parliamentary Conferences (CPC) of the Commonwealth Parliamentary Association (CPA) were held, was a tremendous experience for us. Our travels gave us the opportunity to interact with many impressive people from a range of different nations. There was a great deal of formality and ceremonial protocol during our trips. In England, the Lord Mayor of London would host a dinner with much pomp and ceremony. On one visit, we stayed in Scotland, which was quite beautiful, and we were welcomed by our hosts in traditional attire and shown around their enchanting castles.

LoP: Challenging the BJP on Facts

The years 2007–12 were relatively stable in Goa. Digambar Kamat managed to pull off that rare feat for Goa's CMs, namely, to last a full term from 8 June 2007 to 9 March 2012. But despite Kamat's steadiness, the Congress lost the 2012 assembly polls and the BJP–MGP alliance won a big victory with 24 seats. Manohar Parrikar again became the CM.

Parrikar proved himself to be an astute and open-minded leader of Goa. Even though he was a member of the Sangh Parivar, he built bridges with the Catholic community and in 2012 even gave tickets to Catholics in the Congress bastion of Catholic-dominated Salcette. In fact, many of Parrikar's BJP Catholic candidates became giant killers and defeated entrenched Congress Catholic candidates in their bastions: leaders like Luizinho Faleiro in Navelim and the

Alemao family in Benaulim all lost. It was a remarkable achievement by Parrikar. As a result of Parrikar's bridge building, the BJP was able to come to power with a significant majority in 2012, the first election in which the BJP won such a decisive mandate. The BJP has not won such a mandate since.

In 2014, the Narendra Modi-led BJP came to power in New Delhi and Parrikar departed from Goa to become defence minister of the new central government. Parrikar's place was taken by the relatively unknown BJP Mandrem MLA Laxmikant Parsekar, who remained CM until 2017.

Pratapsingh was LoP from March 2012 to March 2017, throughout the Parrikar and Parsekar chief ministerships. His stature in the assembly was such that when he stood up to make his speech, all the other members would fall silent. He would challenge the government on facts and policies but never create an uproar. Pratapsingh was never one to rush into the well of the house, shout and scream, abuse others or raise any kind of hullabaloo.

Instead, as a lover of Goa's precious wild places, where forest, fields and rivers can breathe without human interference, places that today are in danger of disappearing, he raised urgent matters of public interest, such as the alarming rise of illegal construction activity in Goa. In 2013, he delivered a strong speech against illegal construction activities going on in Goa, even drawing on personal examples. 'I was shocked to learn that a native of Karnataka had started building a house on my property without my knowledge.' Pratapsingh pointed out that even the panchayat had been powerless to stop this person, and the matter had finally been taken to the High Court. He had scathing words about the manner in which panchayats themselves were aiding and abetting illegal construction activity in Goa.

Pratapsingh had played a big part in establishing vibrant Panchayati Raj institutions across Goa but now took them to task. 'If you offer them ₹50,000 you can get electricity, water connections etc. to your illegal house. And village panchayat secretaries have become kings. They are advising innocent sarpanches on how to circumvent the rules.'

He also spoke out against some repressive practices of the Parsekar government. In a speech in 2015 on the activities of the Goa police, he said in the assembly: 'There has been some leakage of information which is defaming our members. I would like a strong statement from the chief minister if you believe in the democratic ideal of the country and its Constitution.'

His style in the assembly was always constructive rather than destructive. In 2021, a Supreme Court panel rejected the proposal to double-track the South Western Railway from Kulem in Goa to Castle Rock, a village in Karnataka, on the grounds that such activity would destroy the biodiversity of the Western Ghats. Opposition politicians jumped to their feet in the assembly and demanded the government provide explanations on why such a project was proposed. As a passionate advocate for protecting Goa's green cover, Pratapsingh raised his voice: 'Our rich forests are God's gift to Goa,' he argued. Pratapsingh proposed a solution: railways should run along the coastline. That way they would not destroy wildlife or forests. He also suggested that a wildlife museum be set up in Goa so younger generations could develop an interest in and attachment to Goa's landscape and wildlife. Arguments for their own sake were not enough; constructive suggestions were needed too.

Since Pratapsingh's interventions in the assembly were reasoned and substantive rather than loud, there were those who found fault with his style. Some partymen wanted more theatrics and bombast; they wanted to oppose the government simply for the sake of it. But Pratapsingh, the constitutional democrat, would never take on a government simply for the sake of it and had even supported some of the Manohar Parrikar government's legislations if he felt they were in Goa's interest. For Pratapsingh, Goa mattered more than party, the people mattered more than scoring political points.

Some Congress people unfairly called him 'ineffective', but for Pratapsingh, Goa and her well-being and development was way above narrow party interest.

Tragi-Comic Theatre of the Absurd

In February 2017, the assembly elections in Goa—the last elections Pratapsingh contested—produced a hung assembly. The Congress managed to win 17 seats in Goa, the largest tally among parties. The BJP got 13. The unusual events that followed these elections have gone down in the annals of Indian elections as a tragi-comic theatre of the absurd.

With both parties short of numbers (the Congress less short than the BJP), there was a need to bring allies into the fold. The Congress needed just four MLAs to form the government, the BJP needed eight. Senior Congress leader Digvijaya Singh, general secretary in charge of Goa, flew in from Delhi. Talks began with Vijai Sardesai of the Goa Forward Party (Sardesai was a former Congressman with whom the Congress had refused a pre-poll pact), but negotiations faltered because there was no unanimity on the choice of CM. Would it be Luizinho Faleiro? Would it be Digambar Kamat? Several names were in the mix. As the Congress dithered, the BJP dashed onto the scene. Union Minister Nitin Gadkari flew into Goa bringing armfuls of the allurements of power.

Two power centres jostled for supremacy: the Congress's Digvijaya Singh with his circle in the Mandovi Hotel and the BJP's Nitin Gadkari holding court at the Cidade de Goa. Gadkari proved too fast for Digvijaya. Almost as soon as Gadkari arrived in Goa, Sardesai drove into the Cidade de Goa, as did MLAs from the MGP. The BJP paraded all their MLAs before Governor Mridula Sinha, who invited the BJP to form the government. The Congress cried foul and rushed to the Supreme Court arguing, with some justification, that the party with the larger numbers should have been invited first. The Court directed the BJP to prove its majority. By now, Parrikar had resigned as defence minister, fixed a time for the swearing-in and hurried to take oath as Goa CM. With Parrikar as CM, the BJP easily won the floor test. A shell-shocked Congress was left wondering how the rug had been pulled from under its feet so swiftly and surely.

In 2017, too, I was disenchanted at the Congress High Command. Even though the Congress did not win, Pratapsingh had led the Congress to a 17-seat haul. Yet, he was not appointed as LoP, the post going to Chandrakant Kavalekar, who later joined the BJP. Some leaders in the party's Delhi leadership once asked Pratapsingh, 'Mr Rane, you were a bad Opposition leader, how did you last for so long?' Pratapsingh replied, 'I spoke on issues. I kept my promises. That's why I lasted.' Truth to tell, these New Delhi-based leaders of the Congress in recent times have repeatedly failed to do justice to Pratapsingh or respect his stature. Although he has remained loyal to the Congress, Pratapsingh has been disappointed by the manner in which the Congress High Command has chosen to neglect some promising younger leaders too.

Although he became CM in 2017, sadly, Parrikar could not complete his term. Afflicted with pancreatic cancer, he passed away on 17 March 2019. Parrikar was replaced by the young second-time MLA Pramod Sawant, as Laxmikant Parsekar, the previous BJP CM, lost the elections from Mandrem.

Chief Minister Pramod Sawant subsequently led the BJP to victory in the assembly elections of 2022. In this 2022 election, analysts opined that the presence of the Aam Aadmi Party, the Trinamool Congress and the Revolutionary Goans Party split the votes in the BJP's favour, leading to a BJP victory with 20 seats. Yet, however bitter the political battles, an easy camaraderie between parties has always existed in Goa. Long may it continue to flourish. 'Whatever the party affiliations, Goa is like one big family,' says Pratapsingh. 'There is a canteen in the secretariat building where we all meet and enjoy meals together. We have very friendly relations with the polite and well-mannered CM Pramod Sawant. The first time he met us, he said, "Please don't call me Mr Sawant, please call me Pramod."'

End of the Political Innings

On 14 March 2017, Pratapsingh's tenure as LoP came to an end and so did the last of his official responsibilities. He was 78 years old, but still undefeated in elections and still in the assembly as an MLA. He was spending more time at Golden Acres, although we also maintained our flat in Panaji.

Often Pratapsingh would divide his time between mornings in Sanquelim and afternoons in Panaji. Our neighbour in Panaji was Dr Rita Paes, principal of the Nirmala Institute of Education. 'I remember Mr Pratapsingh Rane as a complete gentleman, unassuming, quiet and always courteous,' says Dr Paes. 'Our flat was opposite his and our paths would invariably cross when he was entering or leaving his flat. He always had a smile and a kind word. As former CM, Speaker, LoP, he was and is a giant figure in Goa, but there were never any airs about him. He extended great help to us whenever we needed it, particularly in getting us associated with the Cambridge International Diploma in Teaching and Learning and helping us become Cambridge-certified teachers.' Paes recalls her visit to Sanquelim and how much at peace Pratapsingh seemed to be in the countryside with his beloved plants, animals and farming activities.

In 2022, Pratapsingh completed half a century as an MLA. On Thursday, 6 January, the BJP government in Goa led by CM Pramod Sawant conferred lifelong cabinet minister status to Pratapsingh Rane, Goa's longest serving legislator and longest serving CM. On this occasion, Sawant said, 'He [Rane] will always be an inspiration to people across strata. I look forward to his continued guidance as we work towards the welfare of the people and the development of the state.'[13]

The previous year, a special mention had come Pratapsingh's way. Prime Minister Narendra Modi said on X (formerly Twitter) on 24 March 2021:

> **Narendra Modi** ✓
> @narendramodi
>
> Congratulations to Shri Pratapsingh Rane Ji on this momentous feat of completing 50 years as MLA. His passion for public service and Goa's progress is reflected in his work. I remember our interactions when we both served as Chief Ministers of our respective states.

Source: @narendramodi, X (formerly Twitter), 24 March 2021, 6.16 p.m., https://tinyurl.com/msumfwzt. Accessed on 11 September 2023.

Prime Minister Narendra Modi and Pratapsingh belonged to different political parties, but they often worked together. At national forums in New Delhi, they sat side by side because both ran states beginning with the letter 'G', with Goa placed just before Gujarat. They shared a friendly rapport and every time the PM visits Goa, he unfailingly asks after Pratapsingh's health.

Pratapsingh decided not to contest the 2022 assembly polls, choosing to retire from public life. In fact, he had been weighing the decision to retire since 2021 when he turned 82. 'There comes a time when we must step back and let other younger people take over. There comes a time when a man requires rest and time to look after himself. I had a very good academic career, I excelled in sports, I came back to my land to do my duty, which I did to the best of my ability. I kept my word to my father that I would

---

[13]'Goa CM Decides to Grant Lifelong Cabinet Status to Pratapsingh Rane to Honour His 50 Years of Public Service', *ANI*, 6 January 2022, https://tinyurl.com/5xnbt56x. Accessed on 4 August 2023.

always look after my ancestral homelands, and I kept my word to the people of Goa who kept electing me and giving me an opportunity to serve them. There may be those who criticize me and say I didn't do enough. All I can say in my defence is I tried my best.'

In our farmhouse, Golden Acres in Kulan, in the wooded, green haven of Karapur village, his days are full of people. This is where his life's work has been, this is where he feels most at home and most valued. 'I served in public life for 50 years since 1972 when I first became an MLA. Fifteen of those 50 years I was CM. I take satisfaction from the fact that I did my duty.'

It is the people's love that matters most to Pratapsingh. He never sought out power; instead, power sought him out. Writes veteran journalist Gurudas Singbal in the January 2006 edition of *Goa Today* magazine, 'Power has always walked into his [Pratapsingh] embrace uninvited. There is an elegant charm in his manner and a quiet dignity and sense of rectitude in his public doings which make him stand out as a politician of a different kind.' Singbal also writes, 'Rane has never been a big hit with the Press due to his somewhat taciturn nature. He is at times also curt with them when they become too "nosey" in the quest for controversial news.' Always one to look at life's positive side, Pratapsingh has no time for unnecessary negativity, nor does he care about publicity or the media claptrap.

His loyalty to the people of Sattari—his constituents who have sent him to the state assembly in a record 11 successive election wins—has never faltered. Over these last 50 years, his development works in his constituency have improved the lives of thousands. The GIM is a recognized national management college. He has established hospitals in Bicholim, Sanquelim and Valpoi. Modern bridges have been built: Hedode Bridge, Veluz Dhabos Bridge, Poriem Bridge and Codal Derodem Bridge. Other structures have come up: the Honda Bus Stand, the swimming pool at Sanquelim, a hygienic and modern building for the fish and vegetable market in Sanquelim and the Morlem community hall. He runs two schools and one higher secondary school, the Bhumika Higher Secondary School. He also runs an Industrial Training Institute (ITI) specializing in hotel management. Currently, he is busy with plans to set up a nursing college. Pratapsingh is keen that the Rane ancestral home, just 4 km down from Golden Acres, the heritage house where so many years ago Bhausaheb Bandodkar arrived to convince Pratapsingh to join politics, be converted into a museum and be opened to tourists and the public. 'We have a gun in our collection that was used by one of the American rebels in the Boston Tea Party [an eighteenth-century protest in Boston against colonial rule],' Pratapsingh points out. Rich in artefacts and memorabilia, the sprawling Rane wada is a piece of living history for younger generations.

The Ravindra Bhavan at Sanquelim has become a lively cultural centre, where local youngsters as well as visiting troupes regularly stage performances of a remarkably high standard. 'Along with industry and education, entertainment and leisure activities are extremely important. Once incomes increase, opportunities for public entertainment must also be provided. That's why I built theatres all over Goa,' he says.

Arangetrams are of particular interest to him, as they are performances which establish that a classical dancer is now fully trained and can literally 'ascend the stage'. Dancers trained in Goa who achieve their arangetrams brings him much gratification. The renowned Goan Bharatanatyam exponent Kshitija Barve, who joined the Kala Academy in 1996, recalls how Pratapsingh once asked her why Kala Academy students did not stage arangetrams more regularly. Coincidentally, Barve at the time was preparing two of her students for their arangetrams and invited Pratapsingh to attend and even deliver a speech. 'He said he would read books on Bharatanatyam to be able to deliver the speech,' Barve says. She remembers how Pratapsingh not only came for the arangetram but remained in his seat through the performance. She also recalls how he would visit the Kala Academy every Friday punctually at 3.00 p.m., often accompanied by visiting distinguished guests. 'He would show them [the visiting VIPs] the ongoing classes, auditoriums, library and art gallery with interest and pride, yet take care never to disturb us,' Barve recalls.

What message would he like to give to new generations of Goans? 'Keep the peace. Let us enjoy the beauty of Goa in all its forms, the beauty of its landscape as well as its cultural traditions. It is Goa's beauty that fills us with so much peace. Let's develop Goa as a model state and always try to live in harmony with each other and the beautiful natural world that Goa is blessed with. There is music in the air of Goa. Let us make sure that music never fades.'

Legacy of Hands-on Work

The man is also the message. Pratapsingh's personality is one that new generations can learn much from and emulate. Not many politicians today are like him: unassuming, understated and quiet, yet hard-working and disciplined, an administrator and manager of terrific skill, with the gallant charm, inborn etiquette, sensitivity as well as the love of life and music that marks all Goans. Delicadeza and decencia.

As his active public life drew to a close, I would like to mention a few incidents and vignettes to highlight the spirit and style Pratapsingh brought to his long tenure.

In 2007, when accompanying Pratapsingh on the election campaign, Malojiraje Chhatrapati noticed Pratapsingh's capacity to listen. Even on a hectic election tour, Pratapsingh stopped to listen in detail to what people were telling him. 'He was a very good listener, never saying much but always listening. I realized that this is how he must be proceeding with his development work, by listening to people.' Malojiraje also remembers the manner in which Pratapsingh first started building a road in the remote village of Surla, located high in the Western Ghats. Surla is an idyllic spot with gushing waterfalls and thickly forested slopes, rich in birds and varieties of trees. It is a sparsely populated place, and though breathtakingly scenic, access is difficult. Pratapsingh took it upon himself to construct a tarred road to Surla, persisting with his efforts until the hilltop village acquired a motorable road.

'It was a learning experience to see Pratapsingh Rane labouring so hard in putting up road infrastructure for only a small group of people who lived in Surla,' recalls Malojiraje. There were no vote bank concerns or publicity campaigns here. Only the conviction that even a small village of little political significance in a remote region had the right to modern amenities like roads and communication. No one was to be neglected, even if it meant a big personal effort. 'Mr Pratapsingh Rane is endowed with a listening ear and kept his ear to the ground,' says former IAS officer Rajeev Talwar.

Pandharinath Bodke was Goa state registrar and head of notary services. Bodke's father, the late Shrinivas Sinai Bodke, popularly known as 'Bodke master', worked with the Rane family, including with Pratapsingh's father, Raoji Satroji Rane, in sorting out property matters, and the Ranes in turn provided help to the Bodke family in gaining education and employment. Pandharinath recalls an incident that shows how even as CM, Pratapsingh never stopped listening.

One day, an elderly gentleman timidly approached the CM's office (CMO) to meet Pratapsingh. He did not have a prior appointment. A senior company executive, who did have a prior appointment, had already arrived and had been shown into the CM's room. It was a busy day for Pratapsingh, packed with meetings. Still, his personal staff sent him a message saying that an elderly man of modest means had come to meet him all the way from Cotigao in Canacona. Almost immediately, Pratapsingh emerged from his room, ushered the elderly gent into another chamber, asked about his problems and directed his office staff to look into his needs.

The senior executive who was waiting, was surprised, aware as he was of Pratapsingh's office discipline and what a stickler he was for punctual appointments. Curious, the executive asked the office staff: did CM Rane know this elderly man personally that he's giving him so much personalized attention in the middle of a hectic day? No, replied the office staff, CM Rane doesn't know him. But since the old man had come all the way from Canacona and is a man of humble background, the CM made it a point to meet him. Says Bodke: 'Mr Rane's heart was always with Goa's poor. He pays maximum attention towards the difficulties faced by farmers. Being a farmer himself, he knows how hard they have to strive.' The words of the wise Bandodkar stayed with Pratapsingh always. *However high you reach, never lose touch with the people.*

Rajeev Talwar, arriving in Goa as young SDM was shocked to find that the CM could be addressed by name or even as '*tu*' or the informal 'you'. In Goa, members of the public could approach the CM and demand: '*Tu mhajea khatir kidem karta?*' (What are you doing for me?) In North India, bound by feudal mores, such directness was unthinkable. Perhaps this innate dignity and egalitarian spirit of the Goans can be summed up in these lines by the writer Manohar Malgonkar in his book *Inside Goa*. He writes: 'The Portuguese, no matter how intolerant and repressive they were in the first half of their reign, permitted their subjects a much greater self-respect [than the British colonialists]. The poorest farmer did not quite have to quite go on his knees as he presented a petition to the local Administrator…no official was too grand to take a drink with you and toast your health…a *mamlatdar* [like a tehsildar] and taxi driver [could] shake each other by the shoulder as though they were brothers…because [they] came from the same village.'[14]

This spirit, this 'non-aggressive individualism', as the Goan

---

[14]Malgonkar, Manohar, *Inside Goa*, Directorate of Information and Publicity, Government of Goa, Daman, and Diu, 1982.

writer Maria Aurora Couto describes it, is also the result of a distinctive feature of Goa, namely the *gaunkari* system. The gaunkari system—which later came to be known as the *comunidade* system—is a practice by which, in Goa, there has flourished a long tradition of self-ruled village communities and village associations over common lands. Although different imperial dynasties ruled Goa, the gaunkari system of self-rule and of equal stakes in the land persisted in villages. This traditional norm of self-rule gives the Goan a sense of his own individual dignity, a sense of brotherhood with his village folk, however high or low, as well as an egalitarian attitude to rulers. The Goan is not one to bow and scrape, nor do Goa's leaders demand feudal self-abnegation from citizens. Pratapsingh fully imbibed this spirit of equality. Never self-important or pompous, he would walk and talk with a wide variety of people, share a glass of feni with village folk and interact as a brother with elders in Sanquelim.

Pratapsingh's outlook is refreshingly open. He believes in welcoming the world to Goa. In the early 1980s when only the hippies would descend on the beaches, Pratapsingh presented Rajeev Talwar with a plan (which Talwar still preserves) laying out his ideas for large-scale tourism in Goa. 'That Goa is today identified as a prime tourist destination is a tribute to Pratapsingh Rane,' says Talwar. 'Mr Rane was able to persuade politicians and the public of Goa that the state could be developed into a haven for tourists all over the world and in turn raise the employment potential of Goa besides its GDP.' Some criticism has been directed at Pratapsingh for amending laws permitting offshore casinos, but open-minded as he was, to him, this was another feature to boost Goa's tourism potential.

He made strenuous efforts in setting up the Automobile Corporation of Goa Limited (ACGL). The undertaking was to be a public limited joint venture between the Goa Industrial Development Corporation (IDC) and Tata Motors (then known as

Telco). Pratapsingh had a long association with Sumant Moolgaokar, the visionary chairman and MD of Telco, having worked briefly at Telco in Jamshedpur. Pratapsingh was keen that a Tata plant be established in Goa. The ACGL was established in 1980 and today the facility is so advanced that it produces thousands of buses each year for export and domestic markets.

Senior Tata Motors executive Vivek Annaswamy recalls how Pratapsingh visited the Telco factory in Pune to inspect the vehicles and took a personal interest in the expansion of the ACGL project in Goa. 'He called me to accompany him to scout for land [for the expansion of ACGL],' remembers Annaswamy. 'It was just Mr Rane in his gum boots, with an umbrella in hand, and me on a drizzling day, looking for the land for the proposed bus body division. We spent a full day together as we walked along the slushy fields in Bhuipal, just 2 km from Honda where the ACGL Press Division was located. At the end of the day, we found one suitable plot. The paperwork for the allotment of land was done immediately and on time to start construction work. That was Mr Rane's commitment to industrialize Goa.' In the drive to create industry, jobs and enterprises, Pratapsingh was sure of his goals. When the ACGL plant was faced with labour union troubles, he made sure to support the factory so that it did not face any disruption.

Mining activities have recently been stopped in Goa and the state's iron ore industry is at a standstill. Pratapsingh, however, remains convinced that mining is one of Goa's foremost industries and should be encouraged and not stopped. 'Mining industries allow us to make use of the treasures below the earth to create industries and jobs. If we can export the ore, we earn foreign exchange, and this benefits us as a whole. All industries should abide by the law of the land, but mining should definitely be allowed in Goa.'

Talent attracts more talent. Pratapsingh was quick to spot talent and, when he saw it, made every effort to encourage it. Vijay Kumar

Verekar is a high-school science teacher at Progress High School in Sanquelim. Verekar's father worked closely with Pratapsingh in the MGP. Verekar recalls how he was interviewed by Pratapsingh for his first job in 1977 after he graduated with a degree in science. 'My father insisted I try for a teaching job at the same school where he was teaching, although I would have to clear the interview. I applied for the job of assistant teacher and was called for the interview. Mr Rane was the chairman of this school and sat on the interview board. During the interview, he asked me a direct question: "How does iron rust?" I answered in detail and he seemed impressed.' Having asked a straight empirical question and received a detailed answer, Pratapsingh lost no time in telling the school principal that not only should the young Verekar be appointed but should teach the higher classes. Not only that, Verekar was also tasked to tutor the young Vishwajit, then in primary school. Verekar recalls the one instruction we had given him: be very strict with the boy. Once Pratapsingh trusted someone's abilities, he put all his faith in that person and expected him or her to live up to his high standards. Those secure in their own talents always encourage others to give off their best.

To encourage officers to be as productive as possible, Pratapsingh used a mix of discipline and leniency. 'He was neither too tough, nor was he overly friendly or familiar,' recalls Dr Mohammad Modassir. 'He had that all too rare quality among politicians of not interfering too much. Once he trusted you, he gave you autonomy and liberty to work but always kept a check.'

Modassir recalls a telling incident. In 1981, Modassir was appointed administrator of the Goa State Co-operative Bank and worked as a final authority in sanctioning loans to farmers. One day, he received a call from the CMO: come immediately. Such peremptory summons from Pratapsingh were unusual, and Modassir hurried to the CMO, which, in those days, was located in Panaji's Adil Shah Palace, a beautiful heritage building with a characteristic

Top: Honouring the Goa freedom fighter Mohan Ranade in 1986
Bottom: Pratapsingh, Vijayadevi and others at the inauguration of the operation of the spillway gates of the Anjunem Irrigation Project in 1987

1987—Celebrating Goa's statehood. Pratapsingh and Vijayadevi with PM Rajiv Gandhi and Sonia Gandhi.

Top: At the inauguration of the Pandit Jawaharlal Nehru Stadium (Fatorda Stadium), 1989. Bottom: Pratapsingh riding one of the army horses which came for a Military Tattoo ceremony in Panaji in 1989

Top: Pratapsingh and Vishwajit Rane with film stars Rishi Kapoor and Rekha in 1990
Bottom: With Pratapsingh's close friend Hans Dieter and his family in Stuttgart, Germany, in the early 1990s

Top: Hosting an official lunch for President Shankar Dayal Sharma and Mrs Vimala Sharma in 1996
Bottom: With Sonia Gandhi at the CM's official residence in Panaji in 1998

With West Bengal CM Jyoti Basu in 1996. Pratapsingh invited Basu for an official dinner to the CM's residence.

Top: Inaugurating the Konkan Railway with then Railway Minister Ram Vilas Paswan in 1998
Bottom: Wedding of Vishwajit Rane and Deviya in May 1998. Daughter Vishwadhara and son-in-law Vishwajit on extreme left and extreme right, respectively

Pratapsingh Rane at the wedding of Vishwajit and Deviya

Top: With PM Atal Bihari Vajpayee in 2000 at the inauguration of the Goa Assembly complex when Pratapsingh was Speaker

Bottom: With Lata Mangeshkar at a function to honour Pandit Deenanath Mangeshkar in 2000. Also seen in the photo is then Goa CM Manohar Parrikar. Pratapsingh was Assembly Speaker at that time.

Granddaughter Aishwarya's naming ceremony and first birthday at Golden Acres in 2000. In the centre of this family photo is Rajmata Sushila Devi Ghorpade.

Top: With PM Dr Manmohan Singh in Delhi in 2005. Pratapsingh was CM at this time and led a cabinet delegation to meet Dr Singh.
Bottom: Provedoria function at Sanquelim in 2005

Bottom: Chief Ministers Bhupinder Singh Hooda (Haryana), Narendra Modi (Gujarat), Pratapsingh Rane (Goa) and Nitish Kumar (Bihar) at the Conference of Chief Ministers and Chief Justices in New Delhi in 2006. Credit: Rajeev Bhatt/*The Hindu*

Top: (From left) Chief Ministers Nitish Kumar (Bihar), Pratapsingh Rane (Goa), Narendra Modi (Gujarat), Bhupinder Singh Hooda (Haryana) and Virbhadra Singh (Himachal Pradesh) at the Conference of Chief Ministers and Chief Justices in New Delhi in 2006. Credit: Rajeev Bhatt/*The Hindu*

Top: Seeking father's blessings—Swearing in of Vishwajit Rane as minister for the first time in 2007
Bottom: With President Pratibha Patil in 2011. Pratapsingh was Speaker of Goa Assembly at this time.

Top: With Shrinivas Dempo in Sanquelim, 2016
Bottom: Pratapsingh and Vijayadevi with the Dalai Lama during his visit to the Goa Institute of Management, Sanquelim, in 2018

Golden Acres farmhouse

Pratapsingh and Vijayadevi—Happily married for over 50 years

slope-tiled roof and wooden verandahs. Modassir arrived and was immediately shown into the CM's room, where a visibly angry Pratapsingh said: 'Mr Modassir, at such a young age, have you become corrupt?' Taken aback, Modassir asked why he felt so. Pratapsingh gestured towards a local politician from Pratapsingh's own area of north Goa sitting in his room, who had brought a complaint against him.

Modassir sought a few hours to investigate the matter. He rushed back to his own office and, looking through his files, found that he had in fact rejected this particular MLA's bid for a loan. He had written the word 'rejected' on the file in capital letters. 'I think I was in a bad mood about the poorly drafted application and wrote "Rejected" in a bold way.' The MLA had complained against Modassir out of a sense of pique. When Modassir showed Pratapsingh the evidence that had led to the accusation, the CM was quick to apologize to Modassir for making an unjust accusation. He also told the MLA who was still in his room, 'You must never again speak so irresponsibly about my officers.'

Bureaucrats were to be held accountable, but equally, if their integrity was unfairly questioned, the CM would stand by his officers and protect them to the last, even if it meant telling off fellow politicians. 'Mr Rane always came down heavily on any rumours of dishonesty among officials. Everyone had to stay alert and be very careful,' remembers Modassir who remained closely associated with us and served as an ex officio member of the Bal Bhavan and Sanjay School, where I served as the chairperson. We enjoyed a good working relationship. 'Mrs Vijayadevi Rane is every bit as principled and tough as Mr Rane, and an equally good administrator,' Modassir says of the days we worked together. Pratapsingh has fond memories of the bureaucrats he worked with. 'The IAS in my time was full of top-notch officers,' he recalls.

Whether swimming with his officers or gunning his self-driven jeep through dirt tracks and village streams where there were no roads, Pratapsingh's love of adventure marked his chief ministerial years. As a sportsman himself, he was also keenly interested in sports.

Brahmanand Sagoon Kamat Sankhwalkar from Taleigaon, Goa's football hero, was captain of the national football team from 1983 to 1986. The tall, whippet-thin Sankhwalkar is considered one of India's best goalkeepers ever. Sankhwalkar recalls how Pratapsingh kept encouraging him to scale new heights in training and coaching. He also recalls how, on one public occasion, the CM even gave him a lift home in his personal VIP car so the footballer could remain safe from being jostled by fans.

'Mr Rane went all out to encourage sports,' says Sankhwalkar. 'His signatures flowed when it came to sanctioning sports facilities for Goan sportspersons.' In 1982–83, when Goa won the national Santosh Trophy (along with Bengal) and the football team returned to Goa in glory, Pratapsingh drove out to the Four Pillars spot on the airport highway, along with several senior ministers, to welcome the victorious team home. A motorcade was organized for the players, and, as they drove along, Goans lined the streets to shower rose petals. In 1983–84, when Goa again won the Santosh Trophy, this time on its own, the Rane government announced plots of land for each of the footballers. It took six years for the administrative formalities to be completed, and, by the time the allotments came through, it was 1990 and Pratapsingh's government was about to be unseated. But despite the fact that his government was teetering on the edge, Pratapsingh called Sankhwalkar to his office and made sure all the team members got their allotment letters as promised. 'In spite of the turmoil all around him, he made sure he kept his commitment to us,' Sankhwalkar says. Once Pratapsingh gave his word, he would remain true to it, whatever his own circumstances.

Sankhwalkar recalls when the foundation stone-laying ceremony for the Pandit Jawaharlal Nehru Stadium in Fatorda in Margao took place on 30 May 1988, he found he was not in the list of invitees. He relates the following account. In spite of not being invited, Sankhwalkar still went along for the function. Soon the various dignitaries, including the CM, sports minister Francisco Monte Cruz and Margao MLA Uday Bhembre arrived, and the foundation stone laying ceremony and *bhoomi* puja began. After a few seconds, Sankhwalkar recalls, Pratapsingh turned his head and asked, 'Where is Brahmanand?' Hearing his name, Sankhwalkar called out that he was there. Pratapsingh gestured for him to come forward and take part in the ceremony, asking the gathered officials, 'Why has Brahmanand not been called for this?' As the cement for the foundations of the stadium was laid, Sankhwalkar reached into his pocket and—as is the custom for auspicious beginnings—planted a 25 paise coin in the concrete. 'My coin lies buried in the foundations of Fatorda Stadium,' says Sankhwalkar, 'because the CM made sure to involve me in the foundation stone-laying ceremony.'

The Fatorda Stadium was completed in record time and inaugurated by then Vice President Shankar Dayal Sharma in January 1989. It was a grand opening with Navy jets flying overhead and an international football tournament—the Nehru Gold Cup, the first international football tournament to be held in Goa—kicking off to thunderous applause. The Fatorda Stadium became an iconic sports ground hosting many national and international sports tournaments. For his part, Brahmanand Sankhwalkar from Goa went on to win the coveted Arjuna Award for exceptional sportspersons in 1997.

Another aspect of Pratapsingh's governance style is revealed by Govind Kale, former curator of the Kala Academy library. Every year, the Kala Academy organizes the classical dance festival in Mardol town, featuring dance performances in Bharatanatyam, Mohiniyattam, Kuchipudi and other forms. Every year, both Pratapsingh and I would visit the dance festival over the entire duration of three days and watch all the performances beginning at 7.00 p.m. and carrying on until 9.30 p.m. Kale once asked Pratapsingh, 'Why do you come every day for the festival and give so much of your valuable time here?' Replied Pratapsingh:

'I come here because the people are here. We, who are elected representatives, must always be with the people and be seen to be among them. That is how bonds are built.'

Tramping through mud, trekking up steep hillsides, always listening to the people, and sitting for long hours with audiences during dance performances, imparting an aesthetic sensibility to his work, these features form the legacy of hands-on work and public involvement that Pratapsingh has bequeathed to the CMs who came after him. He was not a CM whiling his time away in politicking or intriguing in party offices with party folk. Instead, he was a hard-working chief executive of great stamina and physical fitness who was not afraid to be on the road, forest and hillside, as he poured his energy to secure Goa's future and build dignified ties of mutual respect with Goans of all creeds.

I believe Pratapsingh's tenure saw a carving out of a complementary role for the wife of the CM. I think I set a new template for the CM's wife: of making the most of the position I had to carry out as much public welfare as I could.

In my own way, I contributed to Pratapsingh's chief ministership with my work. I learnt on the job and became an efficient administrator too. I gained a reputation for being able to take projects to completion and to their heights, so I was entrusted with more responsibilities. Apart from my work in the Bal Bhavans and the Sanjay School, I also worked in women's football and did a great deal of work in providing medical assistance to those in need. People would come to me with complaints; I would take a look at their reports and assess what their health problems were. I grew so adept at reading medical reports that, in later years, a senior doctor told Pratapsingh: 'Mr Rane you have a resident medical officer (RMO) in your home.'

Once I had perused the reports, we would pass the hat around and try to collect as much as we could to send patients to Mumbai. I happened to be on friendly terms with a few doctors there and they always helped me out. Pratapsingh used to find any means possible to fund healthcare. Donations by rich childless donors to the provedorias were used to fund patients.

Big Shoes to Fill

No telling of the story of Pratapsingh's later years is complete without recounting how our son Vishwajit has taken up his mantle. Vishwajit first became an MLA in 2007 when he contested as an independent from the Valpoi constituency and became health minister in CM Digambar Kamat's government. Vishwajit resigned as an independent and joined the Congress in 2010 and won from Valpoi as the Congress candidate in the by-poll of 2010 and assembly polls of 2012. For the 2012 assembly polls, however, the Congress party's policy of one-ticket-per-family was reversed and both Pratapsingh and Vishwajit won from Poriem and Valpoi, respectively, on Congress tickets.

In 2017, however, Vishwajit resigned from the Congress and joined the BJP. After statehood in 1987, Sattari was divided into two constituencies—Valpoi and Poriem. Pratapsingh always won from Poriem. Today, Vishwajit is the MLA from Valpoi and our daughter-in-law Deviya is the MLA from Poriem.

Vishwajit idolizes his father and looks up to him as a role model and pathfinder. As he writes: 'I relate to my Baba at many levels. As a farmer, I am amazed to see his passion for the field and the animals. He taught me that there are questions you can best ponder about in the greens that sometimes have no answers in books. As a political leader, he has held his head high through the rough and tumble, always being a man of principle and values. The respect he gets across the political spectrum is something that very few statesmen are capable of.

'There is so much to learn from his forthright and straightforward nature. Whenever I'm in doubt, all I have to do is think what he would do and the situation becomes crystal clear to me. There is a thin line in making your child feel special and privileged. He made us feel special but always made sure we had our feet firmly grounded. Baba was equally supportive in my decision to take up public life and helped with words and in deed. My father is more than a father—he has been a guiding light in my life.'

Vishwajit has done magnificent work in the healthcare sector in Goa. He has established the Goa super specialty hospital as well as upgraded the emergency and casualty departments across hospitals. Recently, when Pratapsingh underwent a cardiac procedure, the surgery was performed in Goa. In fact, while recovering from the operation, Pratapsingh mistakenly assumed that he was in a Mumbai hospital because the surroundings were so up to date. Vishwajit has inherited his father's capacity for tremendous hard work and for single-mindedly pursuing the development of Goa. The fact that he is a minister in charge of major portfolios in the Goa government today—Health, Town & Country Planning, Woman & Child Development, Forest and Urban Development—shows the faith that the party leadership has in him.

Vishwajit is always bubbling with energy. He is a doer, someone whose switchover to the BJP was driven by growing disillusionment with a status-quoist Congress leadership unwilling to give ambitious new talents opportunities to grow or take their own decisions when required. Today, he is on his way to proving what an asset he is to the BJP, carrying as he does the tremendous legacy of his father. Of course, Vishwajit has big shoes to fill. Living up to expectations as the son of a towering figure brings its own challenges.

Pratapsingh belongs to the old school of politics, where economic development was the main point of debate, when there were grave deliberations in the assembly and the party system was based on principles. Friendships across party lines were common and politics was played in a somewhat rule-bound manner. Vishwajit is a leader of a new kind of politics where loyalties are more polarized and there are burning identity issues of religion and caste to deal with at every stage. Vishwajit is an adept practitioner of twenty-first-century politics in India, in a way that perhaps Pratapsingh could never be. Perhaps the baton passed from father to son at the right time.

Yet although there has been a generational shift, Pratapsingh's ideas on governance and public administration are timeless and remain as a rich treasure trove not only for Vishwajit but also for new generations of leaders and administrators. It is to these ideas that we now turn.

SEVEN

THOUGHTS: LOOKING BACK, LOOKING FORWARD

'I believe in free enterprise.'
'The best government is a government of laws.'
'Religion is a personal matter in which governments or politicians should not get involved.'

The life and career of Pratapsingh Rane, in important ways, is also a history of Goa after Liberation. Events unfolded rapidly in the life of the UT, the state and its CM. He had a hectic pace of work. Together, he and Goa achieved many milestones. Along the way, as CM for 15 years and an MLA for 50 years, he developed many ideas which shaped not only Goa but, today, also provide insights for governance and administration in democratic India.

Born of decades of political and administrative experience and hands-on dealings with people, his insights into public life and governance are very useful. He not only served as MLA and CM but, over the years, also served on a range of Legislative Assembly committees, from the Business Advisory Committee to the Select Committee on Code of Criminal Procedure. His ideas and thoughts would help readers glance at the past and also gaze into the future.

A Free Economy and Free Society

Politics is defined as the pursuit of power. But how is the pursuit of power of one individual a public good for society as a whole? Pratapsingh says: 'A politician should not seek power for himself. For example, when I came back to Goa, I was US-educated and had been looking forward to working in a corporate job. I was 26 years old. Then my younger brother died. My father was shattered by the loss, and I gave my father my word that I would stay in Goa and develop Sattari and Goa. When Bhausaheb D.B. Bandodkar offered me a ticket to contest elections, I decided to pursue politics but my aim was to develop Sattari and Goa.'

Power in itself is not important. It is how you use power that is important. The best use of power is for development. Power should not be used to forcibly demand respect or declare 'I am this and I am that.' It's not the 'me' factor that matters in politics, the 'we factor' does. It should be 'we' instead of 'me'. Sadly today, many in public life believe power is everything. But power is nothing if you're not going to utilize it for the benefit of the people around you. Power is for the people. For Pratapsingh, the politician holds power in trust for the people.

Pratapsingh has never pursued the politics of the 'me' factor and is the most self-effacing of leaders. When the Goa Assembly conferred on him the title of 'Legislator of the Millennium' in 2001, MLA after MLA stood to lavish praise on him and appreciate his work for Goa. Acutely embarrassed by all the paeans, in his speech of thanks, Pratapsingh, then Speaker of the Assembly, said: 'How much of these praises I deserve shall be judged by the generations who agree with me, and the generations are full of expectations. I thank all of you. It is very embarrassing to sit here and hear praises. I was put in an odd situation. I would rather have faced a no-confidence motion than to get these praises. I don't know whether I should put this motion to the vote of the House. I take it that it's adopted.' Amidst laughter and table thumping, the motion was adopted.

A politician who dislikes being praised may seem like an oxymoron in today's times. But that's exactly the kind of politician Pratapsingh is. He dislikes flattery. 'Pratapsingh Rane was one exceptional public figure, an unusual politician who never promoted himself,' says former IAS officer Shailaja Chandra. Pratapsingh's view on power echoes Gandhi's beliefs on ends and means. For Gandhi, unless the means to achieve power are just and honest, the goal (of power) can never be used to deliver just or honest governance. Gandhi believed once the ends are achieved, the means shape the nature of the victory. Without the benchmark of moral and ethical means, the ends often degenerate into an anything-goes power lust.

To understand the pitfalls of power is the duty of every public servant. Speaking for myself, Pratapsingh would always tell me never to be carried away by official positions but to keep myself grounded at all times. He would say: be careful or else you will get hurt. I understood only in 1998 when he lost office what these words meant and how certain people who called themselves our 'friends' disappeared. He was extremely good at assessing people and was always wary of those who saluted the rising sun. When it came to his dealings with people, he lived by the motto 'be cautious'. He had two invisible compartments, one for his true friends and one for those who were his 'friends' because he was powerful.

He would make it a point never to inaugurate projects on his own birthdays, as so many politicians are wont to do, nor would he take personal credit for projects being paid for by the government and therefore the taxpayer. He did not believe in yoking a government achievement to his own persona. Instead, on his birthday, he would remain at home to meet all those who came to wish him and be at the disposal of people. People came first, not building a VIP cult around himself.

This strict separation of state affairs and personal life stemmed from his conviction that power was held in trust for the people, to bring improvements in the people's daily lives. It's the people, big or small, who matter, and it was his duty to make each person who he came into contact with feel special. 'Everyone wants to feel wanted, to be seen and heard and to feel as if they matter,' he says. 'As their chosen representative, it is my duty to make them feel that way, to remember all their names and take an interest in their lives.' I imbibed this spirit. By way of a small example, when visiting constituencies or weddings, I make it a point to wear the saris that have been gifted to me by those to whose homes I visit. I treasure those saris not just for their looks, but for the thought contained in them.

Power in itself is irrelevant for us both, and until this day, Pratapsingh, himself low-key and understated, cares two hoots for big names or self-styled VIPs tooting their own horns or making a big show simply because of the chairs they sit on. He has always believed that respect is commanded, not demanded, and respect must be given freely. Throwing one's weight around is no good. It is the work you do and the real welfare you deliver that matter above all. When anyone who has ever worked for us, or anyone from the constituency, comes to visit us, they always sit down for a meal with us at our family table. People tell us, 'You are such simple, down-to-earth people and you give us so much love and affection.' That's because we have been brought up never to look down on anyone else and to respect the dignity of labour. I can say that we both love people and greatly enjoy meeting new people. Today, many remark on a luminous quality that Pratapsingh seems to carry, a sort of inner glow that draws people towards him. It has nothing to do with official positions since he does not hold any. That glow comes from his constant care of people and from enjoying people. It comes from nurturing relationships.

If power is an instrument to be used in the service of

development, what about ideology? Don't political parties believe power is to be used to spread and propagate their own ideology to win hearts as well as minds of the public? Pratapsingh believes the following:

'Political parties decide on their own ideology. They decide whether they want to propagate socialism, communism or capitalism. But in governance, we cannot be prisoners of an ideology, theory or any ism. A government ideally should not impose socialism, communism or even capitalism because any form of imposition is wrong. You can't use the state apparatus to push a certain ideological point of view. In a democracy, you cannot go about dictating to the people, you can't do this and you can't do that.'

There should be as much freedom for citizens as possible—a free, liberal society and free enterprise.

India is a participatory democracy. Progress and change are achieved through a constant process of consultation with the people. 'In a participatory democracy, you can't be so deep into a particular philosophy or an ideology that you ignore the people's real needs. Why else do we stand for elections? We stand for elections precisely to know the mind of the people and find out what the people support or do not. If one is a prisoner of theory, one can't understand what the people want.'

What is his approach when it comes to ideology? 'I believe in a people-centric approach. People come first. Their needs come first.'

Yet, one could argue that one of his most admired leaders—Indira Gandhi—was deeply ideological. In pursuit of socialist ideals, she pushed through the nationalization of 14 commercial banks in 1969; she abolished privy purses or monies paid to India's royal princes in 1971; and she moved to dilute fundamental rights by asserting Parliament's right to amend the Constitution. It was also Indira Gandhi who inserted 'socialist' and 'secular' into the Preamble. Indira's laws were challenged in the famous Kesavananda Bharati case of 1973, in which the Supreme Court ruled that Parliament did not have unlimited powers to change the Constitution. Did Indira Gandhi not push through the so-called 'Indira revolution'—that is, an attempt to take the social and economic structure of India in a left-oriented ideological direction?

Pratapsingh says candidly: 'I admired Indira Gandhi, but I have always disagreed with her socialist model. I did not like it. I believe in free enterprise. There is no such thing as socialism in Goa. Here, we always enjoyed a society which has laissez-faire or a free economy. In fact, in Goa, people became rich overnight when they got licenses to mine iron ore. Goa has always had a culture of people freely travelling abroad for work. Many Goans down the generations have gone to work in Europe and Africa. They have worked overseas and then come back to enjoy the fruits of their labours. Goa has always had free enterprise, and today, in Goa, you have some of the richest people.'

Here the views of Pratapsingh seem to chime with those of C. Rajagopalachari, former CM of the Madras State and former union minister, who famously broke with the Jawaharlal Nehru-led Congress, and, in 1959, founded the free market–oriented Swatantra Party. Rajagopalachari believed in free play for individual enterprise. He said: 'Talent and energy [must] find scope for play without having to cringe and obtain special individual permission from officials and ministers, their efforts [must be] judged by the open market in India and abroad…statism must go…and the Government reduced to its proper functions.'[15]

Mahatma Gandhi placed his faith in individual freedom when he said: 'It is individuality, which lies at the root of all progress.'[16]

---

[15] Ghose, Sagarika, *Why I Am a Liberal: A Manifesto for Indians Who Believe in Individual Freedom*, Penguin Random House India, 2018.
[16] Ibid.

The Economic Liberal

Pratapsingh's views on the role of the government and State and that freedom must be given to individuals have more in common with those upholding the values of openness, rather than with those who believe state power must always be supreme. For Pratapsingh, a free economy is vital to growth, albeit with intelligent regulation and carefully established norms. His openness to establishing tourism; the leisure industry, even casinos; bringing in international talents to Goa; steering clear of any kind of prohibition on liquor all point to his belief in freedom for the economy as well as freedom in society.

'When Mrs Indira Gandhi was in power, she saw to it that land reform laws were passed throughout India,' says Pratapsingh. 'She wanted to be seen as pro-tenant. In some ways, her position can be understood because she was, at the time, under great pressure from the communists who were trying to snatch away her voter base. She kept bending leftwards herself primarily to ward off the threat from the communists. Given the left orientation of the central government, governments and administrations across India were under pressure to enact pro-tenant laws. Goa's rent control act was enacted under Bandodkar in 1968 in the form of the Goa, Daman and Diu Buildings (Lease, Rent & Eviction) Control Act of 1968, and Rules. However, Goa held out against a full socialist orientation. Until today, there is no land ceiling act in Goa.'

He believes emphatically in the following: 'The state [or government] should not control the economy. Instead, the government should maintain law and order so that industries are encouraged to do business. However, we can have a parallel economy, by which government corporations coexist with private ones. When I was CM, I kept public works with me, with the government.' The government must not give up on its duties to deliver welfare. When Goa attained statehood in 1987, the Pratapsingh Rane government vowed to create a welfare state in the true sense and carry administration to the doorstep of the people. Governments need to play their designated role but not stifle business or enterprise.

Pratapsingh set up the Kadamba Transport Corporation or State Road Transport Corporation in 1980, which was a government corporation to run buses. But private bus operators were also allowed to remain and bus services were not nationalized. There was no nationalization under Pratapsingh Rane like in other parts of India.

Pratapsingh believes that although governments must provide for basic amenities, it is rare to find state-controlled industries achieving global standards of excellence. It is India's entrepreneurs who have achieved international standards of excellence. 'But however big the Tatas and Birlas are, they have to eat the same food as all of us, drink the same water and enjoy the same electricity. This is where the work of the government comes in.' His degree in business management from Texas A&M University has made him a robust proponent of industry and open markets. At the same time, his experience in government has made him acutely alive to the reality that governments can never abdicate public welfare responsibilities.

Pratapsingh's close friend, Goa-based eminent industrialist Ramnath Govind Kare or 'Ramnathbab' as he is called, former president of the Goa Chamber of Commerce and Industry (GCCI) from 1991 to 1995, testifies to Rane's all-out drive to bring industry to Goa. In 1991, as then president of the GCCI, Kare kept urging Rane to get an appointment for the GCCI with then Finance Minister Dr Manmohan Singh. At that time, the perception in India was that Goa didn't really need any industry as its per capita income was already so high. 'This was a complete misconception,' says Kare. 'The fact is, other than mining, there was very little industry in Goa, and unemployment was massive. Attracting industries to Goa was an urgent need.'

Pratapsingh echoes a similar sentiment, 'In Goa, there was little employment available except for government service. So, we had to industrialize to create opportunities for the young. Some Goans became rich by getting iron ore licenses. But a handful of iron ore tycoons did not create a level playing field for jobs.'

Pratapsingh secured an appointment with Dr Manmohan Singh, and the GCCI delegation flew to Delhi to meet the finance minister. 'What a wonderful person Dr Manmohan Singh is,' enthuses Kare. 'Courteous, deeply learned, eager to listen to us. Instead of the 15 minutes allotted to us, Dr Singh spent close to half an hour with the Goan group.' Later that year on Pratapsingh's invitation, Manmohan Singh arrived in Goa and held talks with the GCCI. He also held a public meeting with Pratapsingh Rane. The following year came a bonanza for Goa: Manmohan Singh announced a five-year tax holiday for all businesses in Goa. 'We were overjoyed,' says Kare. 'Industry started to come into Goa. Hotels, pharma companies. My business grew so fast that I fell short of workers and had to bring in more from Dharwad and Ratnagiri. There is no doubt that these changes happened because of the rapport between Pratapsingh Rane and Dr Manmohan Singh and their shared common interest in industrial growth and private enterprise.'

So, is Pratapsingh a supporter of economic reforms of the Manmohan Singh variety, does he endorse 'Manmohaneconomics'? 'If reforms are for the good, then I certainly support them, but if I feel change will do harm in the long run, I will not support them. But the 1991 liberalization of the economy by PM P.V. Narasimha Rao and Finance Minister Manmohan Singh was great. I fully supported it. It was the best thing. The old "License Permit Quota Raj" had become too corrupted because of the massive discretionary powers of governments [or politicians] to pick and choose business houses. "Manmohaneconomics" is good; in fact, it is excellent. The 1991 reforms strengthened our nation economically. There was more turnover, more investment, more exports going out so we earned more foreign exchange. When I first joined politics in Indira Gandhi's time, I remember India was starved for foreign exchange. The Americans were helping us. You could say that I am a supporter of the economic reforms and in that sense, I am an economic liberal.'

Upholding Secular Values

Liberal on the economy, is he a liberal also on traditions and religion? 'I am totally secular when it comes to religion,' says Pratapsingh. 'We are a secular country, and religion should not be interfered with by governments or by political parties.' Goa is the best model of secularism, he says, because each religion and culture enriches the other.

'As far as my personal beliefs are concerned, I have faith in one God. I go to my temple, but I also visit churches and mosques. God is One. I, or anyone else, cannot claim to have ever "seen" God, so He must exist everywhere and in every shrine. I'm not much of a ritualist who believes in rituals. I am not at all superstitious. I believe when people lack deep faith, that's when they run behind rituals and all forms of elaborate and sometimes nonsensical practices.'

He was always an inclusive figure, rising above Goa's divisions of Hindu or Catholic or Bahujan or Brahmin or Marathi speaking or Konkani speaking. He harmonized all these identities in himself because, above all, he believed and practised constitutional and democratic values. He is a proud Goan and he is a proud Indian.

Does he call himself a modernist? 'I'm not a modernist in the sense of scorning traditions. Many traditions are of great value and have evolved over time. Many traditions represent time-tested practices. Traditions are built over years and they emerge from experiences of elders. For example, I take an active part in the customs of the Shri Vithal-Rakhumai temple where I am the custodian. But some traditions may be wrong. I would never support atrocious and backward practices like sati or slavery or untouchability. Traditions must meet the standards of the times.'

This belief of Pratapsingh bears repetition: *Traditions must meet the standards of the times.*

'Goa is a place of peaceful coexistence, where all customs are honoured and nothing is imposed,' he says. Goa is a perfect place for this sense of God-in-everything. Every family has a kuladevatha or a family temple. There is pride in each temple, that it was preserved from Portuguese assaults and deities were protected through centuries of Portuguese rule and the Inquisition. There is pride that Hindu families clung tenaciously to their old ancestral faith in spite of Portuguese hostility. But Christianity in Goa, too, became a kind of bhakti, as it was shaped by the landscape of Goa. Christianity is a folk religion in Goa, rooted among the people. Whether it is the Feast of Our Lady of Miracles or the Chaitrotsav at the Shri Vithal-Rakhumai temple, whether we place offerings of flowers and candles at white painted crosses in fields or place coconuts, paddy and oil at the feet of a goddess, the presence of the other-worldly is everywhere.

In starlit nights, far out to sea, ships pass like ghostly presences in the dark. Thick forests beckon so that lost souls may find forgiveness and redemption under the shade of ancient trees. Rivers meander gently, their still waters washing away conflict and anger. The presence of the spiritual perhaps gives the Goan his dignity: an old-world courtesy, a certain finesse even among country folk, innate refinement, respect for others and respect for the law. Perhaps this is why it is said that Durga, when she had slain the demon Mahishasur, came to Goa to become Shanta Durga, or goddess of peace.

Recalls Jason Abraham: 'In 1990, the Babri Masjid was partially damaged by alleged Vishwa Hindu Parishad (VHP) volunteers and violence broke out across the country. This coincided with my NSS camp in Sanquelim. I had over 150 students, mainly girls, at the school, which was adjacent to a temple. I was very concerned for the safety of my students. I took a taxi and drove out to Mr Rane's farmhouse to meet with him. He was not expecting me but met with me briefly when I showed up. He was very calm. I explained my situation and expressed my concern given the level of violence that had broken out. He calmly told me that he knew his people in Sanquelim and that they were peaceful. He assured me that nothing was going to happen in Sanquelim or Goa for that matter. Based on his calm and confident assurance, I went back to the camp. He was right, nothing untoward happened for the duration of the camp. The leader sets the tone and example. Mr Rane was not one to use religion or other partisan political tools to succeed as a politician.' Abraham says that because Pratapsingh always adopted a measured, rational tone and an even keel approach, the people responded similarly.

'I have always visited churches,' says Pratapsingh. 'Whenever I am invited, I go to Church. During the Francis Xavier expositions in Goa, which take place every 10 years, both of us go for the Mass, even though of course we don't take the host. I have often been to Mass in America, and all my American friends were Christians. My uncle Krishna Rao Rane is married to a Christian, her name is Victoria, and their son Yashwant Rane is one of our favourite nephews who keeps in regular touch with us.'

'It was a unique honour to welcome Pope John Paul II and Mother Teresa to Goa,' he recalls. Pope John Paul II's visit to Goa in February 1986 was a spectacular event. A gigantic public mass was held at Panaji's Campal grounds and John Paul II spoke in Konkani. Mother Teresa's organization Missionaries of Charity has worked in Goa since 1964, and Mother Teresa herself visited Goa several times. She visited Pratapsingh in March 1986 when he was CM, and he was impressed by her devotion to her work. As the founder of Missionaries of Charity and later canonized by the Vatican as St. Teresa of Kolkata, Mother Teresa's sense of service made a profound impression on him. In 2015, when unfortunate remarks were made about St. Teresa, then LoP Pratapsingh sprang to her defence, saying remarks against Mother Teresa were improper. An Albanian nun coming all the way to India to dedicate her life to the service of the slum dwellers in Calcutta can only be called selfless, he said.

'We, all of us Goans in Goa, live like a family,' he says. 'We share feast days, traditions, cultures, icons, music and art. Goans grow up with a strong sense of religion, yet we all share the belief that God is one. We all have a deep connection with the landscape and locality. That is probably why we have never had communal riots in Goa. Governments should not exploit or divide people for narrow causes like religion.'

Except for one small communal flare-up outside a madrasa in 2006 in Curchorem-Sanvordem, there have never been communal riots in Goa. In fact, Goa is a model for inter-religious harmony. It is an extraordinary thing, says Pratapsingh, that such a pious place as Goa has almost no religious violence or open conflict. 'Today false thoughts are being put in the heads of people. Issues of the sixteenth and seventeenth centuries are being dredged up. It's as if we are back to the Portuguese era, when invaders came in the name of spreading religion but all they wanted was power and to exploit people. Politicians should take care to keep religion out of politics.'

An important reason for the communal harmony of Goa, Pratapsingh believes, is the fact that Goa has a common civil code or what the Portuguese called Código Civil Portugues. Goa follows the Uniform Civil Code in pursuance of Article 44 in the Constitution (Directive Principles of State Policy) Part IV, which holds that the state must seek to ensure for people a uniform civil code across India's territory. The Civil Code or laws in place since Portuguese times lay down laws for property, marriage and succession which apply to every Goan, irrespective of religion.

Some sections of the Goa Civil Code are highly progressive: for example, at marriage, the wife becomes co-owner of her husband's property and cannot be divested of this right.

Pratapsingh says: 'When you lean too far to accommodate minorities, the majority begins to feel aggrieved. Instead, all communities must be governed by the same laws. Here in Goa, there is no Hindu Code Bill or Muslim sharia law. Hindus, Muslims and Christians all live under the same law; it's not as if Muslims are allowed to have more than one wife. The Goa Civil Code has worked very well for 150 years. It has taken away a lot of resentment that majority communities may feel in other parts of India. Nobody has objected to it and it is a very positive legacy left by the Portuguese which has brought harmony to Goa. It is a model that the whole of India should adopt because it's been tried and tested in Goa.'

It was also rather fitting that, at the end of 2002, when PM Atal Bihari Vajpayee wrote his 'Musings from Goa', he used the vantage point of Goa to mount an argument for genuine secularism and also, at the same time, argued against any narrow-minded reading of Hindutva cultural nationalism. The Goa model of religious co-existence is an example for other states.

What is the importance of religion, in his view? In Pratapsingh's words: 'Religion is important because it teaches people ethics. It teaches the difference between right and wrong, respect for others religions and customs, compassion, honesty and truth. For example, on my land there is a cross. I see it as sacred and don't disturb it. In Valpoi, part of my constituency, there are sizable numbers of Muslims. Some of my medical attendants are Muslims. But in Goa, all have an inner confidence in their own beliefs. We don't want to go out and harm others or try to convert people to your beliefs. Whatever your own religion is, follow it peacefully, do not impose it on others or use any form of violence. I am a secular person and believe in secular values.'

Respect for all religions, secular values, strict non-interference by government in religious matters and a common set of laws for all, make up his mantra for impartiality in administration. He says he believes in the wise words of Queen Elizabeth I of England uttered in the sixteenth century: 'I have no wish to make windows into men's souls.' The ruler should not interfere in private beliefs. The government is concerned with the material realm, not the spiritual.

Government of Laws

What is the best form of government, according to him? 'Government must be a government of laws. The people—or elected representatives—make the law and the government implements it. It must be a government that follows laws, upholds laws and implements laws in a fair manner for the betterment of the people. There may be certain flaws in the laws that have been made, and these can be corrected. On labour, industrial development, the government must proceed according to the laws laid down. There may be some state laws and some federal laws. But it is essential that the law prevails. If there is fear of the law, there will also be ethics in administration.'

Ethics is distinct from moral policing. The government should not attempt to be a moral policeman, such as imposing prohibition or trying to over-regulate dress or recreation or other individual choices. He says: 'Today we have plentiful supply of liquor shops in Goa, but have you ever seen any Goan drunk on the road? Abundant supply creates rational behaviour.'

Pratapsingh says: 'I remember once Morarji Desai came to Goa and made comments to the effect that Goans are all drunkards. Immediately, one of our MLAs Roque Santana Fernandes, who had been a great freedom fighter for Goa and later became a Congress MLA, disagreed with Morarji vociferously and said, "You will never be able to impose prohibition in Goa."' Pratapsingh believes that prohibition just cannot work in Goa. Such a policy would hit the small man who, in the cashew season, opens hundreds of small distilleries and makes a good living.

Similarly with the hippies who run around in scanty clothing on Goa's beaches. 'It's best to ignore them. In my time, nobody bothered about them. Some of them I remember were young Americans who had run away from the US to escape being enlisted in the Vietnam War!'

How did Pratapsingh approach his tasks as an administrator and what is the secret of his success? 'First,' he says, 'you have to familiarize yourself with your portfolio and do the work that you have been allotted. Towards this end, you have to build trust with bureaucrats, be helpful to them and try not to get caught in red tape. You need to prepare yourself with all the facts, so bureaucrats know that when they come and meet you, they should not talk in the air but give you specific facts. Making proper appointments is key. Give your officers a certain time that they can meet you and stick to timings.' In fact, while he was CM, Pratapsingh was known to be a stickler for appointments as well as dealing with officers fairly without any unnecessary pomp and show. He built a sense of shared values with his officers so his ministries became akin to well-run firms with a good corporate culture. 'He had no time for intrigue or ego games or any of that. All he cared about is that the work got done,' says Shailaja Chandra. 'One of the crucial ways of managing an administration is to lead by the power of example. If you are always on time, your officers will be too.'

Even his political colleagues acknowledge his administrative skills. 'Pratapsingh Rane was someone who worked for progressive development at all times and implemented many of the resolutions passed in the assembly for roads and hospitals,' Luizinho Faleiro says. 'On development sites, he would come personally in his construction helmet with all his officers and actually get the work done. He may initially have become CM as a consensus candidate, but he proved his mettle.'

R. Mihir Vardhan says governance under Pratapsingh was so efficient because of the air of authority he carried. Bureaucrats had to work hard to earn his trust. 'He enjoyed a good reputation even in neighbouring states and his name carried a lot of weight.' When the CM draws his reputation from his work, his bureaucrats are motivated to do the same.

Pratapsingh believes that for effective governance work, a good educational background is essential because you must be able to read a wide range of subjects and come to your own conclusions. The weaker sections of society will always come to you for help and you have to make time for them. If you're not a minister and an MLA, you need to study what the people are lacking and approach the relevant minister to inform him or her on whatever is needed in your constituency. 'Not all politicians are bad people,' he says. 'You have to constantly build trust with the people and many are able to do just that.'

When agitations take place, the administrator must try to ascertain why people are agitating and whether the demands are genuine or simply being whipped up by vested interests. During the Konkani-language agitation in 1986, Pratapsingh says that he ceaselessly tried to find a solution and even tried to reach out to the agitators. In the end, a solution was found according to one of his formulae for resolving conflicts: nobody should win and nobody should lose. In trying to achieve reconciliation, he is guided by the words, 'Let the best not become the enemy of the good.' We may not achieve perfection, but we can achieve something widely acceptable.

'During public concerns on the Konkan Railway, I appealed to the people's good sense. I said, "Here is a railway line to Bombay by which you will be able to send your children for education, for employment and for medical care. You will have a means of transportation at your doorstep." We have to communicate as well as we can and take people into confidence. We have to reassure people that we want to maintain their particular cultural traditions and way of life and not jeopardize them in any way. We should explain to them why we are supporting a particular development project.' The most achievable realistic goal has to be focussed on, not some impossible, utopian vision.

Pratapsingh warns that agitations and protests are bound to crop up against governments. 'You have to be calm and not lose your shirt. You have to establish a process of give and take, and somewhere impress upon the agitators your point of view. After a while, things settle.'

When the Anjunem Dam was being built, many voluntarily came forward to surrender their land. The Anjunem Dam rehabilitation process has been widely seen as setting the standard on how to build trust and rehabilitate people. He was able to win the trust of all those affected by the project that he would do right by them and ensure they were properly looked after. He believes strongly that whatever the issue is, people must never be left with a sense of injustice or having been wronged. If governments abide by the law, then it follows that the government won't violate the law or the Indian Constitution. 'Above all, you have to be just. And you have to be seen to be just.'

If a protest movement is strong, the state must back down, and even recognize the leadership potential of protest leaders and draw them into the ambit of democracy. In 1983, serious protests erupted in Panaji and Sanquelim over an engineering college to be set up by the Vodithala Education Society of Andhra Pradesh. The admission structure of the engineering college was perceived to be highly discriminatory against local Goans, as only 10 per cent seats were reserved for Goans and the rest of the seats were to be open to all Indians with a high fee structure. The perception was created that admissions were going to be made on the basis of payment or capitation fee and not merit.

Students held meetings and morchas in protest. Vijay Kumar Verekar took a leading role in these agitations. Pratapsingh, never one to take any decisions that were unpopular among people, quickly cancelled the project. Yet, at the same time, he was struck by the leadership potential of Verekar and suggested he contest elections from Pale constituency. Although Verekar's candidature never did materialize, it showed how alive Pratapsingh was to the public mood and to those who succeeded in giving voice to public sentiments. This is how democracy is constantly replenished and given new energy.

No Substitute for Democracy

What about democracy today? These days there is talk of 'elected autocracy'. There are many leaders around the world who have been elected by democratic means, but are increasingly turning their backs on democracy, and functioning like authoritarian leaders. They are called 'illiberal democrats' or 'elected autocrats'. What does he feel about this trend?

In Pratapsingh's words: '*There is no substitute for democracy in India. Democracy has to be there.* It is stupidity to want to be like China, or any other authoritarian country, without being aware of the many mammoth sacrifices those people have been put through. In India, we have opted for democracy and decided to develop and progress with the cooperation of the people and not by coercing people.'

When he was CM, Pratapsingh was sometimes accused by his rivals of being 'indecisive'. This is an unfair criticism. His decisions were slow because he believed in the correct processes of democracy, adhering to the gradualist norms of democratic functioning, of first building consensus and then deciding on a course of action. Decisions cannot be taken in a flash, to play to political galleries or to generate sensation or drama. Decisions in a democracy are taken with a view to ensuring that the peoples' long-term needs and interests are addressed. Therefore, policy decisions must be taken after studying all the relevant facts and bringing as many people as possible on board.

'Authoritarian or autocratic leaders are not geniuses that they somehow know what the difficulties of people are. Elected representatives are better placed to know what the people want because every five years, we have to go to the people and face the people. And the people ask us: "what have you done" or "these are our problems that have not been addressed". We can't have one-sided development in India. I also believe that if we want to run a participatory democracy, we must have talented people. If we stifle the voices of talented and intelligent people, they will not stay in the country and this is not good for our future. As a country, we must try and retain our best talents.'

He believes that autocracy or any form of dictatorship through a personality cult is detrimental for development. Adolf Hitler guided the Germans so wrongly that they were led into a war and appalling and unimaginable pain. Those who only look to their own greatness inevitably fall but also create colossal suffering for their own people. 'For example, I can't go about thinking that all of Goa is going to be my personal fiefdom. Instead, I have to have a broad vision: what I am going to do for Goa, what Goa should be in the future.

'Democracy is of the people, by the people and for the people. Whatever its flaws, I will always prefer democracy over any other system. What is the alternative to democracy? It is only a dictatorship. Dictators rule by bullying people or rule over people by exploiting an area where people have strong beliefs, such as religion.'

He adds: 'Today the most powerful nations in the world are democratic nations. Even Russia today is technically a "democracy", although Vladimir Putin operates like a quasi-dictator. Dictators are those who, like France's eighteenth-century queen Marie Antoinette, advised people to "eat cake" when they did not have bread. That statement has become a catch-line to show just how out of touch dictators are. No dictator has so far been successful in creating growth and welfare for all. Democratic institutions are pre-requisites for economic growth.'

But what about the quality of democracy today and the kind of leaders who are emerging today, who seem to only want to work towards their own self-interest?

'Democracy is not sustainable without mass education. We have to educate the people, in fact, educate the masses, not just the elite. When a man is educated, his vision increases and develops a broad vision. This is the reason my father sent me to the US. Democracy was new to Goa in the 1960s; we saw it as a moral and public good. But to participate in democracy, people need to be educated and aware. I agree—the quality of people who come to power can become the biggest weakness of democracy as all kinds of mafia can get elected. Therefore, we must have an enlightened population which knows what is right and wrong, and elects the best possible representatives.'

Quality mass education for all is a must for democracy to function although the rampant quota-ism of today worries him. The first rate, the talented and meritorious, the 'best men and women', are vitally needed for the country's development, whatever their background. Injustices must be corrected, but the correctives must not become empty tokens. 'Certain measures must be taken to uplift those who have been historically exploited, but after a particular date, quotas should be done away with. Quality education must be provided to all irrespective of background.'

Democracy doesn't only mean a representative government; it also means a transparent government. A government must always be kept on its toes by the people's right to know. He believes Goa's RTI Act, 1997, is a 'wonderful law'. Why so? He explains: 'Citizens can get whatever information they want. The government cannot be secretive about decisions or about appointments.' He says he is proud that he brought in Goa's RTI law and believes wholeheartedly in this particular legislation.

What about those who say that citizen's demands for information hold up governance? 'Absolute nonsense,' replies Pratapsingh sharply. 'If, for example, the assembly is not in session, and you want to question a government decision, you can use the RTI to get information. It opens up everything for people to see. I know several cases where the RTI has been used to get redress. Only recently, a nurse being harassed over her property was able to use the RTI to get justice. The RTI ensures that justice is available to the people.' He says, in any case, Goa is such a small place that everyone knows everything anyway, and neighbours know what is cooking in each other's kitchens!

What about the freedoms available in a democracy? Are these freedoms absolute? 'No, freedoms are not absolute in a democracy. I cannot go into a movie hall and, just because I am free, shout "Fire! Fire!", causing people to run helter-skelter or cause a stampede, leading to loss of life or injury. There have to be restraints on freedom. If there are certain books and movies that create ill-will or disharmony between communities, these books and films should not be allowed. If there is too much obscenity available or if the minds of students are being unduly affected, there is cause to see if such items should be allowed. There is an independent censor board. Movies have to be cleared by them and only then can they be screened.' Did he ever ban books? 'Never. In fact, I am an enthusiast of the arts. I think good books, good art or music or painting can never create disharmony. They always uplift people.' He concedes, however, that in the need to both preserve democratic freedoms and at the same time maintain law and order, governments must walk a tightrope. To do this, he believes it is best that each issue is dealt with according to its specific requirements.

Corruption in public life greatly bothers him. 'The monied men try to bribe politicians. Corruption thrives in democracy. I would never accept money; nobody dared offer it to me. It was the one thing I never did. I did not need to. I have vast lands; I have more than enough.' Leading Goa industrialist Audhut Timblo, Pratapsingh's friend, affirms: 'Pratapsingh Rane would never touch money. He is incorruptible to the core.'

What would he like to see more of today? 'Federalism is an important feature in our national structure. India is a multiracial and multilingual country; there is no alternative to a federalized government. Strictures cannot be imposed from New Delhi. All central governments have to be federal because India is a federation of states. The very first line of our Constitution reads: *India, that is Bharat, shall be a Union of States.*'

He believes that not only federalism, but greater decentralization needs to be built into the system. As Gandhi said, 'Democracy cannot be worked by 20 men sitting at the centre. It has to be worked from below by the people of every village.' 'No one at the top can be so knowledgeable that they know exactly what is going on at the ground level in different parts,' says Pratapsingh. Decentralization enables the system to receive information from people on the ground.

Is he hopeful of today's India, despite all the flaws in its democracy and the conflicts and divisions between people? 'Of course, I am hopeful. There are many good reasons for hope. India has a glorious future. It may not seem like it, but we are a very strong democracy. Nobody can impose an Emergency in India today; democracy has become too strong.'

What is his personal motto in governance? What motivates him to work as hard as he does for the people? 'My motto is: growth is happiness. To create growth, to create development is to make people happy.' Happiness comes from development and his own sense of fulfilment comes from making others happy. To quote the nineteenth-century American humanist Robert G Ingersoll: 'The way to be happy is to make others so.' My brother M.Y. Ghorpade once wrote: 'Remember! To be the dawn is to be happy and to make the whole world happy.'

Towards this end, he is a believer in incremental, planned change, to keep making small and gradual improvements over time, through a process of dialogue, until there is significant transformation. *Growth is happiness.* Happiness for those who create it, and happiness for those who receive it

However, as he worked long hours for Goa, what about his own personal happiness and the happiness of his family? He once said: 'I must thank my family members who have borne the brunt of the various positions I have held, especially the people of Sattari.' As he toiled hard for Goa, did his life choices take a toll on his personal life?

EIGHT

THE MAN BEHIND THE LEADER

'Above all, I am motivated by a sense of duty.'

In north Goa, the Valvanti runs fresh and clear. Along its banks, tall clumps of hibiscus plants grow in riverside courtyards. Pink and red hibiscus blossoms are abundant. Sometimes they fall into the river to drift and float in the limpid tree-shaded water. This is a place of ethereal beauty, a place of the gods.

Sloping gently up from the Valvanti is a little hillock (once known as Marutigad), on which stands the over 500-year-old Shri Vithal-Rakhumai temple of Sanquelim (or the Vithoba temple as it is also called)—the family temple of the Ranes, who are its traditional custodians. The temple complex is known as the Shri Deva Vithal Panchayatan Sansthan. As the current patriarch of the Rane clan, Pratapsingh takes an active role in the Chaitrotsav temple festival. He has never missed the temple festival over the decades that he has lived in Goa.

During the Chaitrotsav, a richly decorated golden palanquin bearing the deities of Shri Vithal (Vishnu) and Rakhumai (Rukmini) is taken from the Rane ancestral home to the temple and returns to the house for the night. In the evenings, there are cultural performances and a village fair in the grounds of the Rane ancestral wada. Toy shops, food and ice cream stalls are put up at the fair, much to the delight of the village children. On the last day of the festival, a chariot procession—or Rathotsav—takes place. A carved and decorated wooden chariot, which is almost as old as the temple, emerges and travels in stately procession around the temple compound, pulled by the temple committee members. Every year, every day of the festival, particularly for the evening return of the palanquin, no matter how tired he is, Pratapsingh is always there.

He is proud of the management of the temple. Every devotional institution in Goa conducts elections to its managing committee, according to a Portuguese rule. He is always elected to it. On the temple entrance wall hangs a board with the name of the temple committee: his name at the top: Shri Pratapsingh Raoji Rane Sardesai: *adhyaksh* or president (Sardesai being a title for a local notable).

Pratapsingh has many memories of this ancient temple complex. As a boy, he would come to the temple with his family, and sometimes dive into the cool Valvanti for a long and leisurely swim. The venerated holy place, over five centuries old, evolved slowly over the years and was an integral part of his boyhood years. 'The temple draws its devotees from most of north Goa and even beyond,' Pratapsingh says, 'because a visit to this temple is considered to be equivalent to a trip made to the pilgrimage town of Pandharpur in Maharashtra. Some of the smaller idols are believed to have been brought from the modern-day Vithal pilgrimage site in Pandharpur. It's my duty to look after it and to be there for the temple activities. The people of the village and the temple committee expect me.'

Duty is one of his moral ideals. While working in Tatas in Jamshedpur when his younger brother died, he felt it was his duty to give up his job, return to Goa and take up the management of his family estates in his brother's place. 'When I left for the US, I gave my word to my father that I would come back to India and I did,' he says. 'After my brother died, I gave my word to my father that I would take my brother's place and look after our ancestral lands. I have stayed here ever since.'

When Bhausaheb D.B. Bandodkar drew him into politics and he became an MLA, duty bound to work for the welfare of his constituents, he threw himself into his tasks, with the dutifulness of a son looking after his larger family. When he became a minister and swore an oath on the Constitution that he would undertake his ministerial responsibilities without fear or favour, that is what he committed to do for the rest of his life. As CM, he was acutely aware of his constitutional duties. 'When I am given a job to do, I feel I have to do it to the best of my ability. You could say I am motivated by a sense of duty.'

He was a dutiful son and has been a devoted and proud husband. He says of me: 'When I first met Vijaya, I thought she was a bit of a chatterbox. Yet, over the years, she has been my inspiration, sharing my joys and sorrows. She is a greatly successful person in her own right and has always done a lot of social work. I must acknowledge her substantial contribution in being what I am today.' In 55 years of marriage, Pratapsingh has been a kind and loving husband and father, always there for us when we needed him. It has been my good fortune to have been his partner and traveller on the journey that destiny mapped out for him. No woman could ask for a more respectful partner—a husband who has been the wind beneath my wings. In my own way, I too have been the wind beneath his wings. Govind Kale, former programme director of Kala Academy, puts it warmly: 'Pratapsingh and Vijayadevi are like Shri Vithal and Rakhumai. We can't imagine one without the other.'

Goa police officer Sunita Sawant is very close to our hearts. Sunita was born and brought up here in Sanquelim; she belongs to one of the erstwhile tenant families of the Ranes. Sunita's father played football with Pratapsingh and was one of the Sanquelim group that travelled by bus to my home in Sandur to be at our wedding. Sunita recounts this incident, which is a telling story about Pratapsingh's attitude to me as a husband. In past days when we lived in the Rane ancestral home, I used to wear anklets on my feet, which made a jingling sound as I walked. The spacious living room in the old house, hung with portraits, sambar heads and armoury, where Pratapsingh received daily visitors, was up a narrow flight of steps. One evening as I was walking up, Pratapsingh must have heard me coming from the bells on my anklets. As I entered the room, he rose to his feet with the words, 'Ya baisaheb, basa' (Welcome madam, come sit with us). Since Pratapsingh had got up, all the other men in the room got to their feet too to welcome me among them. It was a small but supportive note of respect from a husband to a wife. I am reminded of William Blake's lines: 'To see a World in a Grain of Sand and a Heaven in a Wild Flower.' A lifetime of meaning is conveyed in small gestures.

'Vijayadevi has been a true companion to Pratapsingh in every way,' says our close friend Ramnath Govind Kare. 'She always kept a wonderful home and maintained the CM's residence with taste and great style. She handled his communication, publicity and PR. She looked after visiting VIPs and dignitaries and arranged social functions. All of it was done with elegance and attention to detail.'

Rajeev Talwar would sometimes impishly tell me that I would make a better CM than Pratapsingh because I could, on occasion, be much tougher with people. 'It is incomplete to speak of Mr Rane if we do not mention Mrs Vijayadevi Rane,' says Talwar. 'Not only is she the most warm and charming, her smile and twinkling eyes cannot be missed. She kept away from politics but made her mark through warm social interaction with people from all walks of life. She was the "sounding board". Impeccable in taste, clearly reflective of her princely background, she and Mr Rane provided an unmatched upbringing to their children.' Shailaja Chandra goes so far as to say that often, at parties, it was me who was apparently the 'belle of the ball'! I am warmed by such words from officers who over the years became our friends.

Pratapsingh has always been a workaholic, working long hours in office during the day and touring through towns and villages across Goa, including his own constituency, in the evenings. Always, the mission was uppermost: *let's build, with all our heart and soul, a paradise, here, in Goa.* The mission was all-consuming, leaving him hardly any spare time.

'My wife never let my children feel the absence of their father,' says Pratapsingh. 'Whenever I could, I snatched time to be with my son and daughter. I gave them quality time. I think I was a normal father. I am not one of those who says I have sacrificed my family to do good for the people. To me, that's not a healthy attitude. I was happy when my son went to T.A. Pai Management Institute, Manipal, to do his business management and my daughter went to Sophia College, Mumbai. We sent her because I was holding high office here in Goa and we felt that she would be cramped by all the media attention. We wanted her to experience a wider world. My son was a little bit mischievous. I was not the kind of father to get after my children; I let them choose their own lives,' he says, adding that if he had one expectation from his children, it was that they maintain decent academic standards.

As young people, both Vishwajit and Vishwadhara were great fans of superstar Amitabh Bachchan. Once when Bachchan arrived in Goa for a shoot, Pratapsingh thoughtfully invited both star actors, Amitabh Bachchan and Mrs Jaya Bachchan, to the CM's residence, so all the children of the family could meet them and, as was the norm in the days before selfies, take photographs and autographs. I found Amitabh and Jaya a very informal and pleasant couple.

Vishwajit says of his father: 'Whenever I'm in doubt, all I have to do is think what my father would do and the situation becomes crystal clear to me. As a man of the people, my father taught me to cherish relationships. That times change and people may change, but it is the human bonds that continue to provide strength. He would make it a point to drop me to school. We once went to Commercial Street in Bengaluru and he bought me a yellow car.

We would take many road trips to Mumbai with our fox terrier and poodle for company. I remember how the dogs would run away and Baba and I would go and fetch them. Baba helped me with words and in deed.'

Initially, Pratapsingh wanted Vishwajit to go into the corporate world, but later accepted his decision to join public life. 'Vishwajit was studying during my early campaigns,' says Pratapsingh. 'But later he would get involved. At election time, he would organize all the publicity material. He would have the election posters opened and divide them into constituencies. He would organize different bundles for each area and decide who was to be responsible for each set. He knew most of my key people. They would say, "Baba, give us posters, give us banners." Vishwajit has worked at the grassroots so he knows how to figure out election strategy and who is to be contacted. Vijaya too used to campaign with me, but our programmes were worked out separately.'

When does he campaign? 'I normally go out in the evenings after 6.00 p.m. During the day, my constituents come to my home. Sometimes, there are long queues. I try to meet them all and try to help them with their problems.' However, this practise of campaigning in the evenings has not been without its risks. One night, Pratapsingh returned home at 4.00 a.m. in an agitated state, upset by an incident that night. While travelling for a late evening rally on a dark night, an unknown car had started to follow his vehicle closely. The driver of the car kept nudging Pratapsingh's vehicle and tried to push him onto the fields running next to the road. Pratapsingh stopped his car, and got out to angrily confront the troublesome driver. His supporters overpowered the mischief maker and discovered that he was a local youth whom Pratapsingh had once given a job to. The boy had now joined Pratapsingh's rivals. The idea had been to try and provoke a street fight, get Pratapsingh to strike a blow, get Pratapsingh disqualified and his candidature from Sattari cancelled. After this incident, a rule was laid down at home: there would be no campaigning late at night.

'In spite of his busy life, my father was my rock of Gibraltar,' says our daughter Vishwadhara. 'I have precious memories of when he used to drop me off and pick me up from St John High School in Sanquelim in his grey Mahindra jeep. My father would take us to see coconut plucking. Every Sunday, he would pack us in the car and we would drive from Panaji to our ancestral home in Sanquelim. In 1980, after he became CM, I remember he had told me that if anyone in school ever asks you what your father does, tell them he is an agriculturist.'

Vishwadhara remembers that her father was also extremely strict with her, making sure she woke up early to study, kept fit, stayed vigilant on her tendency to gain weight and went for daily walks around Altinho when we lived there. He also insisted she learn swimming. He would always tell her that in the mornings, she was not to come downstairs in her nightclothes but make sure she changed into track pants and shirts before emerging from her bedroom. He would worry if she stayed out too late, and insisted she keep us informed. Pratapsingh expected her to do well in her studies and hoped she would study law. Vishwadhara recalls the life lessons he once gave her: deal with friends and colleagues carefully and also with understanding. Study a situation first and always take a pause before you speak. Most importantly, he told her: Stay low key, and never feel entitled to things just because you are my daughter. 'My father would say, don't feel you can sit in an airport VIP lounge simply because you are my daughter, because when I am no longer in power, I don't want anyone to throw you out.' Vishwadhara says that while some tend to think she is fearful of her father, the truth is that she doesn't fear him but respects him and his judgement tremendously.

'Baba is a man of few words, but greater actions,' says our daughter-in-law, Deviya. 'He always likes to keep things close to his heart and not divulge much. His favourite words are "Even the walls have ears." We are so proud of all his achievements.' 'His love for the people of Sattari; the time and commitment he gives to understanding their problems and needs; the informal open house he has given them; the strict manner in which he disciplines them; and the pride in his eyes when they achieve success are always interesting to see,' observes our son-in-law, Vishwajit Dahanukar.

For our grandchildren Anandita, Aishwarya and Arundhati, Pratapsingh is the doting grandfather, ever ready to tell stories or, occasionally, to play the piano or show them his old photos of his horse-riding days. 'I look at him as a hero, my hero,' says our granddaughter Anandita. 'He is an amazing man, one that I admire and love,' wrote Anandita for her grandfather. 'All the work done by my grandfather is very systematic and he also makes sure everyone abides by the rules set by him,' says our granddaughter Aishwarya. 'My grandfather was a champion in horse-riding and boxing and also plays the piano. I love my grandfather the most,' says Arundhati. Our three grandchildren bring us constant joy and make us proud. 'Your time begins, as mine draws to a close…,' wrote the poet Rabindranath Tagore. As their lives stretch out ahead full of promise and potential and our days are now lit by the rays of the setting sun, we give them our endless blessings.

Usha Raje Pashupati Rana is the eldest daughter of Jivajirao Scindia (the last Maharaja of Gwalior). Jivajirao was the son of Gajra Raje of Sanquelim, Pratapsingh's aunt, so Usha Raje and Pratapsingh are niece and granduncle. 'Kaka is a very special human being as far as I'm concerned,' says Usha Raje. 'It's difficult to find someone who has the combination of the qualities he has—always very principled in his politics, fought his battles honestly and in a forthright manner and yet remains a thorough gentleman. He is exceptionally soft-spoken and gentle. Apart from all this, he is also an excellent horse-rider.'

Usha Raje says she treasures her moments with her Kaka because he is always so affectionate towards them. 'I remember when they visited us in Kathmandu [Usha Raje is the wife of Pashupati Rana, a scion of the Rana family in Nepal and a former Nepal minister and politician], we spent a lot of quality time together. I would visit him on his birthdays in Goa. I went to Goa for Vishwadhara's wedding. I always feel that the Ranes are a close family, they are a blessing for me.' The nature of our connection makes the relationship more intimate. 'The Ranes are my grandmother's family, and so there is an even closer bond,' says Usha Raje. 'They have always looked after us, had us to stay, made us comfortable and kept up with us.'

Usha Raje recalls our own girlhood days in Bombay when we were young women together in the same social circle. We always enjoyed an especially warm relationship. 'We loved each other's company, although Vijaya was much younger than me,' Usha Raje says. 'And then, to my great surprise, she went and married my uncle! So, I then asked her: Okay, so now that you are my aunt, what should I call you, should I pay my respects to you now? I thought perhaps I should address her differently. But of course, Vijaya Raje wouldn't hear of it, and said: No, no, none of this aunty business! So, while I call Pratapsingh "Kaka", I call her "Vijaya Raje" and she calls me "Usha Raje" and we both pay our respects to each other,' laughs Usha Raje, adding that since her husband was not part of our earlier Bombay connection, he abides by the formalities of the relationship and addresses us as 'Kaka' and 'Kaki'.

Prithviraj Chavan, senior Congress leader, is another close relative. His sister is married to my brother and his wife is my first cousin. Says Prithviraj: 'Pratapsingh is the epitome of gentlemanliness, courtesy and warmth. We used to meet regularly at weddings at Sandur, Goa or Bombay. As a senior family member, he is always unfailingly correct in his behaviour. He is wonderful at interacting with youngsters and is always caring towards the elderly. We have often participated in each other's campaigns. I have come to Goa and he has visited Maharashtra.'

Chavan recalls how, in 1975, Pratapsingh, then a cabinet minister in Shashikala Kakodkar government, was part of the Goa government effort to purchase an official home for the Goa government—the Goa Sadan—in Delhi's super-exclusive Amrita Shergill Marg. It is a stately colonial pillared mansion with art deco features set amidst lawns, but in those days, the Goa government bought it for only a relatively small sum.

Chavan says he was very keen that Pratapsingh come to Delhi through the Lok Sabha elections or the Rajya Sabha but Pratapsingh always emphatically refused. 'I have no wish to go to Delhi,' he would say with determination.

Pratapsingh has no interest whatsoever in the suffocating atmosphere of the capital, with its power cliques and *darbars* or in living in a rented official accommodation where one is only a temporary occupant. He infinitely prefers waking up to the birdsong of the Goa countryside!

Does Pratapsingh miss the fact that he never went to Delhi as a union minister and was not given governorships? '*Shi, shi, shi*, oh no, no never ever!' says Pratapsingh waving his hand. 'Live in Delhi, in that atmosphere? Look at what I have here, these huge lands, my farm, my orchards, my work here. I was asked to go to Delhi in the past, but I refused.' Here, among the forests, meadows, hills and rivers of his ancestors; here, where he spent so many years toiling to deliver the basics of life; here, where he can see the fruits of his labours such as when electricity lights up a village or when potable water gushes from a tap: it is here he is most at peace.

Chavan says Pratapsingh's heart has always been in Goa. 'He is deeply knowledgeable about the state. But I know he is disturbed about the corruption that has come into Goa's politics as well as the degradation of Goa's environment. It is good to see that he still remains active,' says Chavan. 'He is passionate about Goa and its growth, particularly in areas like urban development and protection of the environment.'

Universally Admired and Respected

Many of our friends say Pratapsingh is in many ways the odd one out in Goa's politics today. He belongs to an older era, when gentlemen-politicians could function in politics, when promises were kept, when integrity was prized and politicians impartially pursued public interest.

Industrialist Audhut Timblo insists that Rane's brand of gentlemanly politics has gone missing today. 'Rane was an exemplary politician, well-mannered and reliable,' says Timblo. 'He was the kind of politician who could never be purchased.'

'Pratapsingh is a raja *manus*,' says Kare, 'an aristocrat both in his family background and his outlook on life and the way he conducts himself.' He *is* a misfit in today's politics, he adds. 'He has always been quite apolitical. I can't see him being part of the "Aya Ram Gaya Ram" syndrome or using the kind of language used today or playing the politics of today. I know he doesn't like it. He says he is happy to let others do it. He is happy in Sanquelim in his down to earth existence.'

We met the Kares in the 1970s, introduced by our common friend Dr M.R. Narvekar of Bombay. 'Our first meeting was a small dinner at Fort Aguada hosted by Dr Narvekar,' recalls Kare. 'There were only us three couples, and we hit it off immediately with the Ranes. We became friends and subsequently he invited me for his birthday party in Sanquelim. We became very close.'

Kare recalls visiting us after Bhausaheb Bandodkar died and how Pratapsingh sought his counsel about the disappointing manner in which Shashikala Kakodkar's government was functioning. 'I remember advising Pratapsingh that he must join a national party. I told him that only by joining a national party would he be able to develop Goa, particularly as the central government at the time was the Congress.' Within a month, Pratapsingh had joined the Congress, and Kare came to our home to congratulate him.

In 1980, when Pratapsingh became CM for the first time, he visited Kare's home in Margao to take the blessings of Kare's father who voiced his hope that Pratapsingh would make Goa very prosperous. Towards fulfilling this goal, Pratapsingh told Kare that two sectors were of particular importance to him: industry and healthcare. 'His vision was to industrialize Goa,' says Kare. 'I have no hesitation in saying Pratapsingh was Goa's best CM. Goa has never seen the kind of development that occurred under Rane. Goa had 15 [Pratapsingh Rane was Goa CM intermittently for 15 years] fantastic years, it was indeed a Golden Age.'

It was during Pratapsingh's 'golden' tenure that the European Economic Community Chamber of Commerce invited the CM and members of the GCCI, including Kare, who was then GCCI president, to visit Europe. They visited London and Portugal. Pratapsingh had visited Portugal earlier on the invitation of then President Mario Soares, becoming the first CM of Goa to be invited to Portugal after the Liberation. He had been honoured and welcomed by President Soares, who himself visited Goa in 1992. In 1995, Pratapsingh Rane was honoured by Portugal with the Ordem do Infante Dom Henrique or The Order of Prince Henry, awarded to those who have served public office with distinction. As CM, Pratapsingh also took the GCCI to Hong Kong, Macau and Malaysia to witness the development achievements of those countries and also to study different aspects of urban administration such as garbage and waste management methods.

There were some fun times too. Kare recalls one happy occasion on a trip to Europe when the GCCI led by Pratapsingh attended a magnificent dinner at the Dublin home of Dr Reita Faria, who, today, runs a medical practice in Dublin. Faria is a former Miss World 1966 and the first Asian woman to win an international beauty pageant. Her parents hail from Thivim and Santa Cruz in Goa.

Agriculture has been his lifelong passion and main hobby. He maintains his cashew nut, mango and coconut orchards with great care and efficiency. 'I run a dairy and I used to have a poultry farm but I have stopped that,' he says. Every morning, he takes rounds of his farms, orchards and dairy farm. Rozendo Mendonsa, a horticulturist based in Goa who runs a well-known nursery in Panaji named 'Mr Farmer', has supplied us with our plants for many decades. Mendonsa is a specialist in flowering plants and trees and when Pratapsingh became CM, he used to regularly come to wish the CM on his birthday. In those days, birthday queues to meet Pratapsingh were so long that it could often take two hours just to get a few minutes with him. 'On one occasion when I met him, I presented Mr Rane with a bunch of orchids. Orchids were rare in those days and when Mr Rane saw the orchids, he was immediately struck and called Mrs Rane to come and see. Our friendship began from that day on and has endured for decades since.'

What kinds of trees does Pratapsingh like? 'He likes all kinds of fruit trees, mango, coconut and jackfruit. He doesn't like flowering trees that much. He prefers trees that can provide food. He is very keen on new technologies to grow fruit trees. Recently, he used new state-of-the-art farming technology from Israel to grow mango trees that enables trees to be planted just two-and-a-half meters apart rather than the usual 20. This technology gives a better crop per unit of the area.'

When the Pratapsingh Rane government undertook to build the highway from Porvorim to Mapusa, Pratapsingh gave orders to the forest department to take Mendonsa's advice in planting rows of coconut trees along the road. Almost 200 trees were planted. Busy travellers driving down the highway today find their journey pleasantly shaded by rows of coconut trees, tall, elegant fronds swishing gently as the cars whizz past. Perhaps some local Goans may remember how they were planted and think of good old Rane with his good old trees.

Today, Mendonsa helps us with plants and shrubs in the farmhouse. Both of us enjoy watching seasonals bloom at different times in the year. 'No CM is as respected as Pratapsingh is,' says Mendonsa. 'No one else is as admired.'

The UK-based cardiologist Dr Purushottam Desai describes Pratapsingh as a 'farmer at heart'. Dr Desai shared many conversations with Pratapsingh on dairy farming and even preserving the peacock population. 'My first meeting with Mr Pratapsingh Rane was in 1994, when as a newly qualified cardiologist, I simply drove to his farmhouse and introduced myself. We two had a long chat for three hours that evening. Twenty years later, I was asking my wife, "I wonder how and why he believed me; I could have been anyone making up stories",' recalls Dr Desai. Years of experience among the public has made Pratapsingh adept at assessing people.

Dr Desai says he was struck by Pratapsingh's willingness to stand up for what is right rather than what is easy, even if such stances meant giving up positions in government. 'Mr Rane's social commitment is rooted in his love of people. He dislikes it when people engage in superfluous spending at weddings and gets furious at blind beliefs and superstitions.'

Education matters above all. Good schools, decent homes and creating opportunities for progress—social, material and economic. Sattari sarpanch Udaysingh Rane says the unmatched aura around Pratapsingh comes from his deep love for and interest in Goa's people and their future. According to him, Pratapsingh had an almost obsessive drive to spread education in Sattari. Not only did he set up schools and colleges, he kept urging young people to study hard and excel at academics. Udaysingh remembers how his younger daughter once wanted a reference book from Pratapsingh's library. He not only gave her the book, but also these words of advice: 'Follow your dreams and don't act according to pressures from your parents. Women today are independent and think for themselves. Study well and work as hard as possible in your field. Never be afraid to tread a new path.' Udaysingh says that whenever he visits Pratapsingh, the latter is never sitting still but always doing something. Reading in his library, touring around his farm, practising his piano skills or playing with our dog Bubbles.

'The word I would use to describe Pratapsingh Rane is "noble",' says Sunita Sawant. 'I have never seen an MLA so deeply involved in the lives of his constituents,' she continues. 'He would sit with families, counsel youngsters on education, on career options, taking an interest in children as if they were his own.' As a girl, the tall and strapping Sunita excelled in athletics and in National Cadet Corps (NCC) camps. Pratapsingh urged her father to let her try for a career in the police service. 'Let her apply for police posts,' Pratapsingh told Sunita's father, 'you never know, she may do very well.' A girl in the Goa police force, that too from traditional, rural Sanquelim, was quite unheard of in those days. Sunita's parents were undecided, and her mother was deeply worried about this dangerous career path of chasing criminals that Pratapsingh seemed to be suggesting for their daughter. But Sunita herself was all fired up by the idea of joining the police. She studied hard and cleared the police examination. When she got her uniform, she immediately rushed to Pratapsingh to offer him sweets and her thanks. The first question he asked was, 'You've not given any money, no?' referring to the fact that nowadays so many are rumoured to have simply purchased police positions for large sums. When Sunita assured him she had done no such thing and passed her examination and interview fair and square, Pratapsingh was overjoyed and embraced her and her entire family, exulting: 'Our daughter will be a big police officer one day.'

Pratapsingh's years of sporting excellence in school and college have given him an inordinate capacity for physical endurance and ability to withstand hardship. He was not only a swimmer, horse-rider and boxer, but also an unafraid shikari or hunter. 'I was out of Goa from the age of about six to about 25. In school and college, I loved all sports, particularly martial sports like riding and boxing. I enjoy watching cricket too. I like T20 cricket.' When he was young, he was once gored by a Sambar deer that had gone rogue. 'I had to shoot the poor animal, as it could have harmed others,' he remembers with a wry smile.

He takes pride in his Rane identity and in the warrior traditions of his militaristic Rane ancestors who fought so hard against the Portuguese in the Sattari jungles. The many guns on display at the Rane wada were used not just for warfare against the Portuguese but also for hunting. 'In the old days, I used to go on shikar with some of the village folk and we formed strong bonds as a result.' He is also proud of the Rane sense of *noblesse oblige* or the tradition of philanthropy that his family has been known for. When the 'land to the tiller' laws came in, he simply gave away plots of land to his tenants—an act which won him the lifelong gratitude of many.

In office, Pratapsingh took an interest in almost every aspect of administrative work including furniture for official buildings. Furniture maker and interior designer Valentine Pereira owns the exclusive Damian de Goa furniture outlet in Goa. Pereira designed and fitted out the interiors of the Goa Assembly building. He also created the furniture and designed the interiors of Goa's iconic Cidade de Goa hotel. Valentine Pereira has also designed and made some of our personal furniture at home. 'Mr Rane's tastes are modern and sleek,' says Pereira. 'He likes neat classical lines, with a touch of tradition.' Pereira says if Pratapsingh likes an idea, he goes ahead and gets it implemented without waiting. Once the work is completed, Pratapsingh invariably asks: where is the bill? Payments for tasks are always scrupulously accounted for and correctly made, nothing is left pending. Pereira and his family are old friends of ours. Pereira says what marks Pratapsingh out from other politicians is his extraordinary sense of empathy for all Goans. 'He has this unusual capacity to truly care about people and help them. That's why Mr Rane has had an immeasurable impact on the lives of the people here.'

Canacona-based doctor Dhillon Dessai says he will always be

grateful to Pratapsingh for helping to get a US visa for his daughter: 'Mr Rane is not a demonstrative man. He's not someone to go hugging people or making a show. But he is always there to provide real help to people, which is why he is universally respected in Goa. I can't think of anyone who does not have genuine respect for Mr Pratapsingh Rane.'

Destiny's Favourite Child

In politics, he was destiny's child. Never politically ambitious or a schemer, opportunities fell into his lap. 'Even if Rane falls, he falls into the chair,' Ramakant Khalap famously remarked. Kare points out that Pratapsingh has always been supremely lucky. 'He was lucky in the way he entered politics, lucky in the way he was able to govern, and he was lucky that he completed 50 years in politics at the right time and bowed out just at the right time. He is not like a politician at all. He has never had any political ambitions.'

Pratapsingh was gifted with *rajyoga*, or a tendency to be the leader through a fearless and disciplined disposition. Providence smiled on him every step of the way. The more work and care he showered on the people of Goa, the more fortune showered him with gifts, carrying him onwards to successes which others could only dream of.

On 23 March 2001, when he was Speaker, the Goa Assembly conferred on him the honorific title, Goa's Legislator of the Millennium. The tributes paid to him on this occasion in the assembly by his political colleagues are telling of the gentle colossus that he is in Goa. Then CM Manohar Parrikar called him his role model. 'If we had one upright personality in the state, one who could not be corrupted, it was you,' said Parrikar.[17] Former CM Francisco Sardinha said: 'Although I was chief minister myself I

---

[17] *Goa's Legislator of the Millennium: Tributes to a Speaker*, R. Kothandaraman (ed.), Goa Legislature Secretariat, Porvorim 2001, p. 11.

admit that the governance that there was in 1980–1989 under your leadership, Goa can never dream of having again.'[18] 'I remained your critic,' said Ramakant Khalap, 'I pounced on you at every opportunity. I tore to pieces the budget documents. You did not harbour any rancour or ill will and you took the criticism in your stride in the manner a great Statesman would do. You did not hesitate to accept good criticism, you did not find fault with your opponent…you have earned goodwill…by the balanced attitude towards your friends and foes, and I mean your political foes.'[19]

His regular detractor Dr Wilfred de Souza, who toppled his government several times, said: 'When we have to speak about your achievements, nothing needs to be really said in words because whatever you have done in the last three decades is there for everyone to see. You have always conducted yourself in an exemplary manner and I think you have set the tone for all other MLAs to do likewise.'[20] Churchill Alemao, who first brought down Pratapsingh's government in 1990, related an incident when he floated his own party and had gone to Sattari to ask for votes. Instead of listening to his speech, people kept asking: 'Churchill, why did you overthrow Khashe?' 'They told me I had committed a blunder and affirmed they would re-elect you as their leader.' Churchill also said: 'I realized my mistake in overthrowing a good leader like you.'[21]

Shaikh Hassan Haroon, MLA from Mormugao, said in his speech: 'The language issue would have burnt Goa but at the time you saw to it that a solution came and you gave the Konkani–Marathi formula…you have a stern appearance, but you are soft within.'[22] 'You continued the education policies of late Bandodkar by opening various schools in every corner of the state,' said Ponda MLA and former CM Ravi Naik. 'Due to this literacy has increased

---

[18]Ibid. 12.
[19]Ibid. 23.
[20]Ibid. 26.
[21]Ibid. 34.
[22]Ibid. 31.

tremendously. You were instrumental in developing the villages of Goa...many people work on the principle of dividing the people... but you have never thought of doing evil to others.'[23]

Former IAS officer Shailaja Chandra considers herself blessed to have worked with Pratapsingh Rane. 'There is one word for him, and that is excellent.' Chandra remembers how in the height of the Goa summer with a burning hot sun slamming down, Pratapsingh would trundle off, with her in tow, in his Ambassador car without air-conditioning, all the way to Mormugao or Canacona to check on schools and health centres. On these field trips, recalls Chandra, you got the feeling that he was not just asking questions for effect but because he genuinely wanted to understand. He never had any airs or pomposity. Sometimes, Chandra recalls, when the phone would ring, officers would pick up to hear him say at the other end: 'This is Pratapsingh Rane speaking.' Chandra recalls how, in 1990, the day his government was toppled by Churchill also happened to be the last few days of her Goa posting. Even in the midst of the chaos of his government falling, Pratapsingh took the time to ask if her Confidential Report had been prepared and made sure to sign it before he left office.

Rajeev Talwar recalls that an appointment with Pratapsingh meant you had to report punctually and always be in possession of the facts about matters because he himself was so educated and was able to grasp things so quickly. He would always say: Let's fix an appointment and meet at that time. Fixing an appointment means we both save time. Until today, he is scrupulous about his appointments, noting times and dates and keeping to them punctually.

G.C. Srivastava says Pratapsingh's concern for his officers enabled them to give off their best. Once on a trip abroad at an international airport, Srivastava was finding it difficult to manoeuvre his luggage trolley onto the escalator. Immediately, Pratapsingh lifted Srivastava's

---

[23]Ibid. 29.

luggage himself and assisted him all the way down the escalator. On another occasion, when Pratapsingh was holding meetings on the first floor of the CM's residence in Altinho, a pregnant woman officer was finding it difficult to climb up the stairs. When informed of her difficulties, Pratapsingh hurried out of the room and called down the stairs, 'Why are you trying to climb? Wait there, we will all come down.' The meeting was duly shifted downstairs to the ground floor. When Srivastava lost his wife, Roli, who was dear to us both, Pratapsingh immediately flew from Goa to Delhi to express his condolences. 'I was immensely touched that he came all the way,' recalls Srivastava.

'My two mantras of politics and governance were given to me by Bandodkar and Indira Gandhi. Bandodkar taught me to make people always feel at home, particularly if they came from downtrodden communities. He told me, allow people to meet you, to come to your home and your office. In my time, people would walk into the Secretariat without any fear. The other mantra of governance was taught to me by Indira Gandhi. She told me: just do the work. Focus on development, don't pay attention to dissensions and rivalries and don't give in to pressures. After some time, all of it will cease to matter. Only your work will matter.'

Dignifying Human Relations

What about his philosophy of life? Does he find solace in music, books? The Goan has a rich musical heritage, an easy blend of East and West. From Portuguese *fado*s and Western classical music to Indian classical music and Konkani folk songs, music and musicality is intrinsic to the Goan identity. The music creates its own philosophy, a view of life that is sometimes merry, sometimes melancholic, sometimes full of joy, other times full of tears. Life, after all, is like nature around us in Goa, changeable, playful and full of contrasts, each mood complementing the other.

A philosophical distance from the ups and downs of existence is contained in the meaning of the word '*susegad*', derived from the Portuguese word '*sossegado*', meaning quiet. 'The Goan likes his susegad and his little glass of feni,' says Pratapsingh. Susegad is stereotyped to mean frolicsome Goans having a good time. But the word has deeper resonances. It is not just about relaxation; instead, it has some echoes of the Hindu '*sanyas* ashram' of knowing when to leave off. The job must be done and done well. But after it is done, one must know how to retreat. Retreat into the quiet of the forests to let the beauty and joy of nature soak into one's consciousness. Or sit next to moon-lit temples or twilight-tinted churches and embrace a sense of detachment from material striving.

'We are surrounded by water, mountains and forests, and in the evenings, we like to watch the evening stars come up over the palms,' smiles Pratapsingh. 'But this is not the only reason why there is a unique peace in Goa. It is also because there is a sense of respect for human beings. Respect for another, of not pushing and imposing anything on others beyond a point. You could call it an inborn restraint. Staying within the boundaries.'

'I live by the principle of doing my duty and then coming back into my own world. I love Goa's natural world, its flora and fauna. I like waking up to birdsong and watching the peacocks. I have always loved music. I love Kishori Amonkar, Bismillah Khan's shehnai and Amjad Ali Khan's sarod. I also like listening to Ajoy Chakrabarty, I really admire his voice. I enjoy Mozart's sonatas; in fact, I am a fan of Mozart. I also enjoy playing the piano. I admire Marathi theatre and try to watch the plays that come to Goa.'

What about reading or books? 'I enjoy reading. Some books have been my constant companions. I like to read non-fiction. Fiction is not my cup of tea.' His well-stocked library in our Sanquelim home reveals his tastes in reading: books on the economy, farming, wildlife, many books on Goa and some spy thrillers by John le Carré and Robert Ludlum.

Yet, much as he likes life on the farm, it's not as if Pratapsingh is a solitary person. He loves people and loves having people over to our home. We consider ourselves blessed in our friends; their company is worth more to us than words can say. Ramnath and Sharada Kare, Audhut and Anju Timblo, our dear friend Lucio Miranda. Kare remembers many convivial evenings of good conversation, whisky for the men, gin and tonic for myself and listening to Hindustani classical or Western music together. 'Every time Pratapsingh comes to Margao, he comes over to our place,' Kare says. 'He is not much of a foodie. He eats only very light food, chicken mostly.' Pratapsingh likes his Chicken Xacuti and wild meat and often a slice or two of pizza, but he has always eaten sparingly.

Pratapsingh and Anju Timblo (herself an excellent horse-rider) once started a riding school in Panjim and used to ride out together regularly. We go to our friends' homes at Christmas and they all come to ours for our Ganesh Chaturthi lunch.

I delight in hosting our friends and well-wishers. Our annual Ganesh Chaturthi lunch is a big and happy event. Lots of people, including ourselves, look forward to it. We enjoy serving our guests a good lunch of traditional, vegetarian Ganesh Puja fare. There are always five types of vegetable dishes, dals, freshly made puris, *shrikhand* and other sweets. Hindu and Catholic cuisines vary quite significantly in Goa, but that does not mean we don't relish each other's food. 'The Ranes' Ganesh Chaturthi lunch is an institution,' says Sunita. 'It's an open house with food flowing. There are delicious *karanji* and *peda*s and numerous other delicacies. Their house is decorated with flowers. Mr and Mrs Rane are the most hospitable and gracious hosts, making sure that the guests lack for nothing. It is a joyous *mehfil*.'

After parties at our home, people often tell me that the Taj produces far better catering at our place than at theirs. I believe the secret is the personal touch. After every catered event at our home, I make sure to write personal 'thank you' letters to all the service staff. It's the same principle for domestic staff. Staff at home must be nurtured and relationships built over time through ups and downs—such help is not found; such help is created. The personal touch, making people feel wanted, a polite word, remembering names—these things go a long way in dignifying human relations.

All those who work and have worked in our home have become like our family members. We have tried to ensure they get all the material help they need, that their children find opportunities to soar ahead in life, get the education and training they require and develop their self-confidence and self-esteem. We have tried to ensure that our staff members' employment with us is based on ties of mutual goodwill and cooperation.

Social snobbery or social entitlement of any kind disturbs both Pratapsingh and myself. We have left our so-called 'zamindari' backgrounds far behind and worked for years among people. We have been crucially shaped by our varied experiences among a range of different people. The life stories I have witnessed have been so rich and so inspiring that I cannot help but marvel at the human spirit of those who strive to better their circumstances, often against terrifying odds. To see anyone belittled simply because of their birth enrages us both.

Mandeep Singh is a hotelier based in Goa and proprietor of the Sher-e-Punjab restaurant. His family came to Goa in 1966, and the Singhs have been close friends of ours. Mandeep tells a revealing story about Pratapsingh: 'We were hosting a dinner one evening at home, and some guests were visiting from Bombay,' remembers Mandeep. 'There are two entrances to the dining room, one from outside for guests, and one through the kitchen for the staff serving the dinner. Mr Rane was late in coming, and we were all expecting him to walk through the main door. Instead, he quietly came in through the staff entrance, with no security personnel whatsoever, so as not to disturb the party. He even apologized for being late. I don't think any politician today would make such an unobtrusive entry.'

Kshitija Barve provides another example of Pratapsingh's humility. Once, in the early 2000s, Ustad Rashid Khan, the classical vocalist, was scheduled to perform at the Kala Academy at the Surashree Kesarbai Kerkar Sangeet Samaroha. The Ustad's stay was arranged at the International Centre Goa (ICG) in Dona Paula. However, when Pratapsingh arrived at the Kala Academy to inaugurate the concert, Ustad Rashid Khan was asleep and the liaison officer on duty did not have the courage to awaken the maestro. It became an awkward situation as Pratapsingh had arrived and Rashid Khan was not present. Unfazed, Pratapsingh delayed the inauguration by a few minutes and told Barve in Marathi: '*Gavayibuwanchi zopmod karu naka. Mi thambato.*' (Do not disturb the great singer, I'll wait.)

An Inspirational Life

Today's India seeks answers to many questions. How to manage the East–West encounter? How to forge coexistence between different faiths? How to evolve a charter of rights for the citizen so that she is empowered enough to demand that the government she elects functions for citizen's welfare and not for self-aggrandizement of politicians? Politics in Goa may have become rough and ready, yet Goa's experience can provide solutions to the answers we all seek.

For, here in Goa, Indian and Western have mixed and melded unobtrusively, each absorbing the best of the other, English language and Portuguese etiquette combining with Indian values of respect for tradition and family. The religions that have come to Goa—Hinduism, Christianity and Islam—have followed bhakti traditions, seeping into small shrines and family temples. Riverside processions and evening novenas, mosques and temples, coexist in harmony because they are peoples' faiths. They are civic faiths rooted in villages, untouched by too much politics.

The sense of locality—of comunidade, in which everyone is an equal—and pursuing the welfare of the local community is strong in

Goa. Egalitarianism and the belief in the equality of all humans run deep. This is the reason why every individual, big or small, possesses a self-contained dignity; why every home, whatever its size, is gracious and well maintained. No government can ride roughshod over local panchayats and local councils and hope to be popular in Goa.

Under the red earth of Goa, so dramatically depicted by the painter F.N. Souza, runs a hidden river—the river of humanism. Whatever divisions there may outwardly exist of religion or caste or language, there is an undercurrent of respect which every human being has towards the other. Human calls to human in this place blessed by Nature. This humanism touches religions, governments and citizens. It is sometimes obscured by harsh politics and the cult of money and power, yet this river of humanism exists nonetheless, manifesting in the scores of little towns and villages that contentedly follow their own customs and traditions without disturbing anyone else. Here in Goa, the biggest VIP, the most powerful minister, can be spotted in his village square, sitting with the locals, exchanging a word or two. On winding village roads, with waterfalls of greenery hanging on either side, where bread sellers still cycle slowly past, selling freshly baked *pao*, Hindu and Catholic live in peace. In Sanquelim, the Shri Dattatreya temple sits adjacent to the Jama Masjid Sanquelim across the road. The majestic Basilica of Bom Jesus in Old Goa, which holds the mortal remains of the venerated St Francis Xavier, attracts Goans of all faiths.

All these influences have gone into making Pratapsingh the man, the leader and the politician he is. Pratapsingh, the CM, made a powerful impression on advocate Yatish A. Naik when the latter first met him as a student. 'Mr Rane was the very embodiment of grace and authority,' Naik recalls. 'Regal in his bearing, full of genuine interest in young people, he was a formidable presence.' In his recently published book *Flame of Words*, Yatish has composed a poem on Pratapsingh which sums him up beautifully. I quote the poem here:

Grace Personified

Born into an agricultural family
With a valiant warrior legacy
He dropped into public life
As per Bhausaheb's prophecy

Charismatic and graceful
In approach and demeanour
His attention to detail
Made him an unmatched leader

With high academic track
And rich professional expertise
His vision so profound
And acts so precise

He is an institution builder
With passion galore
A skilful horse rider
A statesman to the core

He kept his slate clean
And won over several challenges
Exhibited administrative acumen
Impeccable in every situation

His ways and methods
So entrenched in law
Clean practices and procedures
Bereft of any flaw

His flair for art
And for music and culture
Mastery in public administration
Is his characteristic feature

A legislator of the millennium
And several other decorations
Decorate him with rich measure
But no praise changed his nature.

His soft and amiable ways
And firm grip on governance
Earned popular respect
From all in abundance

The longest legislative stint
And that of chief ministership
Occupy a place of fame
As blessings upon him heap

His social graces and nuances
Make him an embodiment of dignity
As his worthy deeds
Bring glow to his personality

Pratapsingh Rane's life
Is an inspirational story
Of hard work and discipline
And well-deserved glory.[24]

These days, Pratapsingh Rane spends most of his time at Golden Acres, our modern farmhouse which we built in 1983. It is a two-storeyed home, with windows on all sides and sloping roofs, part fairy-tale Swiss chalet with a turret (which Pratapsingh, I must say, was very keen on having) and part Goan-Lusitanian residence with arched entrances and windows. Inside, a carved wooden staircase leads to the upper floor. To us, the memories, love and warmth that this house contains mean more than the grandeur of its appearance.

---

[24] Naik, Yatish, *Flame of Words: Fifty One Poems*, Broadway Publishing House, 2023.

We are surrounded by dense greenery on all sides; forests and orchards encircle us. A majestic, wild deciduous tree rises from the centre of our lawn, towering over the house, with its leafy branches extending in all directions. It is our very own friendly green giant, almost a living deity. 'My father gave me this property,' says Pratapsingh, 'and we built this house because I always wanted to have a place to come to if my government fell. I felt I should have my own home which is a little distant from Panaji. When we first came here, it wasn't as green as it is now. Slowly, we planted trees and made it the green place it is today.' Pratapsingh has the gift of contentment: the ability to be content with what he has and not hanker for more. Why hanker when fortune has always been kind?

I take pleasure in maintaining a beautiful home and make sure that our house is spotless and well looked after. Says Rajeev Talwar: 'Neither Mr and Mrs Rane ever had any airs; they are both very refined people, and their home exuded this sense of refinement and hospitality.'

Pratapsingh's favourite room in the house is his library on the first floor. On the ground floor, in his study, with big windows looking into the lawns outside, the walls are hung with his certificates and photos with many personalities—St. Teresa, the Pope, Indira Gandhi and President Shankar Dayal Sharma. In pride of place on his study wall hangs an oil painting, framed in gold. It shows a young, smiling Pratapsingh on horseback. He has just won a race, and horse and gentleman-jockey are being escorted off the race course by officials and admirers.

Home life follows a quiet routine. Taking care of our old constituents, visits from friends and family and walks with our beloved glossy black cocker spaniel Bubbles. We are a family of dog lovers. Bubbles is very protective about Pratapsingh. She follows him around wherever he goes and barks in concern and worry if she thinks he is tired or not feeling well. 'Bubbles seems to understand everything he says. He even bathes her himself,' notes Udaysingh. Bubbles is always by Pratapsingh's side. When he takes his morning rounds of the farm and walks along country lanes where butterflies flutter and birds weave about, she ambles behind him, his faithful companion.

'Bubbles is like one of his security guards,' says Panaji-based vet Dr Marilyn Estebeiro, who has looked after our dogs and animals since the 1980s. 'It's as if she takes care of him and protects him.' Dr Estebeiro first met Pratapsingh when she was a girl guide in school in the 1970s and he was the minister in charge of Scouts & Guides. 'I was really impressed by him, as he seemed genuinely interested in the work of the girl guides.' Later, Dr Estebeiro joined the department of animal husbandry in the Goa government as vet and worked with the horses that were owned by the government. 'Mr Rane, as a keen horseman, was always very involved with the horses,' she recalls. Dr Estebeiro says that before getting Bubbles, Pratapsingh was keen to get a German shepherd, but now that he has Bubbles, it seems that she has become as brave, and loyal and protective as a German shepherd in the body of a cocker spaniel!

Dutiful, dignified, reticent and reserved, Pratapsingh detests drawing attention to himself or making a fuss about his own achievements. He has a large collection of photo albums consisting of a wealth of pictures with various dignitaries. Yet these albums seem not to mean that much to him. There is only one precious album that seems to particularly mean a great deal to him, and this is the one he keeps under lock and key. He shows it to only very special visitors. This is a green-backed, yellowing collection of his college photos, photos of his horse-riding days in Pune, photos of friends in Texas A&M University, photos posing in New York in a suit and wearing cowboy boots and a Stetson Western hat with a group of cowboys on a Texan ranch. He particularly treasures photos of himself as a lithe young man racing a horse, vaulting over fences, galloping around the race track and winning prizes in riding competitions. One of the horses he rode was named 'Excalibur', after King Arthur's invincible sword. In those days, in those fleeting moments, he too had been full of the invincible confidence of youth: Pratapsingh Rane, the bold young horseman.

He said goodbye to that life. Said goodbye to his life in America. He said goodbye to his international life, to overseas friends and to friends in the corporate world, many years ago. He chose to come back to Goa and to Sattari and work for his people here. Yet that precious album, locked away in his cupboard, remains as a reminder of what might have been and of a life he might have had.

He came back from glittering Manhattan to rural Sattari and perhaps occasionally still feels a sense of loss. Does he have any regrets? 'Not for a moment,' he says firmly. 'My parents stretched themselves to send me abroad. My father had little education but made sure that I received the best opportunities. I gave my parents my word that I would return and look after these vast estates that my family owned. We are a landed family, and we are rooted here in this land.'

He is an established Goa bhatkar, yet his personal habits have always been simple and spartan. He likes to be well dressed but prefers to wear his safari suits and *bandhgala*s, never anything flashy. He is never slovenly; his shirts and trousers are always neatly pressed and his shoes freshly polished. He wears a Rolex watch only because it was a gift from our son Vishwajit. The only time he bought himself something expensive was when he purchased a Mercedes car on his eightieth birthday. In his working life, Pratapsingh's chariot was either a self-driven jeep or an Ambassador. He has dollops of those virtues which today are considered old fashioned—grit, endurance, the capacity to withstand hardship and crises with a cool head, unassuming manners and humility.

'After 50 years of public life, I have now retired to my farm, to the simple country folk here and to family life. I may have made some mistakes, but I tried to do the best I could for the people of Goa and for public life in democratic India,' muses Pratapsingh as he walks along briskly, inspecting his beloved trees and checking on the livestock.

History will be kind to him. How can it not be? The buses plying through rural roads, the tarred, all-weather roads running through once impassable forests, hospitals dispensing medical care, the proliferation of schools drawing in Goa's young and big dams harnessing the power of water: history is witness to these.

When future generations of Goans walk along the open seashore and see how construction is set back from the water, or wander in orchards where water supply and drinking water are readily available, or gaze on the hilly forests of his beloved Sattari where trees are protected, they may ask how all of this happened. And then, they may remember that there was once a courteous, unassuming yet steadfast and disciplined man, who shunned the spotlight, never drew attention to himself, but who roared like a tiger for his people and spent every waking minute planning for their well-being.

When new generations of Indians come to visit Goa and drive through the carefully planned towns and the tree-lined highways, when they see the industrial estates separated from residential areas, when they see empowered RTI activists challenging the powerful, when they see a senior woman police officer smartly salute, or when they note that whichever party is in power, governments remain more or less neutral to religion and community, they may ask: who started these trends? Who built the foundations?

When they ask these questions, someone may remind them of him and tell them his story: the story of Pratapsingh Rane of Goa.

ACKNOWLEDGEMENTS

My sincere thanks to author and journalist Sagarika Ghose for helping me research, write and put together the chapters of this book. My grateful thanks are due to all those who kindly participated in this book project and gave it their valuable time: (*in alphabetical order*) Jason Abraham, Vivek Annaswamy, Dr Pramod Badami, Shridhar Kamat Bambolkar, Maria do Ceu Barreto, Pandharinath Bodke, Shailaja Chandra, Shahu Chhatrapati Maharaj and Maloji Raje Chhatrapati, Prithviraj Chavan, Shrinivas Dempo, Dr Dhillon Desai, Dr Purushottam Desai, Dr Marilyn Estebeiro, Luizinho Faleiro, Rupesh Kashinath Gawas, P.V. Jayakrishnan, Govind Kale, Ramnath and Sharada Kare, Ramakant Khalap, Mohammad Modassir, Rozendo Mendonsa, Rita Paes, Pandurang Phaldesai, Valentine Pereira, Shashikant Punaj, Usha Raje Pashupati Rana, Udaysingh Rane, Sunita Sawant, Brahmanand Sankhwalkar, Mandeep Singh, G.C. Srivastava, Rajiv Talwar, Audhut and Anju Timblo, R. Mihir Vardhan, Namrata Ulman and Vijay Kumar Verekar. I am grateful to advocate Yatish Naik for being a moving force behind this book. My thanks to the research team of Jeevan Khedekar, Prasad Kalangutkar and Ashwin Souza.

Above all, my gratitude to my beloved family—my husband Pratapsingh Rane, my son Vishwajit and daughter-in-law Deviya, my daughter Vishwadhara and son-in-law Vishwajit Dahanukar, and my dearest grandchildren Anandita, Aishwarya and Arundhati—for their continued love and support.

INDEX

1971 India–Pakistan war 42, 51, 71

Abraham, Jason 135, 158, 159, 192, 193
agitations 53, 68, 110, 115, 134, 198, 199, 200
Agricultural Tenancy Act 52
Alemao, Churchill Braz 112, 124, 128, 129, 30, 133, 146, 153, 161, 223, 224
All-India Congress Committee (AICC) 17, 41, 70
Anjunem Dam xvi, 92, 93, 94, 116, 199
Anti-Defection Act 129, 132
assembly elections 34, 50, 63, 66, 71, 72, 107, 124, 127, 133, 144, 152, 154, 155, 160, 163, 164, 166, 179
Automobile Corporation of Goa Limited (ACGL) 172, 173
awards 48, 101, 115, 121

Bahujan Samaj 36, 63, 67
Bal Bhavan 120, 121, 122, 125, 138, 140, 175
Bandodkar, Dayanand Balkrishna xiv, 36, 37, 38, 39, 40, 41, 43, 45, 46, 47, 51, 52, 53, 54, 55, 56, 58, 59, 60, 65, 70, 72, 73, 89, 92, 100, 119, 150, 168, 171, 183, 188, 208, 216, 224, 225
Bandodkar government 41, 92, 100
Barbosa, Dr Luis Proto 113, 129, 130, 131, 133
Bharatiya Janata Party (BJP) x, 77, 135, 142, 143, 144, 145, 146, 150, 152, 156, 158, 160, 161, 163, 165, 179, 180
Bhembre, Uday 85, 106, 111, 159, 177
Bhumika Higher Secondary School 168
BJP–MGP alliance 139, 160
Bombay High Court 82, 98, 132
boxing champion 13, 146
by-polls 55, 70, 152, 179

Cabo Raj Bhavan 81, 87
Campal grounds 83, 84, 86, 193
Catholics 34, 36, 40, 55, 58, 67, 68, 79, 99, 100, 112, 114, 115, 129, 130, 134, 141, 142, 144, 160, 191, 227, 230
central government 43, 50, 111, 161, 188, 216

Chaitrotsav temple festival 9, 206
Chandra, Shailaja 76, 94, 184, 197, 209, 224
Chavan, Yashwantrao Balwantrao 35, 41, 68
Chhatrapati, Malojiraje 155, 156, 169, 170
Chhatrapati Shivaji Maharaj 3, 113, 125
CHOGM Retreat xvi, 75, 76, 104, 105, 106
Chowgule, Sarladevi 9, 10, 20, 24
Christianity 4, 6, 192, 229
churches 1, 2, 6, 13, 15, 16, 32, 44, 79, 98, 100, 191, 193, 226
civil disobedience movement 18
common civil code 194
Commonwealth Heads of Government Meeting (CHOGM) xv, 75, 104, 105
Commonwealth Parliamentary Association (CPA) 160
Commonwealth Parliamentary Conferences (CPC) 160
communal harmony xiii, 194
Congress High Command 88, 114, 133, 144, 157, 164
Congress (I) 70, 71, 72, 73, 107, 113, 129, 130, 131
Congress Legislature Party (CLP) 82, 133, 136, 141, 152
Congress (Urs) 70
Constitution of India 42, 69, 112, 162, 186, 187, 194, 199, 204, 208
corruption xvii, 88, 203, 215
cultural traditions 2, 169, 199

culture and art x, xiii, xvi, xvii, 4, 5, 12, 32, 44, 64, 90, 98, 99, 100, 101, 103, 118, 119, 120, 121, 135, 151, 156, 169, 187, 191, 194, 197, 203, 215, 218
Cunha, Dr Tristão de Bragança 17, 18, 83
customs 3, 84, 191, 192, 195, 230

Dabolim airport 19, 84, 114, 139
Dada Rane Revolt 4
Dahanukar, Vishwajit 102, 138, 213
Daman xv, 32, 43, 52, 56, 83, 97, 113, 115, 116, 117, 171, 188
dance 85, 98–99, 177, 178
decencia 88, 169
delicadeza 88, 169
democracy 31, 38, 39, 43, 44, 78, 126, 127, 149, 154, 157, 186, 199, 200, 201, 202, 203, 204
Dempo, Vasantrao S. 34, 137, 143
Desai, Dilkhush 148, 149, 150
Desai, Morarji 42, 69, 196
de Sequeira, Dr João Hugo Eduardo (Jack de Sequeira) 39, 40, 41, 42, 43, 53, 65, 66, 150
de Souza, Dr Wilfred 44, 55, 63, 65, 67, 70, 72, 73, 78, 87, 88, 105, 107, 108, 119, 131, 132, 133, 134, 136, 141, 142, 143, 144
Dhempe College of Arts & Science 119, 135
Dinanath Mangeshkar Kala Mandir 100
Dipaji Rane Revolt 4
Diu xv, 32, 43, 52, 56, 83, 97, 113,

115, 116, 117, 171, 188
drinking water xvi, 94, 236

Economic Development Corporation (EDC) Board 138
economic growth 52, 202
economy 17, 37, 94, 187, 188, 190, 191, 227
education x, xv, 1, 7, 10, 23, 39, 86, 87, 89, 108, 111, 119, 122, 123, 126, 136, 144, 165, 168, 170, 198, 199, 202, 219, 220, 224, 228, 235
election campaign 49, 66, 155, 169
elections xv, 20, 31, 32, 33, 38, 39, 41, 42, 45, 46, 47, 49, 50, 51, 52, 55, 59, 60, 62, 63, 64, 66, 69, 71, 108, 141, 144, 153, 154, 155, 160, 161, 163, 164, 167, 169, 179, 211
electrification xv, xvi, 28, 29, 36, 52, 87, 91, 94, 161, 189, 215
Emergency (1975) 57, 59, 60, 64, 65, 66, 204
employment 53, 154, 170, 172, 190, 198, 228
environment xvii, 99, 140, 215
European Economic Community Chamber of Commerce 217

factories and industries x, xv, xvi, xvii, 22, 23, 34, 36, 57, 117, 124, 134, 168, 173, 188, 189, 217
Faleiro, Eduardo 59, 71, 84, 109, 116
Faleiro, Luizinho 63, 73, 107, 111, 144, 145, 158, 160, 163, 197
farming 26, 47, 137, 165, 218, 219, 227

freedom 17, 18, 19, 20, 31, 32, 33, 34, 35, 39, 44, 46, 83, 186, 187, 188, 196, 203
freedom fighters 17, 18, 33, 34, 39, 83
free economy 183, 187, 188
free speech 18, 19

Gandhi, Indira xv, 9, 42, 43, 49, 50, 51, 55, 57, 59, 65, 66, 70, 73, 74, 75, 76, 78, 88, 104, 105, 106, 107, 108, 110, 122, 150, 186, 187, 188, 191, 225, 233
Gandhi, Rajiv 12, 74, 76, 83, 84, 85, 101, 102, 108, 113, 114, 116, 131
Gandhi, Sanjay 58, 70, 78
Gandhi, Sonia 84, 144, 145
garbage and waste management 217
Ghorpade, Murarirao Yeshwantrao 21, 22, 23, 48, 60, 204
Ghorpade, Rajmata Sushiladevi 8, 21, 23
Goa Buildings (Lease, Rent and Eviction) Control Act 52
Goa Chamber of Commerce and Industry (GCCI) 189, 190, 217
Goa Congress 17, 18, 19, 34, 41, 105, 107, 108, 109
Goa, Daman and Diu Buildings (Lease, Rent & Eviction) Control Act of 1968 188
Goa, Daman and Diu Land Revenue Code 52
Goa, Daman and Diu Mundkars (Protection from Eviction) Act, 1975 56

Goa, Daman and Diu Official
  Language Act, 1987 115
Goa, Daman and Diu (Opinion Poll)
  Act, 1966 43
Goa, Daman and Diu Preservation
  of Trees Act 97
Goa, Daman and Diu Public Health
  Act, 1985 117
Goa, Daman and Diu Reorganisation
  Bill 116
Goa, Daman and Diu Town and
  Country Planning Act, 1974 xv,
  56
Goa Industrial Development
  Corporation (IDC) 172
Goa Institute of Management (GIM)
  xvi, 93, 119, 140, 167
Goa Legislative Assembly xvi, 42, 59,
  62, 69, 82, 83, 132, 141, 145, 146,
  149, 157, 159, 183, 221, 222
Goa Medical College 120, 132, 140
Goan Hindus 32, 68, 79
Goan identity 40, 41, 44, 79, 84, 225
Goan People's Party 129, 130
Goa Panchayati Raj Act 154
Goa Pradesh Congress Committee
  (GPCC) 64, 78, 79
Goa Prevention of Defacement of
  Property Act 1988 xv, 120
Goa referendum issue 41, 42, 43
Goa Revolution Day 18
Goa Right to Information (RTI)
  Act of 1997 xv, xvii, 139, 202,
  203
Goa Rural Employment Guarantee
  Scheme of 2006 xv, 154

Goa University xvi, 117, 118, 125,
  138, 140, 154
Goa University Act 117
Gomantak Maratha Samaj 10, 36,
  99, 103
Government of India 19, 53, 94

'half ticket' protests 68, 89
health and sanitary facilities x, xiii,
  xv, 89, 95, 104, 117, 166, 171, 178,
  179, 224
Hindu Code Bill 195
Hindus 2, 3, 4, 5, 6, 32, 34, 36, 58,
  67, 68, 73, 79, 88, 98, 99, 100,
  112, 114, 115, 129, 134, 142, 191,
  192, 195, 226, 227, 230
Hiradevi 9, 10, 20
horse-riding 11, 12, 76, 146, 213,
  220, 227, 234

Indian classical music 101, 102, 225
Indian Union 82, 86
industrial estates xv, 57, 236
infrastructure x, xvii, 29, 56, 104,
  106, 117, 170
International Centre Goa (ICG) 119,
  140, 229
International Civil Aviation
  Organization 139
irrigation xvi, 29, 92, 94, 96, 126

Jamshedpur 21, 23, 24, 27, 119, 175,
  207
Janata Party 59, 64, 66, 67, 69

Kadamba Transport Corporation

Limited (KTCL) xv, 90, 189
Kakodkar, Gurudatt 58, 59, 68, 89
Kakodkar, Purushottam 18, 34, 41, 42, 65, 66, 70, 71
Kakodkar, Shashikala xv, 39, 54, 55, 56, 57, 59, 60, 61, 62, 63, 64, 67, 68, 72, 87, 89, 90, 94, 148, 150, 215, 216
Kala Academy xvi, 100, 101, 102, 103, 122, 125, 140, 159, 168, 169, 177, 208, 229
Kale, Govind 101, 177, 208
Kamat, Digambar 102, 135, 152, 156, 160, 163, 179
Kare, Ramnath Govind 189, 190, 209, 216, 217, 222, 227
Khalap, Ramakant 55, 60, 71, 72, 73, 112, 127, 128, 130, 133, 222, 223

Konkani language xiii, 2, 5, 9, 44, 57, 85, 86, 105, 106, 107, 109, 110, 111, 112, 113, 114, 115, 139, 191, 193, 198, 223, 225
Konkani Porjecho Avaz (KPA) 111, 112, 113
Konkan Railway 134, 198
Kustoba Rane Revolt 4

land reform laws 74, 188

Legislator of the Millennium xvi, 153, 183, 222
liberation xiii, xvii, 14, 17, 20, 31, 33, 34, 36, 39, 65, 76, 91, 99, 103, 111, 112, 116, 182, 217
License Permit Quota Raj 190

Lok Sabha xv, 34, 59, 65, 116, 145, 215

Madho Rao I, 7, 8
Maharaja of Kolhapur 24, 125, 155
Maharashtrawadi Gomantak Party (MGP) 32, 34, 35, 36, 37, 38, 39, 40, 41, 42, 43, 45, 46, 49, 51, 54, 55, 57, 58, 59, 60, 61, 63, 64, 65, 66, 67, 68, 69, 71, 72, 81, 112, 114, 124, 127, 129, 130, 131, 132, 135, 142, 143, 146, 148, 160, 163, 174
Mahatma Gandhi 21, 187, 204
Mahatma Gandhi National Rural Employment Guarantee Act (MGNREGA) 154
Mangeshkar, Lata 98, 103
Marathi language 40, 44, 63, 112, 114, 115, 191
medical care 198, 236
Mendonsa, Rozendo 218, 219
Mihir Vardhan, R. 136, 137, 153, 198
mining 22, 23, 36, 37, 173, 189
Modassir, Dr Mohammad 89, 90, 174, 175
Modi, Narendra x, 161, 166
monsoon 91, 99, 140, 143
Mopa airport xvi, 139, 140, 153
music 2, 13, 28, 67, 84, 88, 98, 99, 101, 102, 122, 124, 169, 194, 203, 225, 226, 227

Naik, Ananta Narcina 58, 62, 63, 65, 66, 67, 68, 70, 72, 78, 79, 87, 88, 106

Naik, Ravi 131, 132, 133, 134, 224
Naik, Yatish A. 154, 230, 231, 232
Narasimha Rao, P.V. 102, 122, 190
Narvekar, Dayanand 88, 143, 150
National Bal Shree Awards 121, 122
Nationalist Congress Party (NCP) 77, 152
Nehru Gold Cup Football Tournament 128, 177
Nehru, Jawaharlal 16, 18, 19, 22, 32, 33, 41, 55, 65, 74, 187
no-confidence motion 69, 105, 129, 143, 150, 183
North Atlantic Treaty Organization (NATO) 19
North Goa xv, 6, 28, 35, 46, 66, 71, 73, 92, 97, 114, 116, 130, 137, 139, 153, 175, 206, 207

Official Language Act 109, 115, 116
Opinion Poll, 1967 40, 42, 43, 65, 74, 111, 129
Ordem do Infante Dom Henrique 217

Parliament 34, 66, 70, 84, 116, 186
Parrikar, Manohar 106, 136, 138, 145, 146, 147, 152, 156, 158, 160, 161, 162, 164, 222
Pawar, Sharad 68, 77
Portugal 4, 6, 14, 17, 18, 19, 32, 33, 217
Portuguese Goa 10, 13, 20, 91, 111
Post-Liberation Goa xiii, xvii, 19
President's Rule 69, 131, 144, 152

Progressive Democratic Front (PDF) 130
Prohibition of Smoking and Spitting Act 1997 xv, 140

Raje, Maharani Gajra 7, 8, 10, 21, 71, 77, 213
Rane family 7, 8, 28, 155, 170
Rane, Jaisingrao 46, 49, 59, 70
Rane, Manoramabai 7, 8, 9, 20, 21, 26
Rane, Raoji ix, xi, 8, 9, 10, 11, 26, 27, 29, 207
Rane, Raoji Satroji 6, 7, 170
Rane revolts 3, 4, 6
Rane, Udaysingh 9, 27, 219, 234
Rane, Vishwajit Pratapsingh ix, 52, 138, 154, 155, 174, 179, 180, 181, 210, 211, 213, 235
Ravindra Bhavan xvi, 103, 140, 151, 152, 168
Revolutionary Goans Party 164

Salazar, António de Oliveira 17, 18, 19, 33
Sanjay Centre for Special Education (Sanjay School) 122, 123, 138, 175, 178
Sardinha, Francisco 113, 145, 146, 223
Sawant, Pramod 164, 165
Sawant, Sunita 208, 220, 227
Scindia, Jivajirao (George) 7, 8, 213
Selaulim Dam xvi, 94, 95, 116
Shahu Chhatrapati 125, 126, 136, 155

Sharma, Shankar Dayal 119, 177, 233
Shashikala Kakodkar government xv, 62, 68, 215
Shastri, Lal Bahadur 41, 42, 55
'Shiksha Samrat' 117, 120
Shri Deva Vithal Panchayatan Sansthan 206
Shri Shivaji Preparatory Military School (AISSMS), Poona 11, 54, 126
Shri Vithal-Rakhumai temple 5, 8, 191, 192, 206
Singh, Bhanu Prakash 132, 133, 134
Singh, Dr Manmohan 154, 189, 190
Singh, Giani Zail 100, 101, 103
Socialist Party (SP) 49, 50
South Goa 59, 71, 95, 112, 116
Souza, Francis Newton 100, 101, 230
Srivastava, G.C. 139, 140, 224, 225
statehood for Goa ix, 66, 74, 81, 83, 84, 105, 107, 109, 110, 111, 112, 114, 116, 126, 127, 179, 188
States Reorganisation Act, 1956 35

Talwar, Rajeev 97, 104, 106, 170, 171, 172, 209, 224, 233
Tata Engineering and Locomotive Company (Telco) xiv, 21, 23, 24, 27, 147, 173
Tatas 27, 28, 146, 172, 173, 189, 207

Texas A&M University xiv, 14, 189, 234
theatre 25, 99, 102, 163, 226
The Chastity Belt 25
Timblo, Audhut 29, 204, 216

tourism x, xvi, 104, 113, 117, 124, 172, 188
Town and Country Planning Act xv, 56, 117

Ulman, Namrata 157, 158

Union Territory (UT) ix, xiv, 31, 32, 39, 50, 64, 82, 83, 86, 104, 114, 116, 123, 126, 141, 182
United Goans Democratic Party (UGDP) 146
United Goans Party (UGP) 32, 34, 39, 40, 42, 45, 55, 62, 65, 66, 72, 87, 114, 141
United Nations (UN) 16, 146
United States (US) x, xiv, 14, 15, 16, 17, 20, 23, 27, 29, 46, 57, 67, 123, 135, 146, 183, 193, 197, 202, 207, 222, 235

Vajpayee, Atal Bihari x, xv, 77, 144, 195
Rane, Vishwadhara 52, 136, 138, 147, 155, 210, 212, 214
Vodithala Education Society of Andhra Pradesh 199

Wadia College, Pune 10, 11, 13
water supply xvi, 29, 87, 92, 94, 95, 96, 161, 236
Western Ghats 1, 2, 89, 91, 94, 162, 170
World War II 9, 16, 19, 37

Zantye, Harish 113, 114, 122, 128